Dione
410-5523521

Path of Promise,

Path of Peace

D1414380

Path of Promise, Path of Peace

How to Hear Your Higher Self Speak

by Barbara Paulin

Foreword by
Michael Brant DeMaria, Ph.D.

Be The Light
With love, Barbara Paulin
Barbara

A·R·E
PRESS

A.R.E. Press • Virginia Beach • Virginia

A.R.E. Press
Sixty-Eighth & Atlantic Avenue
P.O. Box 656
Virginia Beach, VA 23451-0656

Library of Congress Cataloging-in-Publication Data
Paulin, Barbara, 1934-
    Path of promise, path of peace : how to hear your higher self
speak / by Barbara Paulin.
       p.   cm.
    ISBN 0-87604-328-7
    1. Parapsychology. 2. Spiritual healing. 3. Mental healing. 4.
Channeling (Spiritualism)—Case studies. 5. Paulin, Barbara,
1934- . 6. Psychotherapy—Miscellanea. I. Title.
BF1040.P38 1995
133.8—dc20   94-28852

Cover design by Lightbourne Images

For Mabel and May, Bryce and Bernice

The mass of men lead lives of quiet desperation ...

Henry David Thoreau
Walden, 1854

TABLE OF CONTENTS

Foreword

THE TWENTIETH CENTURY HAS BEEN A SPIRITUAL "dark age." We have witnessed the culmination of Newton's dream of the universe being a well-oiled machine. There have been both blessings and curses to this vision. As a culture we have become more adept than ever at curing physical illness and expanding the quantity of years that one may live. At the same time, we have seen a decline in people's sense of meaning, purpose, and spirituality. *Path of Promise, Path of Peace* offers a guide toward reconnecting with the life of the spirit, which more often than not has been repressed, ignored, or denied in the last hundred years. In this experiential guide, Barbara Paulin helps the reader explore the path of spiritual growth from a very personal and genuine perspective. Instead of offering easy solutions or a recipe for salvation, Barbara allows us a rare glimpse into the inner world of true spiritual growth, commitment, and struggle.

Many people who explore the spiritual often become lost in the paranormal or psychic "bells and whistles" that are a natural side effect of spiritual practice. Barbara helps us to remember that "psychic" is not synonymous with "spiritual," but rather is a vehicle to accessing the Spiritual Source. Our eyes help us see, our ears help us hear, while psychic abilities (intuitive guidance) provide a window into other dimensions of our existence, often beyond our usual understandings of space, time, and death. The theories of nonlocal mind and quantum physics show us that the dimensions of space and time are malleable. Right now, this moment, there are radio and television waves passing through the air we breathe. It only stands to reason that many dimensions exist which are invisible to our eyes or undetectable by our ears. The human senses we know only pick up a small part of the spectrum of light and sound. The psychic sense appears well suited to peer into the wrinkles in the fabric of space-time. Barbara gives us exceptional accounts of that realm traditionally and anciently called the third eye of intuition, but she also does much more than this. She gives us a glimpse into the territory and land in which the psychic is a bridge to the Source.

In my work as a psychologist over the last decade, the most valuable practice I've found is a combination of journal-writing, service to others, and meditation. All three take a central role in Barbara's path. Immediately this resonated with my own experience. The central place she gives the practice of sacred Silence and opening to the Source also have parallels in virtually all spiritual paths. Barbara gives this universal truth vivid, vibrant, and poignant life by showing how her love, caring, and dedication to her path brought ever-renewed promise and peace. We readers also have the wonderful opportunity to be nourished by the fruit of her own dedication, courage, and hard work. A guide for all travelers and wanderers on their way home, this book is indeed a "path of promise" and a "path of peace."

Michael Brant DeMaria, Ph.D.

Dr. DeMaria is a clinical psychologist, writer, and artist. He is the author of *Horns and Halos: Towards the Blessing of Darkness* (Peter Lang Publishing, Inc., New York, 1992), and is presently working on his second book.

Preface

THIS BOOK IS ABOUT HEALING, THE KIND OF HEALING that takes time. The kind of healing that requires effort, patience, and perseverance. The kind of healing that is life changing.

This is not a book about triumph over tragedy, a dramatic illness or injury. Rather, it is about the changing of a life lived in quiet desperation into a life of quiet calm and confidence, good health and—more often than not—joy.

As I write these words today, I marvel at the changes in myself, changes not easily brought about. In twenty-some short years, I have overcome codependency, emotional fragility, an addiction to having the approval of others, fearfulness and anxiety, depression, an inferiority complex ("low self-esteem" is not an apt description), and pessimism. Patterns have been broken and released that may have been crippling for generations back in my family, and which, by all current appearances, will not be there to complicate the lives of my children.

If there are miracles in my story, they are small ones, but significant. They are found in timing, contacts, and opportunities presented, the latter often accepted with some trepidation.

The key to healing, growth, and change lies with tapping one's spiritual resources, for we truly are spiritual beings. God would never have placed us in this position—attending the schoolhouse that is Earth—without giving us direct and personal recourse to the guidance of Higher Consciousness. Our psychic and intuitive apparatus is indeed more natural than the physical five senses, which are only present when we are housed in physical embodiment. Our spiritual mode of communication is with us always.

Meditation is the most direct and empowering tool for healing and guidance that one can have. While my techniques and particular paths may not be for everyone, sitting in the Silence and going within *can* be the answer for anyone, no matter who or where.

In moving beyond attunement for personal guidance into attunement on behalf of others, I found that my life continued to be healed and enriched. We are all part of the One, and you cannot help but know this as you come to know yourself.

May this book bring you encouragement as you seek to know who you are, and who you can be.

Barbara Paulin

Acknowledgments

I could not have written this book without the love and support of my husband, Ralph; my children, Lisa, Chris, and Shannon; and my brothers, Barry and Bill. I am doubly grateful, as each allowed me to weave, without restriction, a portion of their personal stories into this tapestry of healing and growth.

I appreciate all of those seekers who graciously contributed guidance from their readings and their hearts for this book. I especially ask God to bless Joy Smith.

Several friends, tried and true, were of inestimable assistance: Nancy Hollen and Linda Stephens, who spent hour after hour reading and feeding back to me what my writing said to them; Jamie Williams and Shirley Clark, who offered insights from their unique perspectives; and Jerry Jackson, who helped me overcome my fear of computers and bailed me out when I was in trouble. Christine Cameron and Pat Turner were instrumental in helping me build momentum in the beginning.

To the many other friends who energized me with their encouragement and endured my limited attention this past year, my heartfelt thanks.

Last but not least, I am most grateful to Pam Thompson, who was pressed into service by the Universe in October 1991 to relay the guidance which resulted in my writing *Path of Promise, Path of Peace.*

Introduction

BARBARA PAULIN HAS WRITTEN AN EXCELLENT description of that hidden dimension of life many of us seek to understand and reach. There are many books which list the steps to follow if we wish to receive inner guidance. Barbara's work, however, goes beyond the norm as she presents this process as an integral part of her growth and self-determination.

The best words to describe both Barbara and this book, which is an extension of her, are "crystal heart." I have chosen this description because Barbara has always been open and above board in terms of her motives and goals, and because she has served Life with the fullness of deeply felt love. From the very start of her search, Barbara had a depth and breadth of compassion that made her stand apart. She has also had the courage to stand alone when that meant standing with the Truth.

When I asked Barbara to counsel convicted felons who were addicted and who had served time in a federal penitentiary, she was quite taken back, but her willingness was typical of her desire to grow and serve. To do either one of these well necessarily involves the other.

Path of Promise, Path of Peace richly portrays this inner process as it commingled with her constantly changing outer activities. This reflective journey of a soul, ever deepening in its growth and expanding in its service, is presented in the clearest language and style, so that all readers may be able to identify with her as they go from chapter to chapter.

While Barbara's odyssey is unique, it nonetheless stands as a powerful example—that of the crystal heart—which can be the basis of inspiration and emulation for the rest of us.

Dr. Roméo Di Benedetto
Department of Sociology
El Paso Community College
El Paso, Texas

To the Reader

To preserve confidentiality and protect privacy, I have not used the real names of the NARA II clients. At the beginning of the NARA II experiment, all clients and staff were advised that guidance received would be included in reports and made available to the public. Several names in subsequent chapters are pseudonyms.

With regard to meditation, it is important for my readers to know that I chose to write about meditation as the natural process it is. There are many fine books on the market today which include the technical and scientific aspects of meditation. Since authors often appear to have slightly different meanings in mind as to terminology, here are the definitions I favor:

HIGHER CONSCIOUSNESS—God, the Creative Force, and Universal Mind; the Collective Unconscious and the akashic records.

HIGHER SELF—That part of you or me which is directly connected to God. Also called our superconscious or Christ Consciousness.

CONSCIOUS MIND—Everyday consciousness; personality self.

SUBCONSCIOUS—Storage facility for current and past-life memories, unresolved issues, and unexpressed emotions. All that is "on hold." Inner child voices may originate in the subconscious.

SOURCE—A specific origin of guidance such as one's Higher Self, the Keeper of the akashic records, or a spiritual teacher.

Path of Promise, Path of Peace offers assistance to the beginning meditator and the discouraged meditator. Connecting with one's Higher Self is not a complicated venture. All that is required is the sincere desire, patience, and willingness to practice. In the practicing, certain choices are normally presented by one's Higher Self to test the meditator's ability to discern. My desire is to help you make the right choices and to recognize the connection with Higher Consciousness as it gradually reveals itself.

For those who are as yet unfamiliar with the mind-boggling ways of the Universe, certain of my experiences may require a stretch of the mental. Some involved a stretch for me as well. Nevertheless, in time and in some remarkable manner, their genuineness eventually was confirmed.

In the final analysis, we each must find our own way to wholeness, using the tools that help us best. Let your intuition guide you as you read this book. Draw upon the advice that feels right to you, and let the remainder go.

The Priest,
the Program, and the Psychic

THE *Please Do Not Disturb* SIGN, OUR SILENT SENTINEL, guarded the entry to the second-floor conference room in which I was to give my eighteenth psychic reading for the Narcotic Addict Rehabilitation Act II (NARA II). I put my purse on the table, slipped out of my shoes, and smiled nervously at the priest. My stomach was, as usual, in subtle motion. Introductions made, I closed my eyes and began to attune to the energy of federal felon Joe Chavez.

Forty-five minutes and many words later, I took a deep breath, wishing fervently that I were anywhere in Albuquerque but the Bernalillo County Mental Health Center, feeling on exhibit and rather spaced out. This was the first reading in which the client sat mute and unresponsive. I couldn't tell if he had listened at all to the encouragement and assessment of his past, his problems, and his potential that had been delivered at length, through me, by my Source—a "voice" no one else could hear.

The invitation to ask questions had been ignored. The priest asked about training opportunities and how Mr. Chavez could avail himself of the help of a spiritual guide. This was given, and once again thundering silence prevailed. Father Di Benedetto reached toward the tape recorder, but I motioned to indicate "don't," and he withdrew his hand. My eyes remained closed, but somehow I knew that our client was about to speak.

Waves of negativity assailed me, and I shuddered. Joe Chavez sat on my side of the table, chair turned toward me, and about ten feet away. The priest was to our left, across the table and halfway between us. I did not know if he could feel the icy, barren, piercing jabs of hostile energy emanating from the client as he voiced his first question: "Will I be able to kill?"

My heart seemed instantly to be consumed by pain, and every muscle in my body tensed as I forced out the words, "Kill what?"

Mr. Chavez: "A human being."

I felt myself plummeting downward, spiraling through levels of consciousness, beginning to hyperventilate, as the Source responded: *"Question is inappropriate."*

The client, perhaps not realizing that the connection had been greatly impaired, asked about a child mentioned early in the reading.

The Source responded: *"Negativity is overwhelming. Must release the instrument."* My hand went to my heart in an effort to soothe the pain. Joe Chavez opened his mouth, but was overruled by a higher authority he could not see.

"Energy expended." And with those words, I was abruptly out, no longer in an altered state.

◆ ◆ ◆

We rode away in the car in an unnatural silence, Fr. Di Benedetto and I. The quivering in my stomach had subsided, only to be replaced by an acute feeling of hollowness in my chest. I had experienced this before, usually when the reading was prolonged and my reserves of energy were exhausted. This time, however, I knew that the images conjured up by the question Mr. Chavez had asked had accelerated the state and plunged me into a dismal frame of mind.

I thought about the other NARA II clients for whom I'd read. Their sensitivity and willingness to listen had made it easy for us to develop a rapport. Each and every one had seemed to want help and encouragement, even if the idea of full health and freedom from addiction was illusory to them, even if what we were talking about eluded their comprehension. Not one had projected malevolence, none but Joe Chavez.

My thoughts went to that eventful day in late January 1972, when Reverend Rita Sellman, a Christian minister and psychic development class teacher, asked me to take her place as the psychic/spiritual counselor for the drug program. She was ill, and both she and Fr. Di Benedetto—the coordinator of NARA II—were anxious to preserve continuity in the project. I had studied with Rev. Rita, as her students affectionately called her, for only twelve weeks. My experience was limited to practice in classes and the brief psychic "messages" given to people in the congregation at the Sunday service. It was not an impressive résumé, and my lack of self-confidence was inhibiting. On the other hand, my drive for personal validation overrode my fear of rejection and failure.

Fr. Di Benedetto's announcement in November 1971 that psychic counseling was available had been received by the clients without enthusiasm. The first reading was given without the subject being present; the second was a very short, in-person reading. It was the third reading that turned the tide.

On January 10, 1972, Rev. Rita Sellman advised Filiberto Yanez not to go out that night with his friend Manny Garcia. Fortunately for Filiberto, he listened and stayed home with his wife. The next morning, Manny was found dead, his throat cut. This event established credibility in the counseling project and from that point on the coordinator had little difficulty in lining up candidates for a psychic reading.

Cooperation notwithstanding, I had so little psychic counseling experience and a total unfamiliarity with the personality of a substance abuser that I didn't know what to expect. In my terror, I visualized sitting across from someone just out of prison and opening my mouth to speak but nothing would come. Largely because of my nervousness, Fr. Di Benedetto scheduled general program readings (without a client present) for the first few sessions, and these went fairly well.

My first face-to-face reading with a client was easier than anticipated, but I remained apprehensive before and uncertain after each session. The challenge of reaching genuine attunement was intimidating and the responsibility involved, overwhelming. As I met with more of the NARA clients, however, their obvious vulnerability and sincerity proved to be a stronger draw than the stress was a deterrent. Until today.

"Are there any more like him?" I asked, as Fr. Di Benedetto turned onto my street.

"A few, but they are avoiding you. Joe is the only one who doesn't see you as having a special 'in' with God. You know that they call you the 'blanca bruja,' the white witch. That's the good kind. After last week's incident with Rev. Rita, they have no doubt that you are working for the Deity. But I'm sorry about today; I had hoped that Joe would listen to the guidance and want to change his life."

The car pulled into my driveway. Before I stepped out, I told the priest I planned to transcribe last week's reading for Olga Salas, one of the few women clients in NARA II, the next day.

"Good. It is certain to have a positive effect on the Dallas and Washington people. It is just astounding enough to get their attention and take notice that there is something worthwhile going on here. So far they've been highly skeptical."

I asked if he was still being greeted with "stony silence" from his own staff and other department heads at the mental health center. His eyes twinkled and a devilish grin came across his beard-framed face. He didn't need to answer. I waved good-by as I turned and went into the house.

The next afternoon, with my two oldest children in school and the youngest down for a nap, I sat at the typewriter, plugged in the tape recorder, and began to assemble the paper and carbons that I would need. I mentally ran through the various offices involved to make certain eight copies were enough.

NARA II was an experimental treatment program created by Congress and funded by the federal Bureau of Prisons. The program had two phases: Incare, which provided service in the federal prisons, and Aftercare, to which the formerly incarcerated felons reported when released on parole status. The Bernalillo County Mental Health Center, in conjunction with the Department of Psychiatry of the University of New Mexico, oversaw the operation of NARA II.

Roméo Di Benedetto was a Roman Catholic priest who had found it increasingly difficult to reconcile his intuitive spiritual philosophy with the existing religious doctrines of the church. When in his early thirties he left the active priesthood with a reluctant and heavy heart, it was with the conviction that he had to live by his deepest principles. In 1970, he became the coordinator of the NARA II Aftercare Program. In late 1971, discouraged with the lack of favorable results from traditional counseling methods, including psychiatry, he requested permission from the national director of NARA II to conduct an experimental research project.

Fr. Di Benedetto proposed that psychic counseling be offered to the addicts and that reports—including transcripts of the readings—be furnished to the national office of the federal Bureau of Prisons in Washington, D.C.; the regional director in Dallas, Texas; the director of the Bernalillo County Mental Health Center; and the chief U.S. federal probation officer in Albuquerque.

Authorization was received for the conduct of a one-year pilot study to determine the value of using psychic/spiritual counseling as an additional alternate rehabilitation treatment therapy.

In a remarkable example of synchronicity, Rev. Rita Sellman and her husband, Dr. Lloyd Sellman, relocated from Phoenix to Albuquerque and announced the advent of their metaphysical church services and classes. Thus began an association and an experimental project that would amend the course of several lives, perhaps most visibly of all, mine.

In my personal meditations and during the psychic development class exercises and church work, I asked to be connected to my superconscious or Higher Self for guidance. As attunement took place, I would hear a soft, gentle, ethereal voice saying, "*I am here, I am ever with you, Barbara...*"

For my work with the NARA II program, however, I was to have a new source of guidance. The introduction was made during my second general program reading, which took place in a private home. Several people were present in addition to the priest and me. Upon opening up, I heard a mental voice distinctly different from that of my Higher Self.

The unfamiliar voice greeted us with warmth and humor and a first name, sounding almost like a gentleman on the other end of a telephone line, someone in physical life. I was caught off guard and my investigative processes were aroused. In response to the group's probing as to identity, we were given a surname which, when tacked onto the first name, was recognizable as having belonged to a man who recently lived on earth. I personally knew very little, however, about this individual's life.

As I relayed his message to the group, we realized that the psychic/spiritual counseling project had not come about in a haphazard manner, but was part of a higher plan. All of us were aware of the need for caution and discernment in psychic communication, and the quality of guidance received that night and through the next seven months convinced us as to the trustworthiness of this source. His humanitarianism and compassion were consistently evident in all of the NARA II readings.

The hum of the typewriter brought me back to the present and I typed: READING TWENTY-NINE. PSYCHIC COUNSELING FOR A NARA II CLIENT, OLGA SALAS. APRIL 18, 1972. I depressed the play button on the recorder, slipped the headphones over my ears, and listened to my own voice speaking from that place of Silence deep within.

It was easy to visualize Olga Salas as I transcribed the description of her former life as an Indian woman and the decision to kill herself rather than face dishonorment in the quarters of white men. Although Olga was of Hispanic extraction in this life, I could see genetic traces of an Indian lineage in her face, her long black hair, and her bearing. Slender as a silver birch and timid like a reed in shallow water, Olga Salas must have been beautiful in the natural setting that once was the heritage of Indian people.

Because the suicide was the result of a cruel captivity— and in recognition of her principles—she was not assigned undue karma. She chose the present life, availing herself of a captivity in drug addiction and vowing prior to this incarnation that she would free herself of this entrapment and lead others through and out of slavery.

I shook her image from my mind and typed on, noting the guidance that Olga was not using drugs at this time and the references to other attributes and qualities. The Source advised Olga to stay with her companion for six more months so that he might further strengthen his resolve to stay clean of drugs by observing her. And then, her time with him completed, she could go on to build her future with another, one with whom she would have spiritual compatibility and more happiness than she had ever known.

The Source then spoke of her courage and fortitude, " . . . *the sensitivity and spirituality which evolved through many lives . . . but were crushed to the greatest degree in the taking of her own life as a Mohican . . . still there in the inner recesses of the soul, but must be brought out through meditation and contemplation. Simply ask God to help you consciously remember and let those soul qualities arise which you will need to carry on this life's work."*

Guidance was given about Olga's children and the difficulties in her current relationship. And then came time for questions.

> Olga: "I need some advice and guidance for Eloy."
>
> (Note: Eloy Ramirez was Olga's friend from childhood days. He was also in the program. By his efforts to stay off drugs and out of trouble, he had earned the opportunity to work as the director of a halfway house located in the southern part of the state. His record had been considered a significant credit to NARA II.)
>
> Source: *"Eloy is fixing on heroin. He is using. He also is in danger from adverse influences . . . "*

As I repeated the words, I realized on a conscious level that if this pronouncement were true, heavy consequences could occur for Olga's friend. The enormity of this responsibility unnerved me, but I stayed connected and the reading continued through several additional—but, thankfully, un-complicated—questions and responses.

The worry engendered by the revelation of Mr. Ramirez's return to the use of drugs apparently consumed excessive energy. My closing statement was simply, "The Light is gone; I've lost it."

As I pulled the last page with its thick wad of carbons and copies from my ancient IBM, I recalled the relief I felt when the coordinator called me the day after the reading to confirm the guidance. Mr. Ramirez, alerted by the NARA grapevine, had responded to his parole officer's request for a urine sample by admitting that he had indeed been using drugs for the preceding three months.

It was this guidance that the coordinator was counting on to sufficiently impress the national and regional NARA II offices and secure authorization of the psychic counseling project beyond 1972.

Although for the most part, liaison personnel in the national and regional offices remained aloof from the project, a few were intrigued enough to send Fr. Di Benedetto personal questions to be asked in their behalf. One liaison person newly assigned to Albuquerque scoffed initially, but later had several personal readings away from the NARA II offices.

Sadly, at least one member of the local NARA II office did not support Fr. Di Benedetto's experimental project, but instead considered the readings to be a "betrayal" of the clients' privacy. Whether this staff member discouraged any clients from having a reading is unknown.

A number of the NARA II clients wanted guidance, but did not want an in-person reading. These clients were invited to give their questions to the coordinator to be placed during a general program reading. Fr. Di Benedetto would relay the resulting guidance to the client privately as soon as possible following the session. The coordinator also took the opportunity to ask in the general program sessions how he could more effectively help clients who had not come forward with questions.

We normally held the readings at the mental health center or in my living room. One reading was held in a guard's office at the Bernalillo county jail. However, the level of anxiety, anger, and other negative energies present created such an oppressive atmosphere that it took more than twenty minutes and intense prayer for a connection to be made with the Source. Maintaining attunement until all of the client's questions were answered was quite a challenge.

Building the conduit, reaching attunement, and delivering the guidance required an inordinate amount of my energy. The Source instructed me to meditate a total of three hours for every hour spent in giving a NARA II reading. This meant that when we held two psychic sessions a week, as was usual, I was to meditate for a minimum of six hours (not all at once) to avoid depleting my energy reserves. I was also to allow a minimum of eight hours, and preferably a full day, between readings.

When a client or participant was depressed or exceptionally tense, or if there was an emotional reaction to the guidance, I often had to struggle to maintain attunement. Fr. Di Benedetto was vigilant in this regard. He supplemented my energy level by holding his hands toward me, palms outward, visualizing the flow of energy for perhaps ten minutes. Nevertheless, I would be physically and mentally tired for an hour or two following a reading.

My frame of mind affected my stamina as well. Long-standing marital stress and my personal insecurities fostered an underlying depression that occasionally rose to the surface. When this happened, it took longer to secure a connection with the Source. Here, too, the coordinator's contributions as a battery were vital.

Time and time again, I would be cautioned that I was not meditating enough nor adequately rebuilding energy through balance in my life style. Sources are not allowed to overuse an instrument, according to guidance I received in a personal meditation. First and foremost, an instrument's well-being must be protected.

Fr. Di Benedetto and I were both advised repeatedly by the Source to avoid emotional involvement in our communications and relationships with the NARA II clients. We were told that personal involvement contributed significantly to the energy drain. We would reach more clients if we could remain *"healthfully and lovingly detached."*

As the summer months of 1972 neared and the school year ended, it became increasingly difficult to find quiet time and space for six hours of meditation a week. I had begun to read for people in the private sector as well, albeit not more than one a week. My days were full, with little time for recreation. In July, caution turned into warning. I was told that if I didn't adhere to the requirement for replenishing my energy, I'd be "shut down."

On August 4, I gave an unusually long reading for the program, with Fr. Di Benedetto and an attorney in attendance. The reading went smoothly, as both men were excellent batteries. On August 7, the lawyer asked for a supplemental reading. Ten minutes in, the Source said, "*The door will now close for the next seven weeks. It will open then only if you follow guidance."* With that decree, the mental communication ended, the force field abated, and attunement dissolved. My return to everyday consciousness was unusually expeditious. I knew I'd been chastised and I knew it was serious. I was more than a little embarrassed.

My personal meditations were also affected during this time. Try as I might, I could not perceive one word or thought while in the Silence. As dismaying as this situation was—and I did worry about permanency—when the door reopened almost seven weeks later, an unanticipated but rewarding benefit had materialized. I was able at last to let go of all doubts about the reality of guidance coming from outside of my own mind. At various times during the previous year, I had agonized over this question.

Furthermore, the sabbatical afforded me an opportunity to pause and reflect on my work with NARA II and the clients. While to my way of thinking, the responsibility was awesome and other challenges disconcerting, when I saw a light go on in eyes that beforehand were dull and lifeless, I thanked God for using me.

I felt led to review the readings I had given for the program from January through July. As I pored over the transcripts, I was increasingly impressed with the range of information received. Guidance frequently addressed both healing the child within *and* rearing the children in the family. More than one child in spirit, perhaps miscarried or aborted, made its presence known to me so that I could assure the client of its continued existence, its love, and—when appropriate—its forgiveness.

Guidance was offered regarding relationships. It was always emphasized that supportive companionship was critical to a client's recovery. A few spouses asked for and received readings. Clients were urged to break with pre-prison associates and to seek new and wholesome friendships.

Reinforcement of strengths and the recognition of talents and abilities, some perhaps dormant or forgotten, comprised a large part of each reading. Most important, and often the most eloquent, was the guidance that encouraged clients to *believe* in their potential, the accessibility of their spiritual resources, and to have faith in their birthright as children of a loving God.

Past-life information was given only when relevant or when it served to explain a client's deeper drives and emotions. The description of a negative life was invariably followed by a positive one. This was clearly illustrated in a reading given in March 1972.

Source: *"Mike Terrazas has been through similar circumstances in several previous lives. One involved opium addiction in a Chinese incarnation in which vapors also induced hallucinatory experiences, but in a subsequent life he conquered another type of narcotic by his own free will, against almost insurmountable obstacles. He overcame that particular enslavement and let himself be used as a guinea pig in medical research, thereby availing his country (the U.S.A.) of ... valuable information. He did so unselfishly and gained much in that life."* It was given that Mike had returned in the present life to show others the way to freedom.

Several readings revealed a thought-provoking correlation between a former life and one's current experience. Raul Rojas was NARA II's loner, isolating himself whenever and however he could. According to his reading, Raul had been a noted Russian author who *"stayed free of entrapment but was exiled by the Russian politicos for ... treasonous attitudes and behavior, but which were in reality the writings and attitudes of an exponent of God's design for freedom of the whole man ... The physical exile promoted bitterness, frustration, and resentment."*

Jerry Ortega had been a Royal Canadian Mountie who needlessly and cruelly used a whip on prisoners. In the present life, he was reaping what he had sown, as he frequently complained about police brutality.

As I turned to the transcripts for May and June, I recollected with a grimace the exasperation that both Fr. Di Benedetto and I had experienced following an unusual psychic session. The lengthy guidance received in this particular reading did not seem to relate to the client about whom we'd asked. During the reading, I was shown the face of a different client, but not being in the conscious state, I did not try to match face with name. I was too busy listening to the Source and concentrating on delivery of the guidance. In the supplemental readings hastily held in an effort to clear our confusion, we were told by the Source that the

mix-up and non-notification of the change were deliberate.

The client whom we had asked about was on his way
back to prison, and the client on whom guidance had been
received was *"in greater need of help."* We were to *"reorder
... priorities and deal not with those on their way to prison,
but with those who can still avoid that fate ... The lesson
here is that when we on this side feel that the time we spend
in communication needs to be directed to a different subject,
we will give you what we feel is of overriding importance ...
communication, while it seems free, easy, and almost always
available, is a precious commodity not to be expended on
cases which cannot be directly helped ... "*

Our discomfiture was ignored because *"We needed to at-
tract the attention of both the instrument and the ...
coordinator, and we seemed to be unable to accomplish this
in any less spectacular way with any degree of effectiveness
... We are chastening both of you now, perhaps too harshly in
your view. But what we are doing in effect is whittling down
two very fine pieces of grand old wood, quality wood, into
exacting, effective, knowledgeable, loving, reliable servants
of God ... "*

The gentle chiding—and on occasion stern admonishment—did not impair the bond that had evolved between
the Source and me. I did not realize the depth of the bond.
At this point in my life, I had not heard the term "codependency," nor was I able to recognize that my emotional
needs were symptoms of deep distress.

On one deceptively peaceful and balmy day in May, the
kind of day that lulls you into confident complacency, Fr. Di
Benedetto came to my home for a general program reading. Toward the end of the session, he asked, as he normally
did, "Is there any general guidance to be given at this time?"

Source: *"Your open-mindedness and understanding
and acceptance of our help without skepticism, with-*

out undue evaluation, has been most gratifying ... because of these factors, we are able to work more closely with you and to bring you more finely accountable and detailed guidance. Have faith. You are all doing your parts; we are very proud and happy. There will be a change of guides for ... "

I was devastated. Although I had not an inkling beforehand, I knew with certainty at this moment that the next words to flow into my head would complete the unanticipated, unwanted announcement.

For seven months, despite the anxiety and pressures incumbent with this work, something wonderful had been happening in my life that gave me a critically needed sense of worth and self-esteem.

That this Source, eloquent, wise, and renowned, had selected *me* to help him contribute in such a unique way still seemed incredible, but I had begun to rely upon hearing his voice as my reason for living. And now I was going to be abandoned. Again. Suddenly, from out of an inner nowhere, I saw my father's face and then my grandpop's face, and I knew I'd been abandoned before.

The emotion that swiftly swept through me threatened to catapult me out of the altered state, disconnecting me from the Source I loved and needed—perhaps forever. And so, although I wanted desperately to stave off the words that I knew were waiting in the wings, I resisted, with all the force I could muster, the elevator ride down to everyday consciousness. I held on, sobbing and wiping away the tears as I allowed the communication to continue.

Source: *"I appreciate the sentiment, but I must leave you before too long to go on to other work of a similar nature. There will be another more highly evolved than I who will continue working with you. I, too, must progress. You have been a most willing instrument,*

anxious to do well and harmonious, more than ad-
equate for our needs. Your (work) is just beginning. I will
not leave you just yet. My thoughts and prayers will be
ever with you and you can call upon me when the need
arises ... "

The impending loss followed me around like a tarpaulin
hanging over my head. But I was determined to grow
through whatever came my way in life, and the love that
enfolded me in the Silence during each day's meditation
helped me to accept the transition. The readings continued
to be given, and the quality of guidance remained exceptional. I did not ask the identity of the new communicant,
but only for reassurance that all was in divine order. This I
received.

In late summer, the director who had originally approved
the psychic/spiritual counseling project transferred into
another job. The new regional coordinator took a dim view
of the project, and Fr. Di Benedetto soon received a letter,
which read in part:

" ... It has come to my attention that in the past we
have been paying for the services of a Mrs. Barbara L.
(Paulin) as a "Medium/Counselor." I regret that I cannot endorse this kind of treatment under the guise of
psychotherapy. Therefore, effective October 1, 1972,
we will no longer pay for services rendered ... "

The coordinator responded with a letter explaining that
the change in compensation from $8.00 to $15.00 per hour
was due to my having taken over the transcription of the
readings to ensure confidentiality. The total bill for seven
months was less than $700.

Fr. Di Benedetto's letter concluded with: "Upon reading
(the transcripts) ... you would quickly become aware of
their lofty spiritual nature and the powerful hope that is

given to the clients. General and very specific recommendations for problem solving are also offered . . . You did not proscribe the utilization of (Mrs. Paulin's) services, and she has generously offered to give of her time and labor without material recompense. Initially, by the way, she did not want compensation. It was I who offered to pay her for the time, labor, and services rendered, thinking it just. I hope to soon discuss this matter with you over the phone . . . "

We continued to request guidance on the psychic/spiritual project through December 1972, holding the sessions in private homes.

Although Fr. Di Benedetto hoped for a reversal of the regional coordinator's decision, it did not happen. In 1973, the priest's contract was not renewed.

In Fr. Di Benedetto's words: "The experience of this pilot study has led me to conclude that each addicted person has a unique reason for having become addicted, and that this uniqueness can be neither identified nor sufficiently understood without examining past lives and the lessons they have come to learn in this lifetime. I believe that a spiritual-psychic rehabilitation program is worth pursuing, even though the obstacles are gargantuan."

In April 1989, more than fifteen years after our collaboration, Roméo Di Benedetto sent me several questions to be asked of Higher Consciousness on his behalf. He was considering writing a book on the NARA II experimental project. I was happy to comply.

Question: What were the best results from the NARA II effort that we can identify and promote?

Source (to Di Benedetto): *"The courage you exemplified and what you learned about human nature. Your ability, at times, to love regardless of the externals . . . (and) to identify with the character flaws, inhibitions, and fears so obviously apparent in people living a totally different kind of life . . . You touched many lives . . . Some of those beings are not there but are here now. While you may not have saved their lives and while they may have buckled under . . . even while you were still there, they are not buckling under now.*

" . . . (Of) the seeds that were sown among the clients: some lay dormant for many, many years; some blossomed minimally; very few seeds blossomed anywhere near the maximum . . . but not a word was truly lost, especially the words of encouragement. Also, there were several in the hierarchy (of the federal structure) . . . whose minds were opened just a trifle, but enough so that when they met others echoing the philosophy you follow, they . . . took notice . . . Two people in particular have been impressed to . . . serve their fellow man with more Light than levity and without judgment.

" . . . We will say very clearly that Barbara Paulin may never have achieved the level of self-confidence that came to her in those years without your assistance and support . . . and the fulfillment as well as the ability to overcome frightful fear, insecurity, and reluctance during that work. In some of the eyes on this side, the work that was done for her in her work, especially in self-concept and self-confidence, was almost phenomenal."

Higher Consciousness was right. When the NARA II psychic counseling project ended and 1972 came to a close, I had indeed gained in self-esteem and confidence. I had overcome my reluctance to risk failure. Although I hadn't quite mastered the "frightful fear" and insecurity, I had turned them from obstacles into opportunities for growth.

But the most remarkable and precious result of my work with NARA II was the inner knowing, with every fiber of my being, that I was doing *what I came to do.* And in the doing, I was putting my life in divine order.

I had found my path of promise, path of peace.

On Walden, War, and
the Wandering Wounded

CONCURRENT WITH MY RECRUITMENT AS THE
spiritual/psychic counselor (replacing Rev. Rita Sellman)
for the NARA II experimental project in January 1972, there
was a comfortable coming-together of a number of people
who were attending the Sellmans' "Gateway to Light" services and classes. We gathered on Friday evenings in one
home or another to share our quest for spiritual growth.
Since Roméo Di Benedetto (who later married) and his wife
were part of this group, it seemed a natural and convenient
setting for several general program readings, the first ones I
gave for NARA II.

We had met for only a few Friday nights when we realized the significance of our mutual interests and goals. Enthusiasm was clearly evident with regard to the readings, the opportunity the coordinator had presented, and his courage in seeking federal sanction of psychic counseling. The initial seven of us rapidly coalesced into a dedicated, united group.

In mid-February, the group was advised by the Source that we had been brought together to "*form an alliance to preclude harassment and to enable the giving of service without fear of legal entanglement.*" It was understood that the organization would sponsor my work with NARA II. We were further guided to incorporate as "*quickly, simply, and quietly as possible.*" Since one member of our cluster of inquiring minds was a practicing attorney (the Universe thinks of everything), this was accomplished in record time.

Settling on a name for our organization took longer than the actual incorporation. The Source was less than impressed with our first choice, "Adults and Youth Against Drug Addiction" (AYUDA). Our second choice, "Metaphysics, Inc.," fared no better.

We then turned to the guidance that had been given. Upon noting that the word *alliance* had been used more than once in reference to our group, we settled on "The Alliance for Health and Wholeness, Incorporated." The Source responded: "*Excellent, excellent! We hoped you would use your heads. (The others) were all right, but spirituality is so much more implicit in the words 'wholeness' and even 'health,' for what is physical health without the health of the Higher Self? We are most satisfied.*"

By March 1, 1972, we were chartered by the State of New Mexico as a not-for-profit corporation with the following purposes:

A. To promote general health and welfare of the society, especially among its most unacceptable, alienated, and rejected persons by use of all knowledge and methods of healing and amelioration of the entire man; methods including, but not limited to, meditation, spiritual healing, and guidance, counseling, and all legally licensed skills and healing arts.

B. To educate by courses of instruction in any of the above which are not so programmed, controlled, or licensed by this state or nation, and to provide recognition and certification upon the completion of such courses which are not under the licensing authority or power of this state or county.

C. To promote by person-to-person and group methods the development of religious attitudes.

On the heels of the instruction to incorporate came startling guidance asserting the need for a *"unique treatment program and drug abuse rehabilitation facility."* The concept excited and inspired us. Our pool of talented and motivated members was growing. We took up the challenge, assigned responsibilities, and prepared to develop a proposal for the innovative treatment concept.

Once again, we were confronted with the need for a name. After reviewing the Source's description of an ideal site for a facility, we agreed upon "Walden," perhaps in an unconscious effort to tap into the serenity for which New England's Walden Pond was known.

What follows are pertinent excerpts from guidance received in 1972 with regard to the Walden Proposal.

> *" Think about this. Would you not want your son to have the most meaningful, worthwhile opportunity for rehabilitation? Would you want him to go through incarceration after incarceration, surmounting no problems, only accumulating more neuroses because of the side effects? Or would you prefer that he have the opportunity to be placed at a facility where people truly care and where he could be taught again to believe in himself and to believe that Christ resides within his*

heart, as He does all men and all women?

"This theme is a simple one, but very profound, and it is at the core of the truth of the rehabilitative process. (The premise is) the building up, the giving back of confidence and faith in self, instead of the constant tearing, tearing, tearing apart of one's morale. In the tearing apart, the guilt grows and grows and is so hard to diminish . . .

"True, there are some patients who would require additional care, perhaps medical or psychiatric help, but basically it will be the spiritual restoration, revitalization, realignment—the bringing forth of the inner knowledge that God is within their very heart and soul, and that they can be just as productive and as happy and worthwhile a citizen as anyone else—that is going to have the greatest effect.

"We would advocate a facility along the lines of a sanitarium in days of old where tubercular patients could recuperate. Much rest, some exercise, and a large dose of meditative opportunity and instruction in same, spiritual and metaphysical teachings to be offered where desired. No coercion should ever be made in this area. The dark night of the soul involves so much personal hell; you cannot expect these men to adjust to 'civilization' as you know it in a few months and in some cases, even a year.

"A country or mountain atmosphere would be encouraged. There should be no community within fifteen or twenty miles outside of any city limits.

"Meditation is the key; we cannot be too strong on this. First, you would have to let them simmer down, quiet down, and think. The addict's physical organism and mental structure has accelerated to such a degree, frequency-wise, that deceleration or realignment cannot be made by shifting sharply from one life style to another . . . There must be a transition period, a leveling

off. Incarceration cannot work because the changes are too abrupt.

" ... Light has a natural inclination to radiate, permeate, and penetrate. It cannot do so in the incarceratory environment. There is a conflict of emotion, a longing, a yearning to be out and free, and yet the soul has inner knowledge that the time must be spent as programmed for the present. It is demoralizing and depressing, particularly when one begins to recognize, realize, and revitalize one's very inner existence and wants to proceed with the ... assignment created, accepted, and embarked upon almost at the moment of conception of the vehicle ... It will ever be so when these men are incarcerated along with others, whose misdeeds, lower mentalities, criminal or deviated minds are thrust upon them as the only companions they are allowed to have.

"Until someone with some common sense and the ability to do something about it, such as to help with funding, to crusade, to support effectively and efficiently in the right quarters, recognizes the need for the spiritual rehabilitation of these men and others like them—even those mentally afflicted through no fault of their own or entrapped in addictions of other kinds— until the spiritual aspects of treatment are recognized and incorporated, and these men and women are given the opportunity for this treatment, you will not see any significant success in any type of rehabilitation program. Period."

The Walden Proposal, with facts and figures as well as guidance extracted from the readings, was finalized in 1974. The proposal was sent across the country to foundations, funding sources, drug abuse program professionals, scientists, parapsychologists, certain psychiatrists, and a few well-respected and successful psychics. One-third of the recipients responded. Without exception, feedback was favorable, but no offers of funding were received.

We went to the Source for guidance about potential funding.

> *"We are reluctant to prognosticate that which has any dependency upon the minds of those involved in the administration of your government in ... Washington, D.C.*
>
> *"Would that we could find more clear, spiritual, vibrant, and willing channels in that city to receive and attempt to effectuate our guidance. But the mist that hangs over Washington is one of such negativity, political intrigue, (the) propagation of self-images, concern only for personal recognition, and exploitation of industrial growth and profit, that it is most difficult to penetrate indeed.*
>
> *"We would like to add that those spiritual guides who are in need of double duty or disciplinary action are the ones that are assigned to the Washington, D.C., areas, and I am most anxious to continue progressing with your group so that I may not be detailed to the land of politicians."*

The Alliance held together for seven years following the demise of the NARA II experimental project. Members served on various community and city councils and committees mandated to inform the public about drug abuse prevention and available treatment options. We visited halfway houses and other drug treatment programs to talk about metaphysical philosophy, teach meditation, and demonstrate spiritual healing techniques.

Whenever our spirits lagged and doubts dogged our efforts, the Source would convey his own special brand of encouragement. *"I speak to those we cherish and on whom we must rely, on whom our very progress depends. Were you not capable—had you all not been leaders—had you all not*

received special schooling for what you are undertaking, we
would not be allowed to spend time with you ... The stuff of
which you are made must not be tarnished, but must with-
stand all stress."

Albuquerque is a fairly progressive town with respect to
differing life styles and religions. In early 1973, the Alliance
obtained permission from a Protestant church to hold a
metaphysical worship service in their sanctuary on Sunday
afternoons. (Rev. Rita and Dr. Lloyd Sellman had relocated
their church to Tucson, Arizona, before the close of 1972.)
The Alliance's Sunday service presented an unexpected and
uncomfortable test of harmony for our members. Where
our teamwork had been remarkable in other endeavors, our
spirit of unity nearly dissolved in the worship service setting.

The next guidance session yielded an admonishment
from the Source: *"Only in unity can there be no division; only*
in harmony can there be no derision ... Forgive those whom
you have wronged as well as those who wrong you. 'An in-
triguing thought,' the instrument is thinking. Think about
it. There is no inconsistency here."

We scurried once again to the early readings on the
group's purposes and brought our primary focus back to
service to others. For the next few years, the Alliance concentrated on offering classes to the public in metaphysics,
meditation, and psychic development. These were very well
received and attended.

Gradually, as members changed direction or moved
away, the Alliance changed in leadership and thrust. All
seven founders as well as Roméo Di Benedetto and his family relocated by the end of the seventies. I've since become
aware that this is typical when a group of people have
bonded and grown while endeavoring to contribute in a
spiritually uplifting way to the community. After a period of
"training by trial and error" and a moderate amount of experience, the workers may be scattered (by Higher design)

to begin anew in dormant terrain. In this context, being relegated to the outposts may indeed be a tribute and could be taken as such.

The Alliance for Health and Wholeness, Inc., remained viable until 1990, when the last board of directors concluded that its work was done. It continues to exist in spirit.

During the period of time that I was connected with the first Source for the NARA II readings, I would often be moved by the depth and intensity of his compassion. This would be conveyed not only by his words, but by the feelings that overshadowed me as I was receiving and relaying. More than once, I sensed his tears merging with my own.

The following excerpts from readings given in 1972 represent a few of the more impassioned passages I will not soon forget.

On the subject of war:

> "Never will there be world peace while one weapon is in position to fire against another country. There is only one way, and it remains in the hearts of many but on the tongues of few — and that is, love toward every other living soul on the planet earth or in any dimension surrounding any planet in any galaxy.
>
> "Until there is no room for anything in the heart of any man but love, we will have strife, we will have war. I cannot help but feel deep sorrow for those who feel that war is profitable in any measure: for the economy, for industry, for employment, for vengeance against those who would ravage an underdog nation, (or) for any reason at all. They are so wrong. If they could just replace that desire for blood, glory, and profit with love for one another, with love for the Christ within each man, what a beautiful world this would be.

"I cannot comment other than this. I am sorely distressed and have chosen to work in another type of war, as I have been (doing) with you now for these months. Please excuse my reluctance to say any more on this subject."

On the war against drugs:

"The problem lies deep within society, deep within the individual will. True, the genuine solutions are very difficult to foresee, and very time-consuming, but there is no better way to resolve the problem than to seek out the cause at the very core and attack it at the core, even if it is the long way around.

"In some instances, just the restoration of a man's self-confidence and belief in himself, and hope for a productive, happy life the rest of this life, is all that is needed—and all of the orthodox psychiatry or incarceration or any other type of mechanical rehabilitation is simply wasted effort.

"The solution lies in alleviating or removing the need for those to return to, to resort to, or to desire the use of drugs.

"It involves a turning back to God, a turning ON with God, in spirituality. It involves removing the stresses. It will take years and years and years, but there is no other way."

On the "wandering wounded," as the Source lovingly called the clients of NARA II:

"He feels completely alienated, cut off from God and many others who would have meaning to him. His gypsy-like existence is a façade manufactured to ensure self-resistance. He cannot tolerate the emergence of the true self. He cannot cope with his innermost feelings,

but then, this is the story of all those addicted.

"He has given up; the fight is gone. He's waiting to be blown by the wind, one way or another—it matters not. He needs hospitalization—long, intensive therapy, relaxation, and restimulation. He needs Walden, right now!

"The damage they have done to themselves is extensive. It cannot be repaired overnight, but with faith and trust in God, the road can become shorter and less cluttered with detours or painful crevices, sharp inclines and declines. They . . . have surely been through hell—a hell of their own making—and one which God would not levy upon them.

"It is a long, dreary road back to God from whence they came. A very difficult, lonesome, dark journey. Even those who seem to decline help want within to call out and accept it.

"It is true that this experience is meant to be a growth experience, but the pull of the earth plane, the pressures put upon them, and too many days in the wilderness are rendering some unable to retrieve the spirituality and awareness without which they are truly in doubt. In other words, not only free will but also environment creates adversity and affects plans. Perhaps strength has been depleted too soon. Many factors affect a soul's sojourn, keeping him from his appointed rounds . . . You do not always nor do those in your environment find the right conditions for what you would hope to accomplish . . .

"The men of whom you speak and many others within your purview are men of such light, basically, although it is temporarily obscured by the gray mists of . . . the environment in which they've placed themselves for the past some years . . .

"Oh, how we would like to help these men . . . if only we could strip away the outer garments, get to the core

of the Christ within, revitalize their systems, realign their thinking, reprogram their brains with the truth. They all feel so hopeless, the world looks so black to them.

"We grieve for these men more than a mother grieves for a dying child, for that child comes back to a spiritual nest and is borne away by angels. We grieve for those who think—who truly believe—that physical death is the end of it all, that once they have gotten into the personal hell and cannot extricate themselves, that living or trying is useless. But, oh how wrong they are!

"For all there is, is of God. And those that we want so desperately to help most likely once offered their love and help to us. If only we could get this message imbedded irretrievably in the hearts of men that all are truly brothers, not one is better than another in the full scheme of things. Only by striving for God-realization in unison—by helping others—can we all expect to reunite with God completely again."

On judging others:

"All who are of God, even the lowest of God, are of God. Do not judge those who sit beside us. Do not judge the man in the bar, the prostitute, the addict, the 'dredges of your society,' as you are inclined to say. A wise man once said, 'But for the grace of God go I.' It is only for God to know what is in the soul ... you cannot and should not clinically analyze the mistakes another has made, but only love him. Give him your hand; give him your cloak if need be. Teach him to inquire at the temple daily so that he may know his personal God. It is well to comprehend the motives behind the problem ... but in so doing, do not judge him.

"You have all been through your own peculiar hells; maybe not in this life, but in another. You have all

brought yourselves through. You all knew when you incarnated in this life what you wanted to do. You brought with you the ability to . . . lead others through what you were able to overcome yourselves, though perhaps not in the same manner. Perhaps it is not the drug problem you struggled with, but you have all struggled nevertheless. Think.

"We are all responsible for our brother's growth and it is only by extending and expanding that hand and that love to our brother, no matter how derelict he may seem, that we ourselves are going to grow. Have we given you enough food for thought?"

Are not we all, at some time in our lives and to some degree, a wandering wounded one—not seeing our Light, not knowing our strength, not looking within for God?

As I listened while the Source guided and encouraged the NARA II clients in the fifty-some readings I gave while I was with the project, I could not help but see my own needs and defenses in a startlingly clear way. While in the altered state, at times—not always—I was able to view myself from a different perspective, almost with objectivity, with detachment. It was as though part of me was engaged in conversation with the Source and another part of me was observing my personality or my life. I could isolate, then, the unhealthy patterns—and not retreat into denial.

All prisons aren't obvious. Many do not have bars, but they are prisons just the same. I began to see my addiction to the presence and approval of certain others in my life as crippling and confining rather than as an indication of my "niceness."

One of the greatest surprises, which proved to be the greatest incentive to change, was my ability to relate with the fears and insecurities expressed by many of the NARA II clients. The only difference was that I was beginning to manage mine and dream dreams, while they were still immobilized by nightmares.

Of the benefits, then, that I perceived through my work with NARA II and the Alliance, I would say that first and foremost, I began my own healing journey within, in earnest.

There but for the grace of God go I.

In Reflection:
My Own Wounds and Walls

I ARRIVED BY HOME DELIVERY ON A CRISP OCTOBER day in 1934, in the midst of this country's Great Depression and between two devastating world wars. My father, John Edward Adams, along with hundreds of thousands of people in the work force, was struggling without job security, benefits, or representation, subject to the whims of foremen and monthly profit sheets. My mother, Mabel Redman Adams, was a homemaker, an "unskilled" member of society.

Home was an apartment in a row house that stagnated in the shadow of a monument erected to commemorate the

1776 Battle of Trenton, in which George Washington scored a crucial victory over the British. New Jersey was very proud of its role in the Revolutionary War. The looming structure was a fitting symbol for the battle of wills taking place within the Adams household. George may have been able to cross the swollen and ice-clogged Delaware in a blizzard, leading his weary and worn-out warriors nine miles to overcome the Hessians—but John Adams, my father, was never able to fully dominate Mabel.

Perhaps, on some level of consciousness, I was aware of the conflicts in the marriage as well as the hard times that had fallen upon our country. I soon tried to go back from whence I came, as evidenced by my baptism in a hospital, with the Episcopal church's last rites being administered at the age of six weeks.

It seems that there was an alarming incompatibility in my blood, which had the doctors baffled since both parents and I tested O-positive. A consulting hematologist finally diagnosed it to be a rare condition that afflicted only first-borns. After much debate, it was decided that my blood should be completely changed, a relatively new, high-risk procedure.

For the exchange transfusions, my father lay on an adjoining table, connected to me by tubes and needles—and whatever bond existed between us at that early stage. The life-preserving fluid coursed from his left arm, slowed, and gently found its way into the heel of my right foot, the inside of my right arm at the elbow, and the base of my spine. Shortly thereafter, I developed pneumonia in both lungs, but once again a stronger will than mine prevailed.

The bond that was forged that day would weaken over the years, yet come full circle and intensify again—ironically, in another hospital.

An auspicious beginning it was not. Added to the illnesses was insult, since I wasn't born with the legendary caul over my face and thus I cannot claim star-crossed psychic status—nor any other silent symbol to presage a charmed or charming life.

My parents could scarcely have been more mismatched. My mother's nature was effervescent and fun loving, although she was not irresponsible. My father was intensely emotional, intensely protective and controlling, and deeply insecure. He worried about everything and took on responsibility for all.

Dad was born in 1906, the youngest of seven children, five girls and two boys. When Dad was two, his mother and an infant boy both died during the birthing process. His father remarried, and the new wife took such a dislike to young John that she did as little good for him as possible and much that was demeaning. She would not buy him shoes, but insisted that he wear his sisters' cast-offs to school. Eventually, as the girls married and moved into their own homes, my father went to stay with one or another until he joined the army at age seventeen.

Following his discharge from the army, Dad went to live with his favorite sister and brother-in-law in Bernardsville, New Jersey. There, at age twenty-three, he was happy and confident, finally able to plan for the future.

One beautiful Indian summer day in 1929, he took a car to the blacksmith shop to make some repairs when a gasoline tank on the rear of the automobile exploded. His left arm was nearly severed at the elbow joint, but skilled surgeons were able to save it. This injury would later be a signal to me in both a dream and a psychic reading given by another person that it was indeed my father who was communicating long after he had died.

The accident did not deter John Adams from pursuing an occupation as an automobile mechanic, a skill and expertise that family and friends drew on until his death. Even when working full-time as a machinist for DeLaval Steam Turbine Company and driving weekends for an armored car service, my father found time to repair cars for other people.

Mabel Redman was born in Trenton in 1913 to a couple who migrated from Yorkshire, England, to the United States soon after they married. She was the youngest of three children. Her father, Ernest Redman, was a stately, handsome man. Kate Fox Redman was a homemaker, as one would expect of women of her era.

Although my grandparents were said to enjoy a little humor, they were somewhat afflicted with the British reserve when it came to communicating or expressing feelings. Their devotion to each other, however, was obvious to all who knew them. The Redman children were raised with care and concern, but largely without permission to cry or complain. "Children are meant to be seen and not heard" seemed to be the order of the day.

Mabel loved dancing, so much so that she and her best friend, May Sweeney, wheedled jobs out of the local Y.W.C.A. in exchange for full use of the facilities—including tap dancing. May wrote me in 1975, in a nostalgic look at their lifelong friendship, that "Mabel never remembered her left foot from her right foot. We couldn't afford tap shoes and we had no money . . . We used to buy soles at the five-and-ten-cent store and paste them on our shoes. We were thrown out of that class, but we did enjoy the pool and working in the locker room . . . "

When Mabel Redman met "Eddie" Adams, as he wanted to be called by friends and family, she was trim but well-rounded, with a full and pleasant face, hazel eyes, and light brown hair. She stood 5'3" in her stocking feet. He was 5'10" with dark brown hair, dark eyes, and a ruddy complexion. His broad shoulders and attentive manner conveyed quite aptly his desire to protect and care for her.

They eloped to Elkton, Maryland, in November 1933, and the appealing qualities that drew them together soon became appalling traits that threatened to push them apart. Mabel wasn't ready for the solemn settling down that marriage meant to Eddie. She felt stifled by his increasing possessiveness and the need to hold the reins. In turn, her need for autonomy and her lighthearted look at life frustrated and irritated him. John Edward Adams had never known what it was to be carefree.

When Mabel wanted to go to work to supplement their income, Eddie insisted she stay home, that he would provide. I was born, and my father took a second job. He prided himself on his sense of responsibility; he seemed to thrive on being "a family man." Dad loved having a baby in the house. They had three children in all, seemingly on a five-year plan. When I was five, Barry arrived. Five years later, Billy came along. Then the production line stopped.

Somewhere along the way, my father's deep-seated insecurities gained a greater hold, and the fear that my mother would someday leave him for someone else prompted frequent arguments. Nothing my mother would say seemed to alleviate his distrust, and it was to pervade the relationship for the rest of their years together.

My father was not physically abusive, but his verbal lacerations were withering. My mother and I bore the brunt of his disapproval and criticism. I'm certain he admonished my brothers when needed, but not with anger or inappropriate comments. He didn't overreact when Barry or Billy misbehaved. When he was displeased with me—and it didn't take much, as I was too scared to rebel—he would say, "You weren't born to us. We found you in a garbage dump, and we felt sorry for you and brought you home."

Once, when I was twelve, I frowned (it was probably more like pouting) when Dad said that I had to go with him and Mom on an errand. Undoubtedly, I didn't make his day, and he drove directly to the rear of the Giant Tiger Supermarket, stopped the car, and told me to go back where I belonged. All around me were huge steel drums full of garbage and rotting vegetables. All I could see and smell was trash. Was that all my father could see in me? I felt humiliated, but for once I did not cry. I didn't know where I was going, but I began to walk away—in the opposite direction of the car. He called me back and insisted that I get in, and reluctantly I did. But I must have thrown him a curve, as he never drove me there again.

About this time, my face began to break out—the first outward sign of the strong emotions within. I was always afraid, always anxious, always unsure of myself. I didn't know why, but I woke up afraid and I went to bed afraid. The word "afraid" would characterize the next forty years of my life.

We were Episcopalian, but Mom and Dad did not attend regularly. Barry, Billy, and I went to various Sunday school classes, always with the encouragement of our parents.

Mabel and Eddie Adams had more than a few friends, people who remained friends all their lives. They helped each other through crises and catastrophes and shared fun times as well. In the late 1940s, television was on the horizon but not yet in every home. On Friday nights, my parents would take the three of us to visit friends, or another family would visit us. The adults would play cards and the kids would play games, go roller skating, or attend a neighborhood movie. There was always an abundance of jokes, laughter, refreshments, and on occasion too much drinking.

There was a genetic predisposition to alcoholism and melancholia in the Adams family. Dad's only brother and one of his sisters were alcoholics, and both died in mid-life. Although I never saw my father drink other than during card games or on extended vacations, I believe that alcohol adversely affected his personality. Conversely, my mother, who did not have the personality traits usually associated with alcoholism, was at least a social drinker.

The best times we had and the best memories we made were the day trips for family recreation. We lived less than fifty miles from the Atlantic Ocean, and I can still visualize our one-car caravan wending its way to the beach at Bay Head, Beach Haven, or Asbury Park.

Dad had an old De Soto, and we'd load that car up with a large ice chest filled to the brim with sodas and sandwich makings, hot dogs, hamburger meat, and condiments. We'd take bundles of beach toys and a ball and bat, blankets, towels, and extra clothes, as well as extra kids from the neighborhood. A huge army-surplus rubber raft and inner tubes, along with the beach umbrella, were securely tied on the top of the car, and off we would go.

We called that car "Old Smokey." Steam invariably rose out of the hood of the car at the same point on every journey. Dad would stop and add water to the radiator, and we'd continue on our way. We usually went to Bay Head in those days, for we could cook on the beach, and it was never crowded. Its beauty was primitive and unspoiled.

Several trips and the better part of an hour were required to unload the car and trudge over the sand dunes to a place on the beach near the water. When we found our spot, the beach umbrella went up, the blankets went down, and the Noxema® went on.

Dad would drive a stake into the sand, put a long rope on it, and tie the other end of the rope to the rubber raft. We kids would sit in that bright yellow raft and ride in the surf to our heart's content. Dad grilled the hamburgers and hot dogs, and Mom dished out the best potato salad in the world.

We fished all the lakes and streams; we crabbed the bays and inlets; we picnicked in state parks and explored historic sites. There may not have been much money to spend, but such memories could only be bought with a love of nature and history, and that our parents had in abundance.

The pleasures of the spring and summer were countered by the strike typically called by the union in the fall. Dad would be laid off from DeLaval for three weeks to three months. With only $35 a week coming in from strike benefits, his part-time jobs multiplied, all juggled so that he had time at home as well. We all tried to make him slow down and stop worrying, but to no avail.

I can remember Mom's efforts to reassure Dad that things would work out all right, and they usually did. He ridiculed her attitude so much, though, that she finally stopped trying. No longer would she react to his brooding or criticism. In her words, she "Let it go in one ear and out the other." My brothers and I saw this change as giving Dad "the silent treatment." It only served to make matters worse, for he saw this as total rejection.

Living with Dad meant walking on eggshells. We never knew what would set him off; usually, it was something Mom said or did. We'd want her to stop ignoring him, and yet we knew she couldn't win the war. The tensions were often intolerable. May Sweeney asked my mother how she coped. Mom said, "I have a little room in my head without a door or window, and that's where I go." The trouble was that Barry, Billy, and I were trapped outside that room as well.

For respite and refuge, I grew closer to my grandparents, staying with them in Asbury Park for part of the summer. Grandpop, as I called him, introduced me to the works of Shakespeare and fostered my love of the written word.

In January 1949, my grandmother died from complications of a stroke. She and my grandfather had never spent a day apart. He was disconsolate in his grief and refused to attend the services. Grandpop moved in with us at Mom and Dad's insistence and spent his days walking the streets, lost in his thoughts and his pain. He had walked those same streets many a time wearing my grandmother's new shoes to "break them in" for her.

One morning about three months later, I awoke especially early for school and wondered where Grandpop was. He usually made oatmeal for my breakfast. Our family occupied the second floor of a brick house on Liberty Street in Trenton. We shared a cellar with downstairs neighbors. Looking for Grandpop, I bounced down the stairs to the first-floor foyer and opened the door to the basement.

Suddenly my legs were very heavy, and I moved down a

few steps in slow motion. I remember thinking that he could have gone to the corner store for supplies. As I reached the halfway point on the stairs, I glanced around, then I turned, and went back up to the apartment. I saw nothing out of the way, or so I thought for the next thirty-eight years.

When I came home from school that day, my father, eyes red and skin blotchy, met me at the door and told me as gently as he could that my beloved grandfather was dead. He had hanged himself with my jump rope from the rafters over the coal bin. That part of the basement was almost directly ahead of the stairs, but slightly to the right. A wall extended from the cement floor halfway up to the ceiling to keep the coal from spilling out of the bin.

My mother had also walked down those stairs, four-year-old Billy in tow, but said she saw him not. Bill remembers Mom turning quickly and prodding him back upstairs. Later, Dad said that the first-floor tenant found Grandpop and called the police.

Mom never spoke of her father's suicide after he was buried, and I never again saw her eyes without seeing the sorrow behind them. I came upon my father weeping in the basement, his hand gently caressing my grandparents' trunk, the only remaining relic of their sail from the British Isles a half-century earlier. My mother couldn't weep. She buried her depression and spent the rest of her life managing its entombment.

We had always been close, Mom and I, but now we became companionable. I was fourteen. We shared friends—age didn't matter—and we shared hours and hours of entertainment, mostly movies, musicals, and dramatic plays. What we didn't share were feelings. She simply could not talk about her heartaches, not with anyone, and I was too self-involved to persist.

About two months after Grandpop died, he called my name while I was walking near the house. I heard his voice, loud and clear, with my *physical* ears. No other words came.

I don't know how he broke through the sound barrier, but he did. The call may have been intended to trigger the grieving process, but I had unconsciously put healing on hold.

Life went on. Dad loved the legends and lore of the Jersey pines. He was always willing to take a Sunday afternoon drive through the Pine Barrens, pointing out old cemeteries and remnants of towns that had lived and died a hundred years earlier. He knew how these towns were settled and how their names came about.

As I moved into my teen-age years, I stopped going to the pines or on fishing trips and Sunday afternoon excursions. Dad continued taking Barry and Billy for many years, endowing them with a treasure chest of recollections.

Somehow, at the same time, I was accruing my Pandora's box of memories. I knew he loved me and I fiercely loved him. I recognized the good in him, but the eggshells and his dictatorial nature were taking a toll. My need to be loyal to both parents kept me from talking to anyone who knew them. In my confusion, I wondered if I was just too sensitive and too emotional.

I looked for God in different churches, different faiths, as though there would be one that was just right for me, and magically I'd stop hurting. Mom and Dad would make their own peace and live in harmony. For me there seemed to be no such magic to be found.

I dreaded my father's disapproval, but when he taught me to drive, he was patience personified. We never concluded a lesson, however, without a few words on the subject of boys and their "sly maneuvers," or sex—plain and simple. He kept telling me that "sex isn't what it is cracked up to be." I couldn't understand why the lecture, since I was not only chaste, but unchased as well.

When senior prom time came around, I invited my good friend Bryce, who attended another school. Dad wasn't worried about my being out with this dear person, as we had been platonic friends for about two years and he was almost part of the family. Bryce and I had a special bond all of his life. He died in 1985 from an AIDS-related illness. He was fifty-one years old.

The prom must have brought me luck, because I began to date soon thereafter. For a few months, I wasn't allowed to go out in a car. We went by bus. Curfew was precisely at 11:00 p.m. I dared not be late, as Dad would be so angry that it would be useless to try to explain. Such emotionally charged confrontations left me drained and distraught. I found I could not stand up to him even when he was wrong, and the internal conflicts continued.

I went to work the day after I graduated from high school and gradually took control over my life. Although the tensions at home were as bad as ever, I never considered moving out on my own. In 1954, I accepted an invitation to visit my friend Helen, who had recently moved from Trenton to Albuquerque, New Mexico. I stayed for six months, enjoying the noncombative atmosphere and my first exposure to independence. Helen introduced me to a pleasant young man in the air force, and when I came home I had an engagement ring on my finger. The courtship continued by mail.

I took a civil service job as a secretary at nearby McGuire Air Force Base and found myself attracted to a young man in the military. This helped me to see that I was more in love with love than I was with my fiancé, and I broke the engagement.

By this time, I realized how much my father's health had deteriorated while I was in New Mexico. His blood pressure was high and he stayed terribly tired, but nonetheless he continued his pattern of overwork and worry. Mom stayed fairly healthy, but had no life of her own. Barry and Bill retreated when the atmosphere was especially charged with friction. Barry, sturdily built and an extrovert, went fishing or out with his best friends, Tommy and Bob. Billy, slight of build and known as the Adams Family Introvert, went to the nearby library and buried his nose in a book.

In 1956, our family moved to a lovely old Victorian-style house in Hamilton Square, a quiet, secluded suburb of Trenton. Mom and I enjoyed our time together, and Dad seemed to be calming down. He and Barry belonged to the Citizen's Rifle and Revolver Club. They went to target practice once a week and fishing or exploring old towns on the weekend. Billy kept his nose in a book.

This reprieve from caustic commentaries and the cold war—Dad's argumentativeness and Mom's retreats into silence—was very welcome to all of us. Dad and I gave Mom a surprise birthday party in May. The old wringer washing machine was filled with ice, beer, and soda. The table was laden with all kinds of marvelous made-from-scratch food. It was a night filled with friends and laughter, one of the last such times for the family.

Early one fall morning, DeLaval called to say that Dad had been injured in an accident and he was on his way to the hospital. He had slipped on a scaffolding and fallen eighteen feet to the concrete floor. When Mom and I arrived at the hospital, we learned that Dad's left leg was shattered in three places. He went into surgery several times to have steel pins inserted and later removed because of infection. He stayed in the hospital for many months, and then was in and out for the better part of a year.

I wish that Dad and I were always as close as we were when he was in the hospital. We talked for hours, each genuinely listening to the other. I was even able to share some of my romantic wonders and woes with him, and—better yet—he didn't malign my mother.

It did not take long for the picture to change once Dad was home but still unable to work. Since he was unused to being "laid up," his pride suffered when he realized that I had assumed his responsibility as a breadwinner. Although the pay from my two jobs barely stretched, we managed. Dad had been well liked at DeLaval, and his co-workers occasionally stopped by with monetary gifts. They told us that Dad was always the first to do this for others.

The winter months were the toughest. We made it competitive fun to think of ways to heat that three-story house, since we couldn't afford coal. The water in the commodes was usually frozen in the morning. I will never forget Barry coming down to breakfast in that large country kitchen and grabbing two hotcakes from the griddle to put under his armpits for warmth. (He ate the rest.)

By the time that Dad was able to return to work, I was engaged again. A longtime friend, Cole was someone with whom I was quite comfortable. My friends were all getting married, and I was weary of the singles scene. I was nearing twenty-three.

The wedding took place in August 1957. I was truly happy that Dad could walk down the aisle of Westminster Presbyterian Church with me. My matron of honor, Wilhelmine Hill, and my six bridesmaids, arrayed in pastel shades, complemented the bright blue and beautiful day.

I no longer had acne, but I did have small pits and large pores as a result of the years of eruption. A month after the wedding, I went to Bellevue Hospital in New York City for an experimental treatment with dermabrasion. A small steel brush scraped the top layer of skin from my cheeks. A week later, scabs formed over the healing skin. The new skin itched terribly, and I picked at the corners of the scabs, thereby sabotaging the treatment and nullifying the results for which I'd hoped.

The optimism and newly gained confidence that my engagement and marriage had fostered were also in danger of erosion. Our relationship had changed very little. While I pictured passion, he pictured a relatively platonic partnership. In place of the companionship I had envisioned, he saw a husband's hobbies and recreation as inviolate and a wife's activities as "her thing to do."

I was bewildered and disappointed, and I reacted in immature ways. At that time, I had no awareness that I was equating physical affection and desirability with proof of my worth. We did not communicate well, but neither did we argue. By late autumn, we were at an impasse, each of us silently determined to make the best of it.

On a Saturday in late November 1957, Mom and I and my best friend Wilhelmine went by train into New York City to see a play on Broadway. We had a wonderful day, arriving home about 11:00 p.m. As I turned onto our street, Mom and I noticed an unusual number of cars parked by the house. I took a deep breath and grabbed her arm to brace us both as we made our way over the ice-covered sidewalk.

Dad came to the door before we got there. His face was drawn and moist with tears. "There's been an accident," he said, "Tommy is dead." Tommy was my brother Barry's best friend.

"My God, my God," my mother cried. "What happened?" I helped her into a chair and sat next to her, my stomach in knots.

"It was a freak accident. Barry, Tommy, and Bob went hunting for rabbits this afternoon. They were planning to leave, and Tommy got into his pickup and . . . " Dad collapsed into a chair, unable to continue. Billy, without making eye contact, moved quietly around the group and out of the room. A family friend handed me the statement that Barry had given to the police, and I read it out loud:

"I walked around to the front of the vehicle holding my Uncle Bill's double-barreled shotgun above my shoulder. As I lowered the gun to the ground, it dropped out of my hands and struck the hood of the pickup truck and discharged. Thomas was sitting behind the wheel and was struck in the face.

"Instantly, knowing what had happened, I jumped in the pickup truck and pushed him over on the seat. I drove to St. Francis Hospital, where I proceeded to pick

Thomas up in my arms and I carried him into the hospital. At that point, he was already dead."

I put the report on the table and went over to my father. All three of us sat silently for a few minutes. The others in the room, all good friends, sat or stood quietly by. Mom asked for Barry.

"He's upstairs, lying down. He's in a state of shock now. The police said that it was the kind of accident that would happen only one time out of a thousand. They told him not to blame himself." Dad shook his head. "It's my fault. I should never have taught him to hunt. I might as well have pulled the trigger myself." Someone told him not to think that way as sometimes these things are beyond our control, but my father did not hear.

I went up to see Barry, but I didn't know what to say or do for him. I just sat there, my hand on his arm, wishing we could start the day over. It was unbelievable that Tommy was dead, and my brother would have to carry this burden, as innocent of fault as he may be, for the rest of his life. He had just turned eighteen.

When I went back downstairs, Dad was standing in the hall, one hand supporting himself and the other holding the telephone. He had called Tommy's parents. The tears were now flooding his face, and he could scarcely speak. Somehow, he said enough to convey his and my mother's caring and pain; he heard enough to know that Tommy's parents blamed no one, and he placed the telephone back on its cradle. Later, he would say again that he felt totally responsible.

As with her father's suicide, my mother kept it all inside. May Sweeney wrote me that when she asked my mother if she wanted to talk about it, my mother said, "If I talked a hundred years about it, I would never forget it. I must go on with my life, and my children's lives cannot be disrupted by our sorrow, which will always be with Eddie and me." And she never spoke of it again.

The grand jury found that it was an accidental death and exonerated my brother. Not so with a few of his fellow high school students who called to him, "Hey, killer, how're ya doin?" as they passed him in the halls.

Tommy and Barry grew up together from age four and were best friends. Tommy's death devastated my brother, made all the worse because Barry was a peacemaker, always gentle to people and pets. The only time he actually shot a rabbit—he was eleven, and he was with Dad—he sat down on a hill and cried. His life was changed forever on that dreadful November day in 1957.

And mine as well, for I vowed before God that night that I'd find a way to bring comfort to people in pain, and I'd never feel helpless again.

The Turning Point

"BARBARA, WE WANT YOU TO MOVE FROM THE gurney to the delivery table now," the operating room nurse intoned, as she stripped the sheet from my pummeled private parts. Modesty was no longer an issue. I barely noticed my exposure.

I clamped my teeth down on my tongue and concentrated on lifting my left hip so that I could heave it onto the rack. A moderately uncomfortable contraction abruptly changed tempo and moved swiftly from the small of my back to the front of my highly visible abdomen, immobilizing me in mid-air. I then gave what might have been my best imitation ever of Carol Burnett's Tarzan call, for suddenly what seemed to be a hundred hands helped me onto the table, rushed the gurney aside, placed my feet in stirrups and the anesthesia mask over my nose and mouth. I'm certain I heard a collective sigh of relief.

I gulped the etheric ambrosia and was instantly transported to paradise, or so it seemed, compared with where I'd been for the previous sixty hours. When next I knew full consciousness—I apparently resisted returning in a timely fashion—I was in the recovery room. A nurse with a look of exasperation on her face checked my pulse. My husband, with a look of excitement on *his* face, asked me if I'd try soon for a son.

We named our beautiful baby "Lisa Carolyn," with "Carol" in commemoration of the holiday season. She weighed over eight pounds and was perfectly formed and healthy. Lisa was Mom and Dad's first grandchild, and my brothers' first hands-on experience with a baby. Thus, Christmas 1959 literally brought a gift of precious new life to a family weighed down by sadness from the loss of life.

The pregnancy had not been an easy one. While I found the *feeling* of life within—the movements of the baby—awesome and thrilling, my unfathomable fear of deformity pervaded the entire nine months. This fear became acute when, two weeks before Lisa was born, a neighbor gave birth to a grossly deformed infant who lived only a few hours.

When back in my hospital room, I saw that my eyes were completely bloodshot. I realized then that my fearfulness could have been responsible for the protracted phase of hard labor. With each instruction to bear down, I must have pulled back instead, subconsciously seeking to avoid the finality of birth.

Whether I had "picked up" on my neighbor's abnormal pregnancy or an influence from somewhere in my past that lingered in my subconscious, I do not know. I *do* know how much happiness my first-born child brought into all of our lives. Yet a scant eighteen years later, Lisa Carolyn would be the catalyst for one of the toughest lessons I had yet to learn.

Mom took care of Lisa when I returned to my job as an administrative secretary for the staff judge advocate office at McGuire AFB. Dad was home until he left for work in the afternoon, and he seemed to delight in having the baby around. Somehow, he and Mom were able to call a truce during those hours, but at other times the atmosphere was riddled with the usual tension and dissension.

My father's illness, diagnosed as hypertensive heart disease, curtailed all activities but his light-duty job at DeLaval and a few local errands. He began to have "small strokes," as they were termed by his physician, Dr. Blair Vine. These episodes, during which oxygen did not reach the brain, intensified Dad's short-term memory loss, erratic mood swings, and anxiety. His antagonism toward Mom became more vehement and the accusations more absurd.

On one occasion, Dad called me to say that Mom had walked to a nearby park and that when she came home, he was going to kill her. I raced to the park, found my mother, and asked her to come to my house. Her response was that he had threatened her before and "it blew over," so she wasn't going to worry now. She insisted upon walking home. I followed in my car and went in with her. Dad's frame of mind had indeed improved, but this did not alleviate my fear that one day he might suddenly and unalterably snap.

Dad was fifty-five at this time and he looked eighty. His skin was ashen in tone, his cheeks were sunken in, his flesh simply hung on his bones, and he looked emaciated. Dr. Vine told Mom and me that Dad's heart would not carry him beyond two more years. This prediction would prove to be accurate.

My father would not stop smoking nor working nor worrying. We all tried to keep in mind how very ill he was and that however difficult he could be, we were still the center of his world.

While Dad struggled valiantly to work and provide despite his near-incapacitating health problems, Barry struggled desperately to salvage and strengthen *his* self-esteem and emotional health.

In reflecting years later on the tragedy that claimed his best friend's life, Barry recalled: "For a long time after the accident, I could hardly write my name. When I went to my senior prom, Thomas was not there. I would ride by his house, and he was not there. When I fished and camped where we had fished and camped together, Thomas was not there. The reason he was not there was because of a person—me—who for one instant was careless. To live with this is very, very hard.

"I felt that I could not be close to anyone ever again. I got along with everyone, but I became a loner, and I remained a loner. Holidays were tough, birthdays were tough, and I thought about Thomas all the time.

"I couldn't talk to Mom or Dad—or anyone—about my accident. I began having migraine headaches. In my heart, I knew I was still grieving. I didn't know how to find peace."

Barry pulled away from us emotionally as well as physically. It must have been stressful to see his pain mirrored in our eyes, and our pain as well. None of us knew how to help each other heal.

Three years after the tragedy of Tommy's death, our brother Billy's best friend Danny died without warning at age sixteen. We learned later that the cause was a rare heart defect. Bill wrote about this event: "Danny's death affected me deeply. I became *again* aware of the fragility and uncertainty of life. It brought Tommy's death vividly to mind."

Both of my brothers had lost their best friends through premature and sudden, tragic deaths.

During the last year or two of Dad's life, Bill bore the brunt of the damage from the explosive domestic atmosphere. A naturally shy and sensitive person, he retreated into books or his own inner world to avoid the turmoil. Bill was terrified of Dad's verbal confrontations with our mother and the scathing remarks Dad made to him that were "just teasing."

Bill's letter continues: "I don't think either of my parents realized that instead of helping me to build good self-esteem, they were contributing to a giant-sized inferiority complex. They couldn't help me to have what they never had themselves. I never saw any real happiness or affection between them or heard any words of endearment. The household was emotionally relieved when Dad was at work and an emotional minefield when he was home."

Bill and I developed several similar patterns that were to adversely affect our lives for nearly thirty years. We both feared confrontation, disapproval, and rejection. We were afraid of authority figures. We were seriously addicted to people-pleasing.

Codependency, or the need for validation through a spouse or another external source, would lead each of us in and out of three marriages. We craved mental, emotional, and physical intimacy, but found it difficult to draw a compatible partner.

We sought careers in which effective communication was vital. Our search for the meaning and purpose of life—and a personal relationship with God—became a drive without respite. Last, but not least, we both developed our psychic and intuitive abilities for the purpose of serving God and helping people in pain.

Conversely, Barry sought stability in marriage, fatherhood, and work. He recognized the emotional scars and his near inability to express feelings and emotions. He tried to *live* what he was unable to express in words. He drew close to God through a traditional form of worship and belief, and he came to hear an inner voice that guided him and helped him heal, much as Bill and I did.

Dad was admitted to the hospital several times during the spring of 1963. Mom, Barry, Bill, and I spent many hours by his bedside in silent communion with him. The bond that had been strong at my birth may have weakened, but it never broke.

My son Christopher John was born on May 3. My father held his first grandson and namesake in his arms for the christening. Dad died in the hospital on June 25, 1963.

Mom, never having worked outside the home, had no marketable skills with which to support herself. At age fifty, she was not eligible for social security. Cole and I asked Mom and Bill to live with us. Barry went into an apartment of his own. I was now working for McGuire AFB as a courts-martial reporter, having graduated the previous year from a two-month legal specialist course at the Naval Justice School in Rhode Island. Mom took care of my children during the daytime. Bill began preparing for his sophomore year at Rider College, where he majored in journalism.

Although I was sincerely grateful for Cole's generosity to my mother and brother, I continued to lament the lack of affection in our relationship. We shared fewer interests than when we married seven years earlier. We communicated only on a superficial level. The void in intimacy that so troubled me crippled not only our physical relationship, but our emotional and spiritual connectedness as well. Not only did I stop growing, but I became controlling and emotionally manipulative as well. I was not happy with myself.

The ensuing year could be likened to a roller-coaster ride. I enjoyed male attention and came precariously close to an emotional involvement. The stronger the attraction, the greater the conflict between my need for physical affection and my conscience.

I began to think about moving away. I rationalized that a

fresh start might be good for all of us. Perhaps my husband and I would work harder on our relationship in a different environment.

Albuquerque beckoned to me. I had loved the dry climate and the exhilarating views when I visited the Land of Enchantment in the fifties. In retrospect, a Higher Mind and Hand must have been at work, setting scenes and pulling strings to bring this relocation about. For not only would I climb mountains, but spiritual heights as well, and thereby be blessed beyond measure.

My husband was drawn to the move; he was ready for a change of scene. Mom, having never traveled far from home, seemed interested, even enthusiastic. Bill chose to remain in New Jersey.

Mom had been spending time with a family friend, a widower. When Russell learned that we planned to move to New Mexico, he proposed. He owned his own home and was financially secure.

I was torn between wanting my mother to come with me and wanting her to have the security Russell offered. Mom deferred the decision about the proposal. She wanted to see Albuquerque first and then return to New Jersey for a while to make certain that Bill did well in college and in living on his own.

A few weeks prior to the move Mom had a simple, but vivid dream about Dad. In it, she watched him "come down from the sky" and walk alongside her through a green, heavily wooded forest. They emerged into the clearing on the other side together. She seldom talked about dreams, but this one both impressed and haunted her.

As the time to leave drew closer, I noticed that Mom was dragging her feet about packing and preparing to go. I became frustrated because she wasn't gearing up as I had expected her to do. When I asked her what was wrong, she sighed and said, "It's as though there is nothing to get ready for." She couldn't explain.

My preoccupation with my own problems and needs blinded me to my mother's need for consideration and patience at this difficult time in *her* life. In her passivity, Mom had been easy to take for granted. In her reluctance to share *her* heartaches and concerns, she had become *my* sounding board. I saw her as strong and invulnerable, and I rode roughshod over her feelings. I cannot judge anyone else for hurting her. Although I loved her dearly, I know that I hurt her, too.

Russell didn't want to chance losing Mom, and so he pressured her into letting him accompany her to Albuquerque. They drove his car and planned to do some sightseeing before going back home.

We arrived in Albuquerque in August 1964. Cole, an exceptionally fine craftsman, went to work immediately as a custom cabinetmaker. We rented a house, notified the movers, and set up housekeeping. On the first night we were able to cook at home, we celebrated with Mom's pot roast and a toast to our new life.

Mom and Russell stayed two weeks, taking day trips to enjoy the beauty of the state. Helen and I and our kids went along on several excursions and had a wonderful time. On the day before Mom and Russell were to leave, she and I had a chance to talk alone. I asked her what she was going to do about Russell's proposal. Although I thought she would be wise to marry him, in my heart I wanted her to come back to Albuquerque and stay with us.

I was surprised when Mom said, "I couldn't live with Russell. He would be as difficult as your father was. I just cannot go through that again. All the security in the world isn't worth it."

That afternoon, Mom bought house plants for our new home. She had a green thumb with plants and a gentle way with birds. I promised myself that before she returned, I'd buy a canary or a parakeet as a "welcome back" gift.

For the farewell dinner, Helen and her husband took us

to a rustic restaurant in a picturesque mountain town, where we were treated to an old-fashioned "mellerdrama." Mom looked especially pretty in a pale aqua dress with a white short-sleeved sweater. She wore the marquise necklace Dad had given her one Christmas.

Mom's face was full and wrinkle-free, just as when she was twenty-one. The New Mexico sun had tinted her cheeks a light pink, and I had tinted her hair a light auburn. (Once before, when she wanted her hair highlighted, I left the color on too long and it turned purple, giving the family grist for weeks of guffaws.)

The full moon that night was splendorous, its soft-hued radiance skating through the evergreens that framed the winding, narrow mountain roads. A sky brimming over with effervescent stars conspired to create a mystical, magical ambience. Captivated, we all withdrew into our private worlds as we traveled home.

My silent reverie was marred only by remembering that Mom would leave on the morrow and how very much I would miss her. I didn't tell her so. I didn't hug her that night, because I knew if I touched her, I would break down. I chattered instead about inconsequential things. The word "good-by" was not spoken.

The next morning, as they had planned, Mom and Russell left before the rest of us woke up. I found a note that Mom had written about caring for house plants. Placed next to the note were a few personal cosmetic items, such as a moisturizing cream she used regularly. I didn't need these, and the gesture puzzled me.

Later that day the children accidentally locked themselves in my bedroom while playing. As the locksmith was leaving, I thought to myself, "Mom will get a kick out of this." I expected her to call that night or the next day.

The call came on September 2, Labor Day weekend, not quite forty-eight hours after Mom and Russell's departure. "Is this the daughter of Mabel Adams?" Before I had a chance to reply, the voice went on: "I need to know what to do with her body."

Every fiber of my being shouted to me to hang up the phone and run, run somewhere where there were no phones. My heart pounded, my stomach churned, and my legs threatened to give way. I slumped into a chair and closed my eyes, praying that this was only a nightmare and the day had not really begun.

The voice introduced itself as a mortician in Waynesville, Missouri. "Didn't the Albuquerque police tell you that your mother was killed yesterday afternoon in an automobile accident? The passenger in the car survived, but he is in the hospital."

I mumbled no and asked the mortician for his number so that I could call him back later. Chris toddled over and held onto my leg. Lisa was in the living room, watching cartoons. I managed to dial Cole's work number before I fell apart.

Helen came immediately and took the children to her house for the following two weeks. Cole and I flew to Waynesville, where we arranged for the transport of Mom's body by train to Trenton. We visited Russell at the hospital. Understandably, he was severely depressed. Within two years, Russell would also be gone.

The accident had occurred at 1:30 in the afternoon. The day was sunny. Mom, an inexperienced driver, was at the wheel, when a double-decker cattle truck started to pass her on the left. Both vehicles were going up an incline on the four-lane highway. Mom was driving about 35 m.p.h. According to the truck driver's subsequent statement, he "nodded off" as his cab reached the front of the car.

The truck began to crowd the car, and my mother veered sharply to the right to avoid a collision. The car went up a small hill, over an embankment, and came to rest headfirst against a tree. Although her seat belt was fastened, Mom was thrust against the steering wheel. Her chest was crushed and she died instantly.

I wept continually, day and night—in the air and on the ground. Immobilized by grief and disbelief, I could hardly walk; I had no energy. All my life, Mom had been a part of my everyday, with few exceptions. She had been a part of my children's day.

Barry, Bill, and I interred Mom next to our father in Greenwood Cemetery. I remained in Trenton a week after Cole left, to talk with two or three pastors. I sought not only comfort, but answers to questions about the continuity of life, answers that would enable me to let go of my mother.

Nothing helped. I was advised to "have faith" that there was an afterlife and that my mother was happy with God. This was all the pastors could tell me. I needed more than that. I needed to know for certain that this life, the physical life, wasn't all. I needed to know that both of my parents— wherever they were—had it easier and were happier than when they were here.

This tragedy made all the more acute my awareness that little I had learned about the meaning and purpose of life had substance to it. Although I had attended many churches in several denominations, Protestant and Catholic, my spiritual understanding and resources were woefully inadequate.

By the time I arrived home, the shock of Mom's death was wearing off and despair was taking its place. Besieged by regrets and bombarded by memories, I grieved from deep within my soul.

I knew that I needed to begin job-hunting soon and to find a good day nursery for Lisa and Chris. The more I thought about what needed to be done, the more exhausted I felt. The more I thought about the future without my mother in my life, the more despondent I became. I felt that a vital part of me had died with her, and I didn't know if I could go on.

At the very lowest ebb in my energy, with grief and despair all that I could feel, I sat on my sofa while both children were asleep and sobbed until no tears were left to shed. A voice—a strong, distinct, nonphysical voice—spoke through my left ear. It was as though someone were sitting alongside me, speaking into a microphone lodged within my ear. The voice said:

"Barby, it's me. I'm here and I'm all right. You have to let go, you have to go on with your life. I want you to go to the library and find a book called There Is a River. *It is about Edgar Cayce. Go now and find it, read it, and believe. Believe."*

There was no doubt in my mind that it was my mother's voice. I wanted to hold onto it, to hear it forever, but it ceased as suddenly as it had come. My heart was beating rapidly, and I pressed my hand against it as though to slow it down. I lifted my head and took a deep breath, daring to digest the message and allowing a semblance of hope and joy to arise.

Before too long, however, I began to rationalize that imagination had been at work, but the abruptness of the experience led me to tentatively trust that something remarkable had happened. I had never heard of the man or the book. I had no reason to anticipate—or even to hope—that Mom could communicate with me now.

An hour later, with two children in tow, I went to the Albuquerque Public Library. Much to my relief and excitement, there was a book entitled *There Is a River* about Edgar Cayce. Author Thomas Sugrue chose his title from the fourth verse of Psalm 46.

I read voraciously for hours that night. For the first time in three weeks, I went to sleep without tears. I returned to the book whenever I could, often rereading passages to be certain that I had correctly understood their meaning. Hope welled up in my heart and mind and helped to assuage the grief that assailed me at those moments when I missed Mom the most.

Early on, I felt good about Mr. Cayce. He was a simple, down-to-earth man, a Christian Sunday school teacher and a gifted professional photographer. Born in 1877, Edgar as a boy demonstrated unusual perception and abilities that perplexed his parents and set him apart from his peers.

One of Edgar's early and impressive feats took place while he was still in school. Having difficulty with a spelling lesson one night, he went to sleep with the textbook as his pillow. When he awoke, he found that his mind had memorized all that he could not retain earlier. This unique method of learning helped Edgar in elementary school. Unfortunately, he had to drop out and earn a living after completing seventh grade.

At the age of twenty-one, Edgar was afflicted with a gradual paralysis of his throat muscles. Fearing the loss of his voice, he asked a friend to help him enter a hypnotic state akin to the sleep that had helped him master his studies in school. While in trance, Cayce diagnosed the malady and prescribed the corrective treatment.

Thus began what was to be Edgar Cayce's lifelong commitment to helping others heal their lives and themselves physically, mentally, emotionally, and spiritually. Local and faraway physicians sought Mr. Cayce's services as a telepathic diagnostician and clairvoyant conveyor of healing guidance.

Edgar Cayce was a deeply religious man, a man to whom the Bible was the word of God and for whom Jesus the Christ was Master. He anguished over the rightness and authenticity of the guidance that came through him in the altered state of consciousness. He had human flaws, but he also had a spiritual integrity that transcended the norm and a deep and abiding compassion for humankind.

The spiritual principles and laws that Cayce described while in the sleeping state were unfamiliar to me, as I had not explored beyond the teachings of the traditional churches. But as I continued to read, I felt a sense of peace-fulness and truth. This came from both deep within me and from without.

For the first twenty-five years of "the Work," as he called it, Mr. Cayce gave psychic readings in which attitudes and patterns in the seeker's *present life* were pointed out as the root cause of his or her illness or disability. But in 1923, Cayce astounded himself as well as others by referring to the *former lives* of the person who had come to him for a reading.

Former lives. Reincarnation. This definition of "eternal life" both relieved and repelled me. A hundred questions flooded my mind, a hundred answers pulsated on the pages before me.

I asked God to guide me in my quest for spiritual knowl-edge. I prayed each night and morning that if I were pursuing a primrose path, I would be shown—clearly and unmistakably—the falseness of this philosophy. But as I read on—not perceiving divine disapproval of the book—I began to see sense and orderliness.

Cayce's primary source of guidance was the Universal Mind, as he termed that aspect of God that oversees *all* life. According to this source, all souls were created in the begin-ning to be companions to Him. When God gave us free will and individuality, we were in effect entitled to a separate existence from Him, if we chose.

In seeking experience apart from God, we sacrificed our understanding of oneness and divinity. By trial and error, we distanced ourselves until we no longer knew from where we had come or why we were on earth.

The purpose of life on the earth plane is to perfect our individuality and to return to God of our own free will. We incarnate many times, often with the same people. Each life presents specific opportunities for growth, opportunities we design prior to rebirth.

The arrangements are ours to make, the responsibility for growth is ours to take. We progress according to the choices we make, the values we cultivate, and the service we render.

In the sojourns between earth incarnations, we live in other realms, spheres, and systems that comprise the spiritual planes. Free of the material body, we experience certain conditions needed for further development. When we are ready, we prepare for rebirth into the physical plane. The earth, in its materiality, is considered to be the laboratory (or schoolhouse) of the universe.

When we have completed our development and *God's will is our will,* we will be ready to become one with Him, and the cycles of our rebirth on the plane of earth will end.

At first, Cayce was troubled by his nonrecognition of such principles in the Scriptures. When the readings referred to former lives as a root cause of his client's current distress, Cayce was in his mid-forties and had read the Bible through for every year of his life. He turned back to the well-loved books and verses and found to his astonishment that they now spoke to him in a different way. Before long, he felt more at ease with the guidance.

When Edgar Cayce died in 1945 in Virginia Beach, Virginia, he left a legacy of over 14,000 psychic readings, all of which are available to the public. The illuminating guidance found in these transcripts continues to help people all over the world.

Mom's introduction to me of Edgar Cayce and metaphysical philosophy may well have saved my life. Although I have never stopped missing her and although it would take years to achieve good emotional and physical health, I found through Mr. Cayce and his work the strength and desire to live.

On a visit to New Jersey a year or two after Mom's death, I spoke to a family friend about *There Is a River.* Her response was, "Your mother gave me a copy of that book in 1961. She said she found it fascinating and felt it offered truth."

According to Cayce, one who has left physical life and is now in the spiritual body can communicate thoughts and impressions by radiating its vibratory force to one still in physical form *with whom it is attuned.* In my deep grief, I had laid my conscious mind aside and entered an altered state, thereby being able to receive my mother's message.

Little did I foresee that God's Other Door would often open that I might convey comfort from a loved one in spirit to a seeker left behind.

Poor Choices,
Painful Consequences

WHEN NEXT I HEARD FROM MY MOTHER—THREE long, lonely months after her "across the veil" message of hope and enlightenment upon my return from her funeral—she was dressed in rags. (Or so she indicated.)

My husband, the children, and I were visiting my friend Helen and her family whose home was nestled on the east slope of the Sandia Mountains near the 8,000 foot level. This relatively short mountain range, which bordered Albuquerque on the east, was wedged between the Sangre de Cristo Range to the north and the Manzano Mountains to the south.

Snow was falling that day, and the two fathers took the seven kids sledding and skiing for the afternoon. The sun, sitting on a backdrop of brilliant blue, cast its bright rays through the random clusters of snowflakes drifting gently down to earth.

Having hailed from Trenton, Helen had known and loved my mother for many years. As we sat reminiscing, I told her again about the message I had received from Mom a few months earlier. Helen jumped up, retrieved a Ouija® board from the game closet, and suggested that we try to contact Mom. Neither of us were familiar with the board—it had been an unsolicited gift—but we were eager to try it out.

We sat with the board across our knees so that our fingers could touch the planchette. I asked, "Mom, are you here today?" It took awhile, but the planchette slowly moved to the "Yes" in the corner of the board and stopped. Suddenly, my mind went blank. I motioned to Helen to ask a question.

After a moment, Helen ventured, "Mabel, what are you wearing?"

The planchette took on a life of its own and moved rather steadily to the letters R-A-G-S. "That has to be my mother!" I laughed, for it was her kind of humor. We decided to get serious and for the next two hours we barraged Old Man Ouija with query after query.

Mom must not have been in the mood to play Twenty Questions—or a Ouija board was not in divine order for me—because that little planchette never moved another fraction of an inch. We relegated the Ouija to the home for senior, silenced sages, never to be consulted again.

I was determined to connect with Mom again, for there was much I wanted to tell her. Over the next few months, I read many books on extrasensory perception (ESP), several by psychics. I spent hours standing in front of a mirror, looking over a candle flame, trying to see something unusual. To no avail.

When I attempted automatic handwriting, I used what seemed like a ream of paper before I spotted my solitary grand achievement: the phrase "Barbaracallagain" in the midst of the heavenly hieroglyphics that swam before my tired eyes.

Soon thereafter, I settled down and let go of my obsession to communicate. Instead, I focused on learning all I could about metaphysical philosophy and spiritual law as described and defined by or through people I respected, such as Edgar Cayce and authors Rudolf Steiner, Allan Kardec, Alice Bailey, and Grace Cooke. I accepted what made spiritual sense to me and I put puzzling concepts on a shelf for future review.

I worked with the principles of divine order and spiritual law, such as the law of cause and effect (or sowing and reaping), however I could. I began to give more attention to what I was sowing in mundane matters as well as in larger issues. Although I was making progress in realigning my attitudes and traits—the depth and intensity of my insecurities and anxieties would require more than *knowing* where my thinking was wrong. Time and tools would be required for the transformation into full health.

Cole and I were reaching the point of no return, at least on my part. He was satisfied with his orthodox religious orientation—and perhaps appropriately so, as his moral and ethical values were above reproach. He was where he needed to be. I knew that *my* drive for spiritual understanding and growth wasn't going to subside.

Furthermore, my need for intimacy or closeness to *someone* had accelerated with my mother's death. Early in 1966, a *someone* came along when my guard was down and my resistance low. He was an air force surgeon on temporary assignment in Albuquerque to study the effects of sonic boom on cattle. We enjoyed an easy and playful rapport and soon found that we had many interests in common.

When we traveled to the project site—an overnight trip—

we moved beyond friendship. In effect, I crossed the Rubicon, as I knew I could not remain in my marriage. The call of my conscience had grown stronger with the spiritual search. Although we both knew that our interlude was as temporary as his assignment and marriage was not contemplated, I asked my husband for a divorce.

The dramatic events of that spring overlapped and I felt frightened. I spent many lunch hours seeking solace—and hoped-for answers—in one sanctuary or another. I united with a large Protestant church and saw a pastor for counseling. Although sympathetic, he had only the usual stock answers, and he agreed these might not be helpful. I remained emotionally unnerved by the turns my life was taking and the choices I was making.

The catalyst for my divorce flew back to his home base. I went out socially with my now-former husband a few times, with and without the children. On one occasion, we were physically intimate, and I suddenly began to sob and could not stop. I felt intense inner conflict, as though my body were betraying my soul.

In late summer, friends introduced me to Marc. He was the most romantic man I had ever met, and he seemed to love and enjoy children. I held back on involvement for several weeks, but the physical chemistry between us was overpowering. Marc admitted that his wife divorced him because of his pattern of infidelity. They were married for almost twenty years and had two adopted children. He was grieving for the children, who now lived in another state. He was also grieving over his damaged status as a Catholic.

When I spoke about my new understanding of spiritual law and principles, Marc was enthusiastic. That the Creator was a God of forgiveness and unconditional love—and that ultimately, we judge ourselves—appeared to bring him much comfort, as did the understanding of reincarnation. We talked for hours about God and metaphysical philosophy almost every time we were together. His ability to open his mind to a deeper truth solidified our relationship.

Marc asked me to marry him. Again, I trekked to churches and chapels on lunch hours and weekends, dousing myself with holy water going in and going out. I wanted God to call down through a megaphone, "Hey, there. You in the third pew, sitting all alone. You don't have anything to worry about. This is the man of your dreams. Your children will thrive. The answer is yes. You may marry Marc."

All of my entreaties for help with this decision seemed to fall on too-faraway ears. I remembered reading that Edgar Cayce advocated frequent prayer and "meditation," the latter giving God a chance to respond.

I sat in the silence in the daytime and at night, whenever the house was quiet. I beseeched Whoever was listening "up there" to please give me a sign that I was being heard. Nothing unusual happened. All kinds of thoughts crowded into my mind, but none were illuminating. I soon lost patience and gave up.

My most serious concern was about my children. I had anguished about the rightness of divorce for more than a year before making that decision. Now I was contemplating bringing a stepfather into their lives. I needed someone Omnipotent to tell me what to do.

As a last resort, I spoke with the senior pastor of my church. His advice—to wait—was sound and sensible, and I disregarded it completely. Perhaps the powers that be on the higher planes—and God Himself—knew all the time that I would only listen to what I wanted to hear, and so they decided not to waste their words. In truth, my neediness overrode my need to know what God's will was.

We were married in November 1966, having known each other four months. Marc's job was relocated to Redlands, California, and we decided to go with it. I yearned for a baby, and he said that he had always wanted a son. His first wife was unable to bear children. When I became pregnant in the spring of 1967, I was elated—and I thought Marc felt the same.

For the first few weeks, my happiness preempted the awareness that the atmosphere around me was changing. Marc had a strong personality, and until now I had only experienced his agreeable side. Until now, our lives had moved in the direction *he* had dictated.

I began to wake up in the morning feeling depressed. I really didn't know why. I rationalized that my confidence was at a low ebb because I didn't have a job. Work had always been my main source of personal validation.

One evening after dinner, I walked into the bedroom and saw that Marc was reading the Bible. He seemed dejected, and I asked what was bothering him. He replied, "Our getting married was a mistake. I should not have gone against church law. When I married you, I thought that it couldn't be a sin to marry a divorced woman and help her raise her children. But now I see differently. Things wouldn't be going wrong if I had lived up to my religion."

I felt as though my heart had been pierced by a heavy spear. I couldn't believe what I was hearing. I hadn't known that anything was going wrong. He would not elaborate, and I was so shocked I could not think. I could only feel.

For the next few days, my movements were zombie-like, while Marc seemed to recover from his woeful frame of mind quite easily.

He did not repeat the exact words that had wounded me so acutely, but he managed to tell me in casual conversation every day or so that we should not be having a baby so soon.

What happened next created a heartache that I would carry in the recesses of my soul for nearly twenty years and a self-assessment of guilt that would almost end my life.

I found myself walking through every day thinking about losing the baby. I was choosing to lose my baby. I chose to lose my baby.

I called a physician in Albuquerque who was known to be a liberal prescriber of amphetamines for weight loss. I suspected that he was liberal in prescribing other medication as well, and I was right. He called my pharmacist and ordered a heavy dosage of encapsulated estrogen for me. The hormone triggered contractions, and I lost the son I was carrying.

One week later I told my husband how I lost the baby and that I would never forgive myself. Marc said, "No. You lost the baby because I willed you to lose it, and I'm sorry. Don't blame yourself." He told me this once more, thirteen years later, when we would separate for the final time. Then and later, I replied, "But I was the one who took the pills."

I wept as I told the rector of our Episcopal church what I had done. He was sincere in his efforts to comfort me, but there was nothing he could say that would help.

Three weeks after the loss, a throbbing headache of several days' duration sent me to the hospital. I was admitted with the diagnosis of spinal meningitis, a serious inflammation of the lining of the brain. (I believe that my depression and the guilt I carried greatly impaired my immune system and rendered it inadequate to combat the illness—or penalty—I had levied upon myself.)

While I was in isolation, grieving over the baby and missing Lisa and Chris, Marc came to the room swathed in hospital garb. He told me he needed me to be discharged as soon as possible as the kids were driving him crazy.

After Marc left, I huddled, weeping, in a corner of the room, absolutely bereft of the desire to live. Someone, somewhere, sight unseen and sound unheard, must have imbued me with a will to survive, for I made it through that desolate night.

The next day, I told the doctor that I had to go home to be with my children. Because the meningitis had proven to be aseptic, or noncontagious, he reluctantly released me early.

Marc and I picked up the pieces and went on. I started work in the legal office at Norton AFB in San Bernardino. I kept busy when at home. I suspected that Marc was occasionally unfaithful, but I couldn't handle a divorce just yet. I believed I still loved him. In my mind, two divorces would have blatantly declared me not only a misfit, but unlovable as well.

When Marc was laid off from his job in February 1968, we moved back to Albuquerque and "away from hard times and heartaches." We had been back only a few weeks when Marc propositioned a friend of mine. I had taken a job with the Bureau of Indian Affairs (BIA). Marc was baby-sitting until a job came through. He called my friend and asked her to spend her lunch hour with him at our house. Lisa would be in school and Marc would put Chris down for a nap, and then he and my friend could "enjoy themselves."

My friend declined the invitation. When I saw my address book open to her name that evening, I surmised that he had called her. She confirmed he had. Sick at heart, I told Marc I wanted a divorce. He offered instead to see a psychologist. I agreed to wait until he had given professional help a reasonable period of time.

After thirteen weeks of counseling sessions, the psychologist called me in. He told me that Marc was insecure about his height (5'9") and his lack of a college degree in engineering, although he performed well in an engineering role.

"Your husband chose to develop an exceptional prowess with women," the psychologist said. "In this way he compensates for other 'deficiencies.' Marc does not need long-term counseling. He assures me that he can bring his proclivities under control."

I was not impressed with the counselor's conclusions, but I took no further steps toward divorce. Although brimming over with conflicting emotions, I resolved again that I would try harder to make the marriage work.

One day in early summer 1968, I had occasion to go to the Greyhound bus station to pick up legal papers coming in for the BIA from an outlying pueblo. I struck up a conversation with the chief dispatcher, a pleasant and attractive man named Ralph Paulin. Ralph mentioned Edgar Cayce and said that he had heard of a Cayce study group being held in Paradise Hills, across the Rio Grande River.

A week later, by "happenstance," I learned that the BIA personnel manager and his wife were the study group hosts. Marc, for reasons of his own, was ready to re-embrace the concepts of a loving, forgiving God and that we are our own judge and jury. We joined the Edgar Cayce study group immediately. This recommitment to spiritual growth gave me a cautious measure of hope that our marriage might work out.

Each study group session included prayer and discussion, followed by a brief period of meditation. Although I could hear the coffee perking in a closet (our hostess hoped to muffle the sound), *I could also hear an energy force field in the Silence.* It was not loud, but it was physically audible. It sounded like a dust devil whirling around on the desert. It seemed to be located to the right of my forehead and about a foot away.

Buoyed by this gentle phenomenon, I was determined to meditate at home whenever feasible. I would sit quietly for twenty to thirty minutes. Invariably, for the next few days I would be less nervous, happier, and better able to cope with pressures or stress.

I began to see a pinpoint of light in the middle of my "inner screen" (the field of vision deep within the mind). This image of a tiny sun would move forward or backward or slightly sideways, but it never expanded its size. Suddenly, it would be gone. I had no control over it, and I didn't know what it represented. I wanted more. Dialogue. The plateau I was on seemed interminable.

One morning when I was particularly discouraged, I sat in solitude and sailed smoothly into the uncharted waters of a higher dimension . . . I saw the pinpoint of light, and I knew it to be my centering point. I held onto it with my mind for a moment, and then I told my mind to relax. I sensed that I was surrounded by unseen companions who were silently guiding me, coaxing me through levels of consciousness, *helping me to release all doubts—and all needs and goals as well.* To just experience.

The pinpoint of light dropped back and then was gone. In its place, cloudlike misty light—indescribable light, light that calmed, light that healed. I knew instinctively that this was the Light of Higher Consciousness, the Light of God, the vital life force, moving and creating. Instilling peace.

I felt safe. For the first time in my life, *I felt completely safe.*

Colors, beautiful, indescribable colors, began to flow into my inner screen, emanating from some place deep within the center. As the colors unfolded and moved toward the perimeter of my screen, the white, misty Light gently evaporated and was gone.

Almost imperceptibly, the colors blended until my screen was filled with tufts of rose hue, seemingly projected toward me by a giant hand that I could not see. The thought gently penetrated my mind that this was the energy, the ray, of spiritual love. Of God's love for me and for all humankind.

When I returned, I knew that all of the physical plane's sanctuaries I had visited and all of the words I had heard and read were as nothing when compared with—

Being there . . . and
all of the peace, the love, and the joy
for which I'd searched for ever so long
had always been *within.*

Meditation as a Way of Life

INTRIGUED AND EXCITED BY THE UNFORGETTABLE colors that had played upon my inner screen, I decided to learn more about color.

I spent the summer of 1968 studying books that described the various hues and shades of energy and the meaning or essence of each. Interpretations varied, but not to a large degree. With thought and care, I designed for my own purposes a tentative compilation of primary colors and the "message" that each might convey in a meditation. Perhaps in doing so, I unknowingly drafted a language by color that my superconscious (or Higher Self) agreed to use.

Although colors did not appear in every meditation and seeing a full spectrum was a rare treat, when a color was displayed on my inner screen I considered it communication. If Higher Consciousness put effort into projecting a ray of color onto my inner screen, I certainly was willing to put effort into interpretation.

Other than the wonderful assurance that I was loved (the rose-hued ray), the message I perceived most often was that I had overlooked or avoided an opportunity for growth or service. An example of this would be to interpret yellow (communication) as guidance to confront or resolve an issue *now* or to share my spiritual beliefs with a troubled person who had approached me for advice. Almost invariably, such messages were timely and appropriate.

Following is an abbreviated version of my chart. The colors I most typically observed are listed first.

(Note to Reader: Your experience and interpretations may differ; follow your intuition.)

PINK/WHITE: God's pure and unconditional love for humanity.

ROSE (pink with purple or a tinge of red):   The outpouring of love to the meditator from all of Higher Consciousness.

PURPLE: Meditator is accessing his or her *deeper* religious convictions, most likely accrued by former lives in religious service.

LAVENDER: Meditator is refining intuition and becoming more *open* to spiritual truth. Discern carefully but continue your quest.

GREEN: Meditator is receiving healing from Higher Consciousness or is being given reassurance of aptitude as a healing channel.

WHITE: Meditator is striving for truth and purity. Higher Consciousness applauds and will guide the search. Protection; peace.

YELLOW: Meditator is learning the art of communication and is to be encouraged. Communication may be a major lesson in this life. Pale yellow also conveys inner peace.

GOLD: Meditator is about to break through to communication with Higher Consciousness. (It may still require months; stay with it.)

RED AND ORANGE: Meditator's life force and vitality is being replenished. Meditator may need to rebuild energy in other ways as well (recreation, exercise, touching in with nature).

BLUE, Light: Meditator is—and should continue—focusing on spiritual aspiration and growth.

BLUE, Dark: Meditator is—and should continue—focusing on *deeper* spiritual knowledge. Dark blue may designate a karmic situation.

BLUE, Royal: Meditator is a teacher, either by earth vocation or spiritual service.

EARTH SHADES: Meditator may be too grounded, security conscious, or materialistic and needs to balance by spiritual growth and service.

RED, Mottled: Meditator may be struggling with—or consumed by—deep anger, jealousy, and possessiveness. Work to overcome.

GREY: Meditator's discouragement or confusion is unwieldy and needs to be cleared through determination, effort, and positive thought.

BLACK: Meditator is severely depressed and may be too critical or controlling. Depression interferes with a direct connection to one's Higher Self. He or she may need professional help. When meditator takes constructive steps and depression lifts, Higher Consciousness will be able to generate further help and healing.

By now, "Practicing the Presence of God" through meditation was a permanent part of my life. Motivated by the progress I had made, I was anxious to experience more. "More" meant hearing a physical or a mental voice while I was in the Silence or having a fascinating out-of-the-body trip. My most important purpose in learning how to meditate was to feel better about myself and to grow in spiritual understanding and strength, but I didn't see why growth couldn't come in delightful ways.

I approached each meditation with unbridled enthusiasm, anticipating that *this* would be the one in which my Higher Self would break through.

A month passed uneventfully. I endured what I termed a "dry spell." My determination dampened but not daunted, I decided that it was time to pause and contemplate what I might be doing wrong.

I thought about the marvelous meditation when colors first appeared on my screen. I had sensed so surely that I was in the company of beautiful beings of light who were impressing my mind with encouragement and suggestions that helped me go deeper within. *I was to set aside all needs and goals while in the Silence.*

I resolved to let go of my ambitions while in the Silence and to let God decide what I needed to perceive or hear. Surely God or my Higher Self knew better than I what I truly needed for growth.

Next, I tackled the question: Does it not stand to reason that feelings such as resentment or negative traits such as judgment of others could also hinder or block progress in meditation? The answer had to be yes. I resolved to work more steadfastly on those errant emotions or negative traits that I clearly saw in myself.

I wrote a letter to my superconscious or Higher Self giving it permission to "order" the dislodgment by my *sub*conscious (as the storage facility) of any *unresolved* issues, wounds, and related emotions. (I placed the letter in the Bible on my night stand.)

This brought results. The identification of blocks came not in the Silence but in dreams, chance conversations, and incidents that triggered old memories. I began keeping a journal, writing with honesty about the revelations and holding the unfinished business in mind until opportunities for healing and closure were present.

In the meantime, I accepted the meditational plateau I was on as being where I needed to be. The subtle benefits of peace, confidence, and a feeling of well-being, as well as occasional guidance through color, were blessings in themselves. But my appreciation of the plateau did not prevent me from continuing to probe my responsibilities in the Higher Self connection.

My belief has always been that we derive from a quest or project in approximation to that which we are willing to put into it. Was I doing my part to facilitate a firm connection? Was I clear enough about what I wanted from Higher Consciousness? Was I clear on what Higher Consciousness could offer through meditation?

I turned to the Bible and found a number of references to meditation in both the Old and New Testaments. The verse that spoke most clearly to me was Deuteronomy 30:14: *"But the word is very nigh unto thee, in thy mouth, and in thy heart, that thou mayest do it."*

Edgar Cayce relayed the following assurance in reading 1782-1: *"Turn within, rather than holding to something above self. For know, the promise is that He shall meet thee within thine own temple."*

These passages confirmed for me that what I believed was true. God can speak to us directly through intuition, the mind, and the spoken word; and there is a place deep within each of us where we can commune with God.

What did I need to do to bring about communion and guidance? The manual used by our Edgar Cayce study group, *A Search for God*, Book I, called to me. Compiled by members of the original Cayce study group in 1942, this slender book had illumined the meditational path for thousands of people. I had only scanned the book on joining the group, as the members were already studying Book II. This time I read carefully. With the advantage of recent meditational experience behind me, I better understood the importance of preparation in Practicing the Presence.

Meditation became an appointment with God, a holy rite of passage, a holy rite of spiritual growth. I prepared for my time in the Silence as one would prepare for receiving Holy Communion in church. I stayed clear in my purpose—to move into wholeness with my Higher Self and to be all that I could be as the child of a loving God.

THE PURPOSE PRAYER

"God has created me to do Him some definite service; He has committed some work to me which He has not committed to another. I have my mission—I may never know it in this life, but I shall be told it in the next. I am a link in a chain, a bond of connection between persons. He has not created me for naught. I shall do good; I shall do His work. I shall be an angel of peace, a preacher of truth in my own place, while not intending it—if I do but keep His commandments. Therefore will I trust Him. Whatever, wherever I am, I can never be thrown away. If I am in sickness, my sickness may serve Him; in perplexity, my perplexity may serve Him; in sorrow, my sorrow may serve Him. He does nothing in vain. He knows what He is about. He may take away my friends; He may throw me among strangers. He may make me feel desolate, make my spirits sink, hide my future from me—still He knows what He is about."

Attributed to
Cardinal John H. Newman
London, 1833

The Greatest Healer,
the Greatest Gift

WEAK AND WEARY FROM THE HOURS-LONG ON-
slaught of yet another migraine, Barry dropped onto his
bed, telephone in hand. When his fiancée Lorraine answered, he said, tersely, "I can't get to church tonight. Go
without me. I barely drove home from work. My head hurts
so bad, I cannot even take a step."

His headaches, always debilitating, were coming closer
together and lasting longer. The only doctor he had seen
did not help him. But then, he hadn't told the doctor
about...

Tommy... How long had it been? It happened in November 1957. Almost six years ago. Would it never get any easier? That terrible time of year, hunting season, was fast approaching . . .

It was seven o'clock. Exhausted, Barry pushed the punishing thoughts away. His mind gradually calmed itself, and the throbbing in his head seemed somehow no longer a part of him, almost as though he were observing someone else lying on his bed . . .

"Get up and go to church . . . GET UP AND GO TO CHURCH."

Startled, Barry sat up and looked around. He had never heard this voice before, at least not so forceful, not so clear. Its claim to authority was unmistakable.

He obeyed. The headache intensified as he closed the apartment door. He drove as if his life depended upon this visit to church. When he arrived, the midweek service was in progress.

When it came time for the altar call, Barry found his way to the front, and there and then accepted Jesus Christ as his Savior.

Thus came Barry's turning point, the event and the decision that changed his life and brought him health.

That night Barry was healed of migraine headaches—not to have another for the next thirty years—and of the guilt and trauma of Tommy's death.

The grace of God once again lifted a burden of grief from Barry's shoulders on the night he learned that our mother had been killed. God's healing heart and hands eased his pain and enabled him to close the door on troubled childhood memories and open the door to a new life with Lorraine.

Many years later, Barry slipped and dislocated an ankle while helping a friend repair a roof. The injury did not heal well, and when he returned to work six months later, he was unable to walk without a crutch or a cane.

A friend, knowing of Barry's interest in the wilderness,

volunteered him for a leadership role in the Royal Rangers. The boy's group was sponsored by the Assembly of God church that Barry, Lorraine, and their children attended. Barry taught the boys skills such as canoeing, backpacking, and camping.

God healed Barry a third time on a particularly rugged backpacking trip in the Adirondack Mountains. The group hiked for six of the planned twenty-eight miles into the mountains and stopped to set up camp for the night.

Barry was hiking with the aid of his indispensable cane. His backpack weighed forty pounds. A leader from the Red Cross asked another man if he thought Mr. Adams "could make it." The man, a member of the church and a good friend of Barry's, said with a smile, "Don't you worry about him. He'll make it."

In Barry's words: "We had a prayer service around the campfire. At eleven o'clock that night, I put my left hand up to praise the Lord. I felt as though a bolt of electricity hit my hand, and a very warm feeling traveled through my arm and down through my injured right leg.

"I heard God say, *'Walk off the mountain on your own.'* I put the cane in the backpack, I continued the hike without it, and I walked off that mountain on my own. I had very little trouble with that ankle again."

The first time Barry heard the inner voice, he didn't try to identify it. He merely recognized its power, and he followed its guidance without hesitation. When the dust of joyous choice and change settled, Barry knew he had heard the voice of God within. That magnificent voice has guided and guarded Barry and his family ever since.

My own healing work was gradual and certainly not dramatic, but, nonetheless, some healing *was* happening. The days of depression were growing further apart. The burden

of guilt and sorrow over the loss of my baby a year earlier—
summer 1967—was finally lifting. I could attribute the
changes only to meditation.

When I entered into the Silence—the sanctuary of the
soul—the most gentle, compassionate, and peaceful energy
would descend upon me and encircle me; in effect, spinning a soft, silvery cocoon in which I could rest and be
renewed in body, mind, and spirit.

No matter my mood or the worries on my mind when I
sat down, I always emerged from the Silence with a feeling
of empowerment. Even without inner dialogue, I would be
able to see problems from a higher, more objective perspective.

I meditated while sitting comfortably in a chair, being
certain not to slouch. I began by taking several deep breaths,
holding each to the count of four before exhaling. (As I inhaled, I thought of God's pure love and vital energy; and as I
exhaled, I released all doubts and distractions.) Next I would
say the Lord's Prayer and a brief personal prayer.

Edgar Cayce recommended holding an ideal or affirmation in mind to calm and center oneself and to raise the
vibrations. When the mental clamor abated, I would let go
of the affirmation and put my attention on the nuances: the
slight sensations in my body, a heightened feeling of confidence, and the subtle and soft sound current that some
people can hear when all is quiet. These signs indicated that
I was moving into an altered state of consciousness.

The body sensations could come as an effortless relaxation of muscles, particularly in the face: an involuntary
smile, a tingling or drawing over the third-eye area in the
forehead, a feeling of weightlessness or expansion, or a
gentle rocking motion. At times, the top of my head would
feel as though a tight band had been placed around it, but
this sensation usually subsided in a matter of minutes.

Typically, I next became aware of the supplemental
sound of an energy force field building either to my right or

in front of me. The force field sounded much like gently spiraling or swirling air. The ever-present sound current could be more aptly described as a low-level, consistent hum. The sound of the *force field* usually lessened as the meditation proceeded, leading me to conclude that it correlated with the accrual of sufficient power, or fuel, for my passage into a deeper state of consciousness.

When I was nestled in this haven of contentment, I had no doubt that I was forgiven, cherished, and loved unconditionally. I knew that no matter what I did, that love would be there for me. The inner peace I felt almost eluded description; again, it was a *knowing* that God was still in charge and all was well.

Knowing that God forgave me enabled me to forgive myself for denying my baby safe passage the year before. I wanted another chance; I wanted another baby. Marc agreed, and in the late fall I became resolutely, irreversibly, happily pregnant.

Soon afterward, Marc left to work for a year in Houston, Texas. When my maternity leave of absence was approved by the BIA, Lisa, Chris, and I joined Marc to await the baby's birth.

As June 27 metamorphosed into June 28, 1969, St. Joseph's Hospital had a power failure. All nonvital surgery was canceled and emergency-generator power was in operation. Electricity was to be conserved. Commodes were not to be flushed. Houston's heat and humidity had been high for days. St. Joseph's level of cooling was low, and temperaments were touchy.

Hospital personnel scurried around, perspiring and commiserating with each other when out of the earshot of patients. As if the conservative contingency plan weren't enough to contend with, the moon was full that night. Women went into labor early to accommodate myth, mystique, and the pull of the tides. The obstetrics nurse groaned with every admission.

Into this frayed atmosphere came our daughter, Shannon Elizabeth, with a frown on her face that didn't dissolve into a smile for months. Tiny and fragile-appearing, she was labeled an "old soul" by the nursery staff and "different" by her sister and brother. Nonetheless, we were enchanted by our delicate, darling baby girl. I watched with warm amusement as Lisa's maternal nature and Chris's protective instincts emerged. We *were* a family.

The year was marred only by Marc's asthma attacks, which began to occur when I became pregnant. He could sleep only when in a sitting position. When a physician was unable to help, I went to my bookshelf. Edgar Cayce, in several of the health readings he gave, had recommended an inhalant with specific and peculiar ingredients. Our pharmacist helped Marc to obtain the ingredients and within a few days, Marc found remarkable relief.

We returned to Albuquerque in January 1970. My job with the BIA was waiting. Shortly thereafter, I was asked to help the Pueblo Indian tribes of New Mexico in their quest for autonomy. I became the assistant director of the All Indian Pueblo Housing Authority, a tribal organization created to administer the HUD-financed housing programs at the pueblos. I loved the Indian people, and I was pleased to be involved in their emancipation.

Later in the spring, I learned that a well-respected psychic from California was in town to counsel, lecture, and teach meditation. Marc and I had a reading, and we were not disappointed. Betty Bethards, with her unpretentious and dynamic personality, proved to be an inspiring teacher as well. She accepted our invitation to start a meditation group in our home.

The Cayce study group meditation had given us a good start. Focusing on an ideal or affirmation while in the Silence undoubtedly helped us to make that statement a part of our being. We *knew* the power of prayer as we directed healing to others following the meditation. We knew that there were intangible benefits as well.

Betty's demonstration and instruction helped us to expand upon the good derived from meditation. Her technique, simple but powerful, was patterned after an ancient Egyptian method taught in the "mystery schools" but hidden from the masses of people.

The process, as Betty described it, consisted of two phases. The first phase was "concentration," whereby the mind was focused on an inspirational thought, such as "God is love." This brought the mind under control. The second phase was "meditation," a free-flowing of the mind in the Silence. Guidance could be received during this part of the process. Betty shared ideas for interpreting guidance and cautioned that continuing discernment was essential.

I was elated with Betty's assistance and the potential I saw for our spiritual growth. Marc and our friends were also enthusiastic. (I thought it interesting that Betty and I were born in the same month of the same year and that we shared the same maiden name, Adams.) We decided to open our home on Saturday nights for this purpose. Anyone sincerely wishing to improve their spiritual life would be welcome. We could not foresee this in 1970, but our meditation group would meet for nearly eight years.

We combined the Cayce and Bethards' methods and called it "Meditation for Guidance and Healing." Keeping the purpose in mind, we maintained a quiet atmosphere before meditation and encouraged camaraderie afterward.

The decision to hold a weekly meditation group in our home brought many wonderful friends and opportunities into our lives. For Marc and me, the next few years would host more rewarding experiences than unhappy ones, a welcome change from prior years.

My personal healing work could not be segregated from the remaining areas of my life, but instead it affected, for the better, my roles as a mother, wife, friend, and employee. Although my responsibilities differed, I contributed the same assets and the same liabilities to each role. As I brought my "rush to judgment" of others—or any negative trait—under control, everyone I interacted with was blessed.

I worked steadily to apply what I was learning about spiritual truth and God's law. I listened to myself talk in an effort to curtail critical or pessimistic remarks or "catch" reflections of a deeper distress yet unrecognized on a conscious level. When I could summon the courage to do so, I asked others how they perceived me. In this way, I discovered that I routinely became defensive when others were merely questioning, not attacking. My insecurities had contaminated my ability to respond with maturity and confidence in most of the areas of my life.

For me, it was truly essential to see and know myself both as others saw me and as God saw me. That God reads one's heart instead of one's lips is an immense advantage.

Of all the tools I used from affirmations through visualization, the most effective was my time in the temple within. When deep in the Silence, I sensed my drive for health and wholeness strengthening, and I *knew* that I could rely upon Higher Consciousness for continuing help. When I missed more than one appointment with my Higher Self, I could see a difference in my ability to cope and in my self-confidence.

Following Betty Bethards's visit, my longing to "hear" or "see" in meditation—to dialogue with Higher Consciousness—surfaced with fervor. For the next few months, I focused so intently on this goal at the beginning of meditation, that I undoubtedly blocked results by knarling up the flow of fuel or energy.

Finally, I decided to "let go and let God." I said to Him, "When I'm ready, I know You will open the door." The breakthrough came on a Saturday night while I was meditating with our friends. I knew that the power of people together seeking spiritual growth and understanding could be phenomenal and that the energy of all was pooled for all to draw on. Nevertheless, I almost didn't recognize that something truly meaningful had happened.

About ten minutes into the Silence, the bland blue of my inner screen faded and the figure of Jesus the Christ appeared. He stood at a distance so that I could see His full body. His arms were outstretched and He wore a white robe with long, wide sleeves. He was not on a cross. His palms were turned outward, facing me. As I was focusing on His face, His mental message propelled itself into my mind with clarity and vigor. " . . . *my peace I give unto you: not as the world giveth, give I unto you. Let not your heart be troubled, neither let it be afraid.*" The words are from John 14:27.

I was startled. This was not what I was expecting. I didn't know why I would visualize Jesus and "hear" a verse from Scripture. Although I revered Jesus as Christed and as a loving Master and Way-shower, I didn't think in terms of religious scripture. I didn't read the Bible regularly. The picture and the words were not *me.*

The scene dissolved slowly and my screen returned to bland blue. I gradually drifted back to the fully conscious state and sat quietly, waiting for my husband to signal the others out of the Silence. Perplexed but unable to dismiss the experience, I pondered its origin. Had it been my imagination? The question opened a can of worms. What was imagination? I'd always been a "word person," seldom able to create a picture in my mind.

A book recently purchased and placed on a shelf abruptly came to mind. As I leafed through its pages the next morning, my eyes were drawn to the following:

> "It is important that we all recognize the value of imagination, because most people are so afraid of being deceived that they draw a heavy curtain between themselves and the real world of spirit. We tell you most earnestly that true and real imagination is the

doorway into the etheric world, into the higher mental world and beyond that, into the celestial or heavenly world, and even beyond again into the cosmic world.

"You will never find what your soul seeks through reading books, unless your spirit is awakened or quickened. The spirit is supreme; the spirit is of God and is God; and man, if he will become as simple as a child, can enter the kingdom of heaven through pure spirit . . . You ask, how can we tell the difference between true imagination and mere fancy or fantasy? *True imagination comes as the result of the reaction on the brain of higher vibrations which have been set in motion by your sincere aspiration and prayer . . . "*

The Jewel in the Lotus by Grace Cooke, White Eagle Publishing Trust, 1973

And then—with a chill creeping up my arms—I realized that the image of Christ with its profound thought-message was indeed the breakthrough I sought.

What better guidance, what better gift could I receive to launch a lifetime of Light? Clearly, my Higher Self knew that my ultimate goal was lasting inner peace and that fear— fear of abandonment, fear of the disapproval of others, fear of the loss of those I loved—had troubled and tormented me for the thirty-some years of my life.

I was excited, and I could hardly wait to meditate again. Disappointed when my solitary meditations that week yielded no images nor thought-messages of any kind, I *knew* that the next group meditation would be spectacular.

When Saturday night arrived, I went into the Silence with two questions on my mind, confident that I would receive answers. No answers came. No acknowledgment of my questions came. Nothing came but *love* and *comfort* and *peace*. I thought again about the meditation of the preceding week. Perhaps I hadn't adequately explored its message;

perhaps I needed to look deeper inside myself.

In my bedtime prayer, I asked God to tell me how to keep the door open to His guidance. That night, I dreamed that I was the target of someone's anger. I couldn't see whose anger it was, but I was greatly fearful. I sensed it was a man. Upon waking, I knew with certainty that this deeply imbedded fear had stunted my personal growth and precluded healthy relationships, particularly with men. When I removed the blinders, I saw the fear of anger plainly reflected in so many of my reactions and patterns, significant and otherwise.

The mundane habits, insidiously self-irritating, were obvious. My routine on grocery-shopping day was to sneak a box of sugared cereal into the kitchen and pour it into an empty health-food cereal box. This I did to give the kids a treat without incurring Marc's censure.

A pattern that was damaging to my self-respect was my reaction to the rather commonplace problem of sexual harassment in the business world. When cornered by a conniving co-worker or executive, I extricated myself by placating or playing head games. I could not comfortably discuss the moral code which had become an integral part of my nature—that we reap what we sow. Neither was I self-confident enough to admit to a man that I did not find him appealing—and I certainly didn't want *his* assessment of *my* appeal. Each time this occurred and I copped out instead of speaking out, I was angry with myself for weeks.

In pondering over my breakthrough meditation, I had broken the lock on Pandora's box and discovered not a diamond but a dagger, a dagger that could cut self-esteem to shreds. I recognized my fear of male anger and disapproval, acknowledged its power in my life, and set out to overcome it.

Shortly after this insight came to light, my favorite former boss, a normally circumspect man, invited me to lunch. I had contributed immeasurably, he said, to the achievement of an important business contract which had just been finalized. On the way back, he turned toward his neighborhood instead of the building in which we both worked. Suddenly aware of his intent, I murmured, "Where are we going?" He replied that his wife was out of town, it was the maid's day off, and he wanted a chance to "make you feel good."

Rather than show my acute dismay, I said nothing but silently and feverishly prayed for help. Lo and behold, as this twice-my-age man approached his house, he exclaimed, "Oh, hell. The maid must have switched days. That's her car in the driveway!"

We went back to the office building, where I made a beeline for the ladies' room to still my quivering nerves. I thanked God and the universe for being with me, for the law of the land was not. This was the last time that I preserved harmony in business and sacrificed harmony in my soul.

Fifteen years and many strides and slides later, I would be *completely* free of the fear of male anger and disapproval.

Two months after the breakthrough meditation, alone and a little discouraged, I sat on my sofa and slipped into a meditative state. I hastily prayed for the white light of Christhood to surround me. The force field (a whirlwind of energy) was especially strong for a solitary meditation. Rather abruptly, my mother's head and shoulders appeared on my inner screen and her words penetrated my mind: *"Barby, it's time to put your house in order."*

Mom's image dissolved. I fought the temptation to call her back. I often talked *to* her while I was doing routine chores, but I had not heard *from* her since she came to me in my grief shortly after her death seven years earlier. Somehow, talking to her seemed all right, but asking her to visit seemed selfish. I knew that my thoughts could reach her without interrupting her progress. I would tell her how much I missed her and that I wished with all my heart that my children could have known their grandparents.

Seeing her was wonderful, as I knew that she came of her own accord. Her message at first seemed odd, but in a short while I understood that she was urging me to pull my life together. Thereafter, whenever my determination to change faltered, I summoned Mom's words to mind to reinforce and accelerate my resolve.

Mom "appeared" a few weeks later, but not in a meditation. I awoke from a deep sleep to see her sitting on the edge of my bed, her hand gently shaking the calf of my leg. She was outlined by a sparkling line of light from her head to her lower torso. I recognized her dress; she had worn it at my wedding. Her facial features were distinctly etched in wispy lines of light. She looked about fifty-one, the age at which she died, but her essence conveyed more peace of mind than I had ever known her to possess.

I kept blinking to see if I were dreaming, but Mom didn't evaporate. As I lifted my head from the pillow, I mentally heard the words, *"Wake up. The baby needs you. Tell her that her guardian angel is with her."* Shannon was indeed crying, as she frequently did in the middle of the night, for no apparent reason (I sensed she was frightened, but I didn't know why). I rocked her and assured her that she had a guardian angel who watched over her the night through. She went back to sleep quite easily.

When I returned to my room, my mother was nowhere in sight, nor did I sense her presence. She had accomplished her mission. From that night on, as long as Marc and I visualized Shannon's bed encircled by the white light of Christhood and her angel present, she normally slept without waking until morning.

The next two months elapsed without dialogue or images when I was in the Silence. Although grateful for all benefits, especially the feeling of well-being, I continued to yearn for solid guidance. I'd read about the helpfulness of "guides," but I wanted to connect with my Higher Self, the voice of my Christ Consciousness.

Then, on October 25, 1970, my "patience" in waiting for an out-of-the-body trip was rewarded. The event occurred as I was drifting off to sleep. Suddenly, a ball of light flooded my inner screen. It waited for me to mentally acknowledge it and then shot backward, off into the star-studded heavens. The light appeared to come from the fireball of a comet or rocket. I was involuntarily pulled up and outward by this light.

We traveled this way, the comet ahead with me "in tow," for what seemed like twenty minutes. I recall thinking what a long time it was taking to get wherever we were going. At last we came to a circular building of gleaming white alabaster or marble, with columns all around the outside. The Doric-design columns supported a portico or walkway. I saw two angels, one on either side of the entrance. The angels were arrayed in light-hued, shimmering robes. I could not recall wings, but I *knew* that they were angels.

I also knew instinctively that this was the Hall of Records, an etheric library that preserves the archives of our world, including the probabilities for what we in the third dimension think of as "the future." Many metaphysical philosophers, authors, and teachers believe that every thought, word, and deed from all of our incarnations is imprinted on the ethers (or "akasha"). Certain "sensitives" are able to access the akashic records when giving psychic/intuitive readings for people.

Thrilled, I moved toward the temple steps.

"You are not permitted to enter at this time." The words echoed through my head. I mentally asked, "Why not?"

"You are not ready." I asked, "Why was I brought here?"

"As an award for entering the world of meditation and to commemorate the beginning of a new phase of life. You will be permitted entrance at a later time."

We must have traveled home by etheric express, because I suddenly became aware of being in bed. I felt physically, emotionally, and mentally exhausted. Although intrigued by the angels' words, I felt myself sliding into sleep, a peaceful, dreamless sleep. It would not be this night's sleep but one nine months later that would provide the key to the *"new phase of life."*

We began to hear favorable results from people to whom we had directed healing on Saturday nights. Our group, which varied in size from six to twenty-two any given week, had met for over six months. The volume of energy accrued while we were in the Silence was remarkable. We *received* in meditation and in keeping with the universal law of balance, we *shared* by way of a healing circle.

People who couldn't attend called to ask that their names be included in the healing prayers. We began by asking God to monitor our requests so that we didn't violate anyone's free will or their divine plan. It was understood that people might need their illnesses for reasons of their own. While the names were being spoken, we held our hands chest-high with palms outward. In this way, the energies could flow more smoothly *through* us toward the center of the circle where the Christ Light was anchored. From that point on, God was in charge.

Distance didn't matter. People in need always received. If the seeker could sit quietly at the time of our healing circle, all the better. We were encouraged by the number of people who felt a warmth suffuse them as they linked up with us and for whom pain lessened and healing accelerated. We didn't need to know the nature of their illness or injury. We asked only for name and location.

It became apparent that as we shared the healing energies with others, we were touched with healing ourselves.

We didn't see miracles, but we saw movement—movement toward health and wholeness.

I had been plagued with sore throats and swollen glands both as a child and as an adult. I often became upset over insignificant events, such as a change in plans or a minor mistake. Nervousness had been a natural state. At work, I was exceptionally organized, but at home I was distracted and restless. I would walk from room to room, starting different chores in each and finishing none.

As of now, spring 1971, after more than two years of steady appointments with Higher Consciousness—about five solitary meditations and one or two group meditations a week—I took stock. Sore throats, colds, and swollen glands were a rarity. My ability to handle unpredictable events or changes in plans was greatly improved. I was no longer naturally nervous, but eradicating anxiety in full would require more complete self-understanding. This would come.

Most beneficial of all, I was building a reservoir of spiritual resources that would see me through the letting go of life as I knew it, to living life as it was meant to be.

GOD, BY HIS GRACE, SENDS HEALING TO MAN

MAN, BY HIS DOUBT, CANCELS IT OUT

From author's reading for a client
April 1992

Meditation for Guidance and Healing

1.   Arrange for privacy and quiet. Sit comfortably but with your back fairly straight. Close your eyes. Place your hands on your lap, fingertips touching or one palm resting in the other palm.

2.   Take several deep breaths, hold each to a count of four and slowly exhale. Breathe in God's light and love, breathe out all negative thoughts or feelings.

3.   Say a personal prayer or the Lord's Prayer, silently or audibly, however you prefer. Visualize yourself enveloped in light.

4.   Mentally focus on an inspirational thought for several minutes, until you sense that the day's duties and distractions have drifted to the background or bleachers. Don't expect an empty arena; it won't happen. A suggestion for your focus: *"I let go and let God."*

5.   When clamor becomes calm, let go of the focus-thought and let your mind flow naturally. Open your hands and let them rest with palms up. You are symbolically saying, *"I am open to receive."*

6.   *Notice the nuances.* Be aware of color, light, and form, sound, and physiological sensations such as a drawing or pressure in the third-eye area. If there seems to be nothing to notice, do not be discouraged. This is a stage some people defer or bypass.

7.   When thoughts come across your mind, do not dismiss too easily nor accept too soon. Simply take note and continue on with the meditation. Soon afterward, write down the key words or thoughts and put them on a shelf for a day. *Always use discernment.* When in doubt, ask your Higher Self to confirm or correct what you have received. Be consciously alert to signals and signs in response.

   a.   The interference by your inner child or subconscious fears, doubts, and wishful thinking will gradually lessen. It is only by hearing these voices that we learn to recognize them. More important, they teach us about our-selves.

   b.   Thoughts emanating from your Higher Self (super-conscious) or Higher Consciousness will be accompanied by an overshadowing of love, compassion, and peace. The lesser-self voices will not.

   c.   If an image or thought occurs "out of the blue" (the topic did not cross your mind during the preceding forty-eight hours), it was most likely originated by your Higher Self for your consideration.

8.   Adeptness in receiving genuine Higher Self guidance takes time, practice, and patience. The rewards are worth the wait.

9.   Healing energies flow during every meditation. You may draw healing for a specific need or simply place yourself in the *Hands of the Most High*. Know and trust that you *will* receive and all will be resolved in accord with *divine order.*

10. At the conclusion of your meditation, it is wise to ask your Higher Self to help you "close down" to protect and conserve your energy. This can be accomplished literally by voicing the request and symbolically by rubbing the palms of the hands together.

Spirit Speaks Softly . . .
in the Silence

PROGRESS IN MY QUEST FOR DIRECT GUIDANCE FROM
my Higher Self finally accelerated in early 1971. The new
"language" involved symbology. My goal, of course, was
words, but I welcomed the supplement to the spectrum of
color that had occasionally graced my inner screen for
nearly three years. As with the various hued rays, effort and
guidelines were needed for a means of interpretation.

Imagery and Thought Messages

The Railroad Tracks

Certain symbols or images—such as calm or choppy water, which reflect the state of the seeker's mind and emo-

tions—apparently are universal. I learned, however, that most symbols or images are customized for the dreamer or meditator.

When in a meditation I saw the image of a *steam engine on a single track being slowed and stopped by a flagman waving a yellow lantern,* I was perplexed. My beloved grandfather had worked for the Pennsylvania railroad. I had traveled across country by rail and back and forth to New York City many times with Mom and friends, but I had no other ties to railroading. Yet, I sensed another connection one day to come . . .

I held the scene on my inner screen as I mused over its meaning. First, I considered the color involved. Yellow traditionally meant caution. My metaphysical study identified yellow and gold as representative of communication. Next, I thought of myself as the steam engine. It then seemed probable that I was being cautioned to proceed carefully in learning how to communicate in the Silence.

As I arrived at this interpretation, a chill raised goose bumps on my arms. This physiological sensation is widely thought to be confirmation from one's spiritual self or Higher Consciousness. It indeed would prove over the years to be a valid indication of correct thinking or accuracy of interpretation.

A few weeks later, I was accorded the image of *a railroad track stretching for miles ahead in a fairly straight line.* As I looked down the track I saw movement, leading me to conclude that the train was moving at a moderate speed. I said to whoever was at the other end of the line, "I give up. I can't figure this out."

A gentle, caring voice, speaking through my right temple, responded:

> *"We are showing you a report card on your progress. Continue to see yourself as the engine and interpret the scene. We will do this every so often."*

Railroading provides a language that is both verbally and visually informative. A simple scene can convey a complicated message and conserve a great deal of energy in the process. For Higher Consciousness, one picture—if the seeker understands its meaning—can save a multitude of words.

During 1971 and 1972, I was treated to a report card generally every other month; thereafter, two or three a year—until the end of the decade, when they ceased. These unique evaluations of my personal and spiritual growth were not only helpful but quite motivating—particularly when the report was unimpressive.

The speed of my travel correlated with the pace of my progress. A steady speed and well-maintained track put me on the honor roll. When I went backward on the track, I knew I was backsliding. Tracks with abundant weeds growing between the ties implied that I was not keeping my life style in good repair. A short tunnel with light filtering through from the other end told me to be especially attentive to guidance. If the tunnel was long or arched and light wasn't visible, I knew that I was facing a test of faith.

Seeing coal tipples and standpipes (fuel and water) alongside the track indicated that I needed more time in meditation to build physical energy, to attain clarity in communication, and to calm the emotional body. Rocks or boulders on the track meant hard work needed to clear my path. Conversely, pebbles meant that forthcoming tests and experiences would be manageable.

On more than one report card, I saw myself sitting on a spur so that baggage could be unloaded before proceeding with further development. Sitting on a siding symbolized a delay in growth, often because I needed to rethink a choice or decision.

At some point in my growth and psychic/intuitive development, I gave up the coal and ran on electricity. This occurred with no fanfare, but I perceived the change as a promotion of sorts.

The railroad track scenario that I liked the best was given in mid-1971. It depicted *an abrupt ending of the track just over a mound of sandy soil that I was about to climb. All around me, I could see nothing but dry, uncultivated terrain or desert.* When this final frame froze on my inner screen, I said to my unseen communicator, "Whoa. Are you taking me out of service? What have I done wrong?"

The same soft, loving voice replied: *"You can lay your own track now. My child, you are ready to become a pioneer."*

Heartened, I asked if I was connected to Higher Consciousness. *"Indeed you are, my child."* I then asked the origin of this particular guidance, hoping to hear that it was my Higher Self. A translucent diamond appeared on my screen as I heard the word *"Thymus."* I asked what or where "Thymus" was. At that, with a burst of light intermingled with the pink/red of love, this enigmatic source closed the meditation with *"All will be well."*

My dictionary gave me nothing relevant. I pulled out a medical book to learn that the thymus was an endocrine gland located just above and in front of the heart. The word thymus was derived from the Greek "thyro," which meant "shield." This helped me to trust in the guidance. I decided to honor the designation as symbolic of a spiritual bond of love and protection, a password more than a name.

Distractions

Inner Child Voices

As I made headway in my efforts to hear my Higher Self speak, I also rushed headlong, at times, into misattunement. This happened when I was haphazard in clearing my mind or calming my emotions. At such times, my deep inner fears, doubts, insecurities, or wishful thinking would try to take advantage of my willingness to listen.

Wishful thinking caught me off-guard more than a few

times, particularly when I *really* wanted the assistance of the Universe with a physical/material decision or goal. Wishful thinking would grab the microphone and blurt out, "Go to it! You have 'our' blessing!" But wishful thinking's voice did not have the ring of authority or authenticity. This inner voice came across as tenuous, as that of a needy child playing boss.

What was missing when unsought, errant voices spoke was the overshadowing of love and peace, and the physiological sensations that accompanied a genuine attunement to Higher Consciousness.

I also perceived a difference in the quality of the voices and the voice of Higher Consciousness. The voices of my vulnerable self spoke with a tone and tenor that clearly conveyed immaturity. The guidance I received from the superconscious had an ethereal, but not melodramatic tone of voice. Every sound, every nuance conveyed compassion and unconditional love.

When I compared fine-tuning in the Silence with fine-tuning a radio, I understood where the static came from. I added to my already verbose prayer, "Please help me to rise above my fears and frailties so that I can have true attunement to my Higher Self."

Remedial Refinement

Most important to achieving a clear, valid connection was the consistent attention I gave to my personal growth. I had been miserable for so long because of anxieties and needs that I was absolutely determined to become healthier and happier. As I gradually cleared out the deadwood, the inner child voices subsided. The inner child was beginning to heal.

As a further safeguard, I took Betty Bethards's suggestion to challenge each source of guidance in every meditation. When I perceived that attunement was taking place, I would use my spiritual password "*Thymus*" and wait for a response.

If I were *properly connected to Higher Consciousness*, the response would be immediate: *"I AM here. I AM ever with you, Barbara."* Next, I asked, "Are you of God?" or "Were you directed by God to communicate with me at this time?" The precise rejoinder was: *"Indeed, I AM of God. You may proceed."* This prompt reply, accompanied by an aura of heightened love and peace, enabled me to trust the source and its guidance.

Even in the early days in my development, I was encouraged to use my spiritual common sense and intuition as communication continued. Several variables that affect a connection are discussed later in this book.

Another valid response that I received was, *"You must go deeper,"* which meant that the connection was not yet firm. I referred to this circumstance as a "false start." In the early years, false starts were plentiful.

When I sensed a presence or heard a voice that was inappropriate, it generally disappeared upon being challenged. This could have been an inner child voice, a telepathic intrusion from someone in the physical, or a thought form lingering in the atmosphere.

Since *Universal Law confirms that like attracts like,* I was never frightened of the Silence. I could draw a being to me who knew as little as I did, but not a being who intended me harm.

According to metaphysical philosophy, our unintentional mistakes and unwise choices do not endanger us in the Silence. Only deliberate harmfulness to others by thought, word, or deed will do so. It is the desire of the heart that defines the true nature of the soul. Thus *right living and right thinking grant us the best protection of all.*

The Proof of the Pudding

Every so often, a meditator in our group became impatient and decided that the Silence was not for him or her. I was sorry to see this happen, for I knew that if *I* could break through, anyone could. I was now being blessed with specific and practical help with relationships, family life, and my personal growth. I carefully considered every question I placed, for I was told by Higher Consciousness that the connection and opportunity were truly *precious*.

I did not always have to ask. Higher Consciousness frequently anticipated my need and came to my assistance with guidance that benefited our entire family and often proved life changing.

Chris

The quality of our family life was enhanced by our spiritual focus. Our friends were family people, and we enjoyed picnics, potlucks, and other get-togethers. We became active members of an Episcopal church. In an effort to be a companionable father to Chris, Marc volunteered to be a leader in a Y-Indian Guide group and to coach a Little League baseball team.

I began to notice, however, that when Marc was displeased with Chris or Lisa, he bore down on them with increasing harshness. He was a stickler for punctuality and disliked levity at the dinner table. Even minimal tardiness and minor infractions of the rules earned lectures which were delivered in a tone of voice that one would associate with the Gestapo. When he was irritated, he walked around the house with a leather belt in his hands, pulling both ends together so taut as to cause a snapping sound.

I protested Marc's intimidating behavior but was overruled. At such times, I wanted him out of our lives, but I was not emotionally ready to act. As a result, I covered up for

Chris and Lisa whenever I could, immensely grateful that neither one courted serious trouble.

Shannon, still too young to irritate Marc, was not too young to be frightened by his domineering demeanor. As she grew, she chose not to chance her father's censure or even criticism. Shannon shielded herself from her father's pattern of mental and emotional abuse by becoming the anonymous child.

Although I was deeply bonded to all three of my children, there was an added dimension to my relationship with my son. It had nothing to do with gender or personality, and everything to do with fear I did not yet understand.

When Marc sentenced Chris to hours of room arrest with the door closed, I would find myself anxiously pacing the floor, wondering what he was feeling and doing. The degree of my distress was out of proportion to the event.

One evening, just before close friends arrived for dinner, Marc sent Chris to his room in tears. The atmosphere was strained while we ate, and afterward I had a strong desire to go into the Silence. Our guests were meditators, and they were quite agreeable.

We barely had begun when the now-familiar, always compassionate voice said:

> "*Do not be distraught. We will tell you why you experience anxiety about your son. You have earned the right to know.*
>
> "*In another life, you and he were related by blood, but not in the same roles as today. You were the younger. You were dependent upon him for unconditional love and support. One day, without warning, he suddenly disappeared. You never saw him alive again, and you never knew why he went away.*
>
> "*You do not need to worry. This will not happen again. It is this fear that troubles you now. Let go and trust in God. All will be well.*"

The guidance gave me mind- and heart-relieving peace, and I was able to let go and trust. I did not consider that my fear of abandonment might relate to other relationships as well. For now, this gift was enough.

Lisa

My eldest child's indomitable will kept her moving forward in her quest for independence. She was a pretty girl, moderately tall, and nicely proportioned. Her personality and sense of humor were distinctive, and she had an abundance of friends and activities.

Following graduation, at loose ends regarding what career to pursue and how to pursue it, Lisa took a courier job with the engineering firm that employed her adoptive father.

On weekends, Lisa often drove 225 miles southward to Las Cruces to visit friends. I'd be on tenterhooks, remembering a telephone call years earlier, "What should I do with the body?" Time in the Silence soothed me, and when I was clear enough, *I would receive assurance of her safety on that particular trip.*

As it turned out, Lisa wasn't courting a driving mishap. A young man from a different race was courting her. When she said that her friend was black, I was stunned. Marc was surprised, but not shocked. He was more concerned about how Lisa was being treated. His attitude would remain commendable.

My mind harkened back to New Jersey and the bigotry around me then. Prejudice against Puerto Ricans, blacks, and even Italian and Polish people. I detested it. Prejudice couldn't be a part of *me*.

But what if Lisa married into another race? Marriage as I knew it was incredibly difficult. Why start out with an extra strike against you? Surely the added stresses would make it impossible to succeed . . .

Several of my friends had daughters who were Lisa's age. Their daughters were engaged or getting married—to Caucasians. I wanted the traditional wedding to a traditional—meaning Caucasian—man for Lisa, and obviously for me as well.

"Wait. This is just a phase," I told myself. "They are just dating. They aren't getting married." I took a deep breath and asked Lisa to bring him home when he came to Albuquerque.

When I met Lisa's friend, I liked him. His appearance was the only aspect of him that differed from the young men dating the daughters of my friends. My initial apprehension was for naught. Their relationship remained casual and in a matter of weeks Lisa met someone new. He, too, was black.

I asked her what she found most appealing in black men. "They are nicer to me and more romantic. They are more attentive than white guys." She paused and added, "It's almost as though I have a sign on my forehead which reads 'Available to date blacks.' If my girlfriends and I go to a dance, they all get asked to dance by white guys. If there is a black guy in the place, he'll head straight for me."

To help me think positively (that her preference would change back to the "norm," young men of her own race), I reverted to my routine of olden days and trekked to chapels and churches at noon time to say an impassioned prayer or two. I replaced the mystery novels I read at night with inspirational material. I doubled my time in the Silence—but I didn't ask questions. I was afraid I'd be chastised for falling short of "true spirituality" as I saw it. My standards and ideals brooked little compromise.

All of my efforts to stay spiritually centered and consciously calm about Lisa's interracial dating helped to a moderate degree, but my first-born child had a mind and a destiny of her own.

After being sidelined by a fractured leg and a bruised ego sustained in an auto accident while on the job, my daughter decided it was time to leave Albuquerque.

In spring 1978, Lisa enlisted in the marine corps, looking at the educational benefits and travel being offered. The USMC didn't offer autonomy, but she reasoned that it was a step along the way. After boot camp, Lisa attended Heavy Equipment Operator School at Fort Leonard Wood, Missouri. She graduated at the top of her class.

One afternoon, she called me "with bad news and good news." The bad news was that she was being assigned to Camp Lejeune, North Carolina, and not closer to home. The "good news" was that she was getting married on October 7, a week away.

Somehow, I got the words out: "Is he white?" She replied softly, "No, Mom. He is black." She told me that the man she was in love with was "quiet, well-mannered, and he makes me laugh. He's my best friend."

Instantly, I summoned up guilt about my self-assessed defects and the relative solemnity of her childhood, but I didn't share these thoughts with her. We talked two hours. I urged her to wait until they knew each other better, but I knew that it was useless.

Once again, I thought about the daughters of my friends and all those traditional marriages. Same-race relationships had so much less to deal with. People in interracial marriages were confronted with cultural differences and prejudice. I thought about the Ku Klux Klan and burning crosses. I even dredged up the recollection of a magazine article I'd read once about the black race's predisposition to sickle cell disease, a serious blood disorder.

The bottom line was my fear that Lisa's children would be ostracized or harassed by other children and much of society. The truly bottom line, when I was honest with myself, was that I wanted the acceptance and approval of society. I wanted approval for my children. I didn't want to be different.

I cried on and off for the next two months. There was no

question that Lisa would *always* have my love and support, but could I love her husband? I would soon know. Lisa called to say they'd be home for Christmas. Was that O.K.? "Of course. We all miss you terribly." And we did.

Up until now, the Source had been mum on my painful predicament. I didn't know if my tears and inner turmoil had blocked the spiritual comfort and encouragement I needed, or if I'd been deserted. I decided to bite the bullet and take my medicine in meditation. Tomorrow.

The next night, as I relaxed in a bathtub of bubbles, I turned inward. With tears streaming down my face, I turned my heartache over to God. Incapable at that moment of constructing a thought on my own, I heard:

> *"My child, what troubles you so? Do you think that your daughter is not under the protection of the Most High?*
>
> *"Know that she is following her divine plan. The time has come for the oneness of humankind to be made manifest in the flesh as well as in the Spirit. There are those in incarnation today who will be as forerunners of the one race to come.*
>
> *"Your daughter has earned the opportunities before her. She will do well. In more than one lifetime, she plowed and pioneered, discharging debts and bringing at-one-ment about. This lifetime is the same. Her journey will bring you joy. Be at peace."*

As soon as Lisa and her husband crossed over our threshold at Christmas, any lingering apprehension was dispelled. My acceptance and embrace of my son-in-law was genuine.

When Lisa called in fall 1979 to say that she was expecting fraternal twins, I was excited. I scarcely noticed the old, familiar apprehension as it slowly surfaced. Nevertheless, as the time drew near for my trip east, I began to wonder how I would feel about my grandchildren, children who were neither white nor black, but both.

Shortly before my departure, I had a meditation that I will cherish forever. An incomparable burst of love enveloped me and a voice imbued with a special sweetness and infinite patience said:

"My child, my child. You worry so. Have more confidence in yourself. You will love these children with all your heart and soul. It could not be otherwise. You have known these little ones before and you will know them again. All will be well."

Devon and his sister Danica were born twenty minutes apart on April 9, 1980. I held each baby in my arms a few minutes after birth, and I knew that God had truly graced my life.

Sadly, in 1983, Lisa and her husband realized that their ideal friendship did not guarantee an ideal marriage. Their time together was complete, and they divorced.

Two years later, while working at a military base in Florida, Lisa met the man who was to be her life mate. Terry was black, but this didn't matter, as I no longer saw the color of anyone's skin. Lisa told me that her former husband had been content with his life, but Terry and she shared similar goals for the future. She added, "The day I was introduced to Terry, I recognized him on a deeper level. I wouldn't say I fell in love with him that day, but I knew we were on the same wavelength."

I asked Terry if he had always known that he would marry out of his race. He answered, "No, not at all. I dated black women at first. I was drawn to Lisa because of her family values, her independent nature, and sense of responsibility. What's really important is to be true to yourself, not to settle for what is expected of you."

Stimulated by our easy rapport, I probed on. "Is it difficult for black parents when their children marry into another race?"

"Sure is. Our race has gone through so much, and the white race caused many of the problems. We're stabilizing now, and when a black marries out of the race, it's as though another brick is lost. The structure is weakened. But once the marriage takes place, the black family accepts it."

Lisa and Terry were married in July 1986. Their challenges proved no different than those of a traditional marriage. Their achievements would be exceptional.

INNER PEACE MAY BE ELUSIVE

BUT ILLUSION IT IS NOT

Meditation
June 1993

Mentors and Milestones

AS THE SEVENTIES SECURED A FOOTHOLD IN THE NEW decade, I secured a telepathic connection with my Higher Self in meditation. Now, I could relax my campaign to break through for the attainment of personal and family guidance. Nevertheless, the vague memory of a vow I had made to myself years before—that I would find a way to help others in pain—wafted through my heart and head.

When I brought the commitment into focus, I saw myself sitting beside my brother Barry's bed on that tragic night in 1957 when his best friend Tommy had died. It was a night when grief knew no bounds.

Was it possible that I could bring comfort from the Higher Realms to people? No, I wasn't worthy of serving in such an important and responsible way. Psychically gifted people were born, not developed. Furthermore, the few truly gifted psychics I knew or read about didn't have to struggle for self-confidence and inner strength. Some were candidates for sainthood, such as Edgar Cayce was in my eyes. No, I didn't qualify for a spiritual calling.

Higher Consciousness, with a copy of my divine plan in hand and an available mentor in mind, was of a different accord. A strong sign was given me through a dream I had in July 1971, which proved to be a herald of the goals and gifts I dared not imagine in my waking hours.

I saw myself walk through the front door of an unfamiliar, ramshackle two-story farmhouse. As I wandered from room to room, each frugally furnished and obviously lived in, I saw no residents. When I came to a kitchen, however, I was struck by its desolate disuse. The shelves and cabinets were empty, in mourning for their purpose of the past. A vintage wood-burning stove, cast iron garnished with rust, soot, and sawdust, stood angled apart from the wall it once graced. Its dismantled and discarded flue lay on the floor nearby. A knife-nicked and color-faded Formica® countertop, propped against another wall on wobbly wooden legs, proclaimed its past with a gaping hole that once held a serviceable sink.

Depressed, I picked up my pace and exited through an archway, dreading the sight of a dining room in a similar state of pathos. Instead, I was astonished to find myself in a second kitchen, a room with hundreds of tiny suns sparkling and bouncing off the ceiling, reflecting on the snow-white walls. The brightness and lightness of every hue in this fully equipped and warmly decorated contemporary kitchen appealed to me and called to me to meld myself in it. Everywhere I looked I saw service, comfort, and nourishment of some kind. I then awoke.

Although I contemplated this dream for days, I could not glean its meaning, nor could I dislodge it from the forum of my mind.

Three weeks later, a friend called to say that a husband and wife ministerial team had moved to Albuquerque. Both were ordained by a Christian denomination with its home church in Phoenix. Rev. Rita Sellman was a gifted psychic. Rev. Lloyd Sellman, a chiropractic physician, also worked with spiritual healing energies.

The Sellmans had announced that they would hold a two-hour service on Sunday afternoons at their home beginning the next weekend. The first hour would comprise a typical Protestant worship service. During the next hour, a number of people would be treated to a short psychic message. Spiritual healing would be offered at the same time. I was intrigued. Marc and I and several friends decided to attend. All week, an unidentifiable sense of déjà vu haunted my thoughts.

Sunday arrived and so did we. Once inside the two-story farmhouse on North Fourth Street that the Sellmans now called home, I remembered my dream. I walked quickly down the hall past two or three open rooms and into the original kitchen. My eyes took in every square inch of the room. No wood-burning stove, no dilapidated countertop nor empty shelves were in view—just a dark, empty room, dismal but not depressing.

I turned toward the archway and squeezed through the throng. When in the clear, I knew for certain that this was indeed the house in my dream. The new kitchen had a textured and heavily glitter-sprayed ceiling that caught the gentle radiance of the afternoon sun as it poured through the windows. By refracting and diverting the rays of natural light, the ceiling finish was transformed into a thousand points of "diamond dust" luminescence.

Almost as bright was Mrs. Sellman herself as she glided toward me, smoothly slipping by people engaged in conversation. She wore an ankle-length dress—a cross between

a caftan and a muu-muu—made from a fabric with surface
sheen. The shade, an opalescent pink, complemented her
light complexion. Rita, as she asked me to call her, wore her
near-white hair in a short, simple style. The soft curls
framed a face that exuded warmth and openness, impressions that were borne out by her personality.

I had to ask. "Why, yes," Rita laughed. "Lloyd tore that old
kitchen up in no time flat. It wasn't until a few days ago that
he hauled that rusty stove and stuff away. Have you seen
the chapel?" With this, she steered me through the throng,
the archway, the original kitchen, and into a newly constructed addition.

The chapel, tastefully appointed with touches of an inspirational decor, was furnished with an upright piano, a
lectern, and sixty folding chairs with padded seats. The floor
was carpeted, the walls were painted off-white, and the ceiling was textured and lightly glitter-sprayed. With fewer
windows, the chapel offered subdued light, an atmosphere
that fostered a more prayerful mood than the kitchen.

From somewhere in the house, a clock struck two. People
hurried into the chapel to find a seat. Rev. Rita Sellman
joined her husband at the front of the room. The male side
of this ministerial duo was about 5'10", broad shouldered
and slim hipped. He had blue eyes and an abundance of
white, wavy hair. Lloyd and Rita Sellman could be considered the two sides of one coin.

The service began with hymn singing. Actually, it began
with Rita's disclaimer: she really couldn't hold a tune. She
led us in four or five spirited hymns anyway. This admission
endeared her to me, as I was not known for having musical
ability either. And I loved to sing.

The fifteen-minute "sermon" was also delivered by Rev.
Rita. The talk, which was on tolerance and compassion, included several scriptures from the New Testament. As she
spoke, I knew for certain that Christ Jesus was the Master
and Light of her world.

Lloyd Sellman then sang my favorite hymn, "How Great Thou Art." He not only held the tune well, but he sang with fervent conviction. His wife's obvious dedication to the Light was clearly matched by his own. I detected no underlying competitiveness in the subsequent repartee, only genuine love for each other and for God.

Since this was their first Gateway to Light service in New Mexico, Rita spoke briefly on how their ministry came about. When she was still in her first marriage, her eight-year-old daughter died as a direct result of receiving the Salk vaccine at school. Rita had refused her permission, but the inoculation was given anyway.

Angry with God and bitter about life, Rita was walking in the rain one evening when she heard church music coming from a small auditorium. Her feet took her into the building. She sat in the back row so that she could make a hasty exit if need be.

The gentleman at the podium was addressing someone near the front. When he finished, he turned his gaze on the sopping wet woman in the last row. Mad at herself for being there, a bedraggled Rita glared back at him.

The man called out: "There's a young girl here—I get her name as Bonnie—who says that she is your daughter. She wants you to know that she's being well taken care of. Stop taking it out on God. It's time for you to get started with your mission."

Rita's mouth flew open, and as she often jokes, "It hasn't closed yet." Her life changed course that rainy night in Phoenix. A little further down the road, she left a bad marriage to move away and begin doing God's will and work.

Rita became aware of her own psychic gifts only after a near-death experience. A pregnant black widow spider bit her over the site where the spiritual eye is said to be located. Quick-acting doctors saved her life. The wound did not heal well and would not close. The hole was half a thumbnail deep. Friends suggested a visit to spiritual healers in Tempe,

Arizona. There, out in the desert at dawn, in the midst of caring, praying people, Rita knew that healing was under way. The wound began to close, and her spiritual eye began to open. A quarter-inch deep indentation remains in her forehead today.

Soon afterward, her psychic abilities inescapable, Rita signed on to serve as a spiritual counselor with several of the small metaphysical churches springing up in the Southwest. Five years later, she and Lloyd met, married, and started the Gateway to Light ministry. Lloyd chose to close the door on a thriving chiropractic business in favor of total commitment to their spiritual work.

"Well, now, I've given you the history of our lives, and it's time for us to go to work," Rita said, as she smiled at her husband—about to leave the room. "Lloyd will be in the front sitting room for anyone who wishes spiritual healing. Just sit in a 'healing chair.' He works on your energy field to remove negativity or blocks. You may be surprised afterward; many people no longer have physical pain. Get up and go in there when you're ready, and come back here afterward. If you're fairly quiet, you won't bother me."

Rita rubbed the palms of her hands together as she walked closer to the congregation. She closed her eyes, said a brief prayer, and opened her eyes again. As she scanned the room, I noticed that her vision appeared to be focused just above our heads. As though she knew what I was thinking, she said, "I look for the light to land on someone's head. Then I know who the Higher Beings wish to address."

I lowered my eyes, not wanting to receive the first message, if indeed I received one at all. With fifty-plus people in the room, I knew that Rita would be hard pressed to read for more than a third. I told myself to be content without.

About sixteen upbeat, often-humorous messages and forty-five minutes later, Rev. Rita Sellman pointed a pink fingernail toward Marc and me, looked directly at us—and yet through us—and said:

"The woman in the turquoise blouse. You are very psychic. In the near future, you will be up here doing what I'm doing now. This is what you came to do, and all that you have gone through was preparation. The time is right. Let go of all doubt. Doubt is your worst enemy. Trust."

She inclined her head toward Marc, waved at me to lean away from him, and said: "I see green rays of healing energy streaming from your fingertips. You, sir, are a healer. The sooner you work with this energy on behalf of other people, the sooner you'll grow into your calling."

We were both quiet on the ride home. I could not imagine how Rita's prediction about me could possibly be true. I had not been born with psychic ability. I wondered if Rita had simply picked up on my desire to help others. Nonetheless, the seed was planted—and in spite of my low self-esteem, it *would* germinate.

I intended to be discreet, but I found myself sharing the recent experience with almost anyone who would listen. When my brother Bill called to confirm his visit the next week, I visualized a captive audience. Bill was well read on religious philosophy, but he had not yet meditated. He'd never had a psychic reading. I made an appointment for him with Rita.

The past few years had been difficult for Bill. After our mother died, he struggled emotionally and financially to finish college. It especially anguished him that he had not had a chance to say good-by to Mom. He missed her very much, and he felt terribly alone. There was little I could do to help except to stay in close touch with him. He said later that my letters kept him going.

Barry and Lorraine had married and were busy settling into family life. Barry offered to help whenever he could, but Bill needed a common denominator, and there was none. Their paths were divergent. Their pain was different. They couldn't talk.

Bill graduated from Rider College in 1966 with a degree

in journalism. His spiritual search led him to convert to Catholicism. Unable to find work in his field, he took a job teaching seventh grade in a Catholic school. In 1967, he was drafted into the army.

A month into a Vietnam tour of duty, Bill had a seizure during a mortar attack at the Da Nang military airport. At a hospital in Japan, he was diagnosed as having had a full-scale grand mal epileptic seizure. He later told me that he'd had several minor seizures in college when exceptionally tired, but did not see a doctor. For the remainder of his enlistment, Bill was assigned to Ft. Knox, Kentucky. He received an honorable discharge in 1969.

Once back in New Jersey, Bill went to work as an editor for the Princeton Packet newspaper chain. His on-again, off-again relationship with the only girl with whom he felt comfortable ended for the final time. Heartbroken, Bill decided the time was right for a change of scene—or at least a vacation. What he didn't know was that his sister was on her metaphysical soapbox, and his brother-in-law had a pretty divorcée lined up to date him.

The first event on the agenda was the psychic reading. Although Bill probably went just to humor me, he found it to be pleasant and interesting. He was told that a young woman would soon enrich his life. According to Rita, "This gal keeps changing her hairdo. And every time I zoom in on her, her hair is a different color." When Bill mentioned this to us, Marc smiled.

The next day, Marc brought Alaine and her six-year-old daughter, Kenna, to meet Bill. Her mother's only child, Kenna was born with cerebral palsy. Alaine was a beautician. A naturally creative person, she blended colors and tried out the new shades on her own hair first. Bill was drawn to Kenna immediately; he fell in love with Alaine a few days later.

On Bill and Alaine's third date, as they talked in my car in the driveway, streaks of light played on the windshield and the hood. There was no accountable source for the strange phenomena. Bewildered, they came into the house and sat on my sofa. Marc and I were already asleep. The bizarre lights then manifested in my living room, dancing on the walls and ceiling.

When Bill described his startling and unnerving experience the next morning, I did not doubt his word. He had always been a conscientiously honest person, and as with many journalists, more than a little skeptical about the unexplained.

We wondered if the light show was designed to imbue a sense of destiny, to keep them together. If it was, it was successful—for two years. (It also brought about his relocation and an opportunity for psychic development.) Bill closed out his life in New Jersey, moved to New Mexico, and married Alaine.

In the meantime, before Bill went home to pack up for the move, he and Marc and I attended a Gateway to Light Sunday afternoon service. The Sellmans had invited another psychically gifted minister to participate.

The guest minister, a Rev. Highlager, wanted to talk about his travels before he "went to work," as Rita put it. While he was discoursing, he became agitated by something—invisible to the congregation—behind him. He glanced to the left, pulled his shoulder forward as though to dislodge someone's hand, and shook his head to indicate no. The third time he did this, he said, "Wait. I want to finish what I'm saying, and then I will let you speak." The mysterious exchange had more than a few of us in stitches. I wondered if Rita had checked the good reverend's credentials.

He finally gave up the travelogue, cocked an ear to the left, and listened to someone for a moment. He then asked the congregation, "Does anyone here know of a lady in spirit named Mabel?"

Stunned, I looked around. No one responded. Marc jabbed me in the ribs. Bill sat mute. I raised my hand and said, "We do."

Rev. Highlager listened again to the persistent Mabel behind his shoulder, then turned to the three of us and said:
"She wants you to know that you are on the right track. Keep
moving forward. You are going in the right direction. Everything will be fine. This lady is very excited. She is jumping
up and down." He readdressed himself to Mabel, asking her
if she was happy now. She must have indicated that she was,
since Rev. Highlager concluded his talk without interrup-
tion.

One of Rita's announcements that afternoon was that her
psychic development class would begin the following
month, September. Marc and I were the first to register. Bill
said he'd join when he returned to Albuquerque. Among the
other students were three former Roman Catholic clergy,
two priests and a nun, who had left the official ministry to
better work for change from the outside. They were Roméo
and Vicki Di Benedetto and their close friend and associate,
Fred McCarthy.

Marc had once aspired to the Jesuit priesthood; it was
only the vow of celibacy that deterred him. He developed
an easy rapport with Roméo and Fred, and I overheard Marc
as he commented, "Once a priest, always a priest, right?"
Both men smiled in agreement.

Rita's technique for teaching could be likened to a "cold
turkey dive into deep water." We took turns—two people
center stage at one time—reading for each other. I found
this an intimidating ordeal. Rita's premise was that whoever
was "on" would be aided by the energy of the group. The pooled
energy should enable the reader to delve into the seeker's
superconscious and above. All we had to do was to audibly
repeat the thoughts and words that came into our heads.

I was certain that when it was my turn, one of two things
would happen: either nothing would come, or all kinds of
dumb, inaccurate information would pop into my head and
I'd repeat it only to be mortified.

My first serious but successful psychic probe was miserable in the making but memorable—for me. I was to read for Fred, who was an attorney as well as a former priest. With my fear of authority figures and Marc's awe of the priesthood—all of his opinions influenced me—I didn't think I had a chance. I took Fred's hands in mine (we sat across from each other in straight-back chairs), closed my eyes, and opened my mouth.

"Fred, you are like a rolling stone which gathers no moss."

I could hear my husband gasp in the background: I had insulted a former Roman Catholic priest!

Well, thank God for Fred. He laughed heartily. "Nothing could be more true," he said. "I've lived in almost every country and seldom have I stayed in a place long enough to call it home."

Meditating for my own guidance was one matter; reading for someone else was entirely different. My anxiety beforehand—and the agonizing replay in my mind for hours afterward—was extreme. My classmates took their hits and misses in stride. I envied them.

I tried to analyze the root cause of my distress. Perhaps it was my need for everyone's approval, my fear of ridicule, or just my lack of self-confidence. Whatever triggered such near-disabling emotions, I knew that I would go on with development. My drive for what I then called "the gift of prophecy" was dominant. This was the first week of October 1971. I had just turned thirty-seven.

An answer came, once again in the middle of the night. Marc and I had decided to follow Betty Bethards's recommendation and set the alarm for a 2:00 a.m. meditation several times a week.

Betty told us that once the "garbage-out" dreams have taken place, the mind is relatively clear and better able to receive. I was concerned that I'd not return to sleep, but Betty assured me that I would. She was right. I woke up at 2:00 easily and was amazingly alert. Afterward, I went back to sleep without any difficulty.

Marc and I alternated in the roles of meditator and battery. When I meditated, he sat at the foot of the bed and directed energy to me from the Universe as it coursed through the palms of his hands. And vice versa.

On my second such session, I had barely closed my eyes when I saw stars—an entire galaxy of stars, all revolving around me. I was out of the body and traveling in reverse. There was no rocket or comet on this trip. It was as though an enormous force were pulling me backward at great speed. Soon—perhaps a minute—I looked down and saw three pyramids.

Instantly, I felt myself being drawn down into one of the pyramids and just as instantly, I was inside a stone sarcophagus. The lid was coming down on top of me. My heart, desperate to escape its fate, hammered violently at my chest wall. I tried to scream, but I couldn't! I couldn't breathe! I heard Marc saying from far off, "Honey, what's wrong, what's wrong?" I couldn't answer him; I wasn't there. I was here, in this death trap.

A gentle, loving voice—a voice I knew and treasured—penetrated my mind: *"Be calm. You are safe. This is only a remembrance. It was essential that we take you back to where it began. You have asked for the gift of prophecy. You had the gift once. You betrayed your vows. You betrayed the people who believed in you.*

"You are again seeking the gift, seeking to help people. If you pursue this path and are granted the gift, you must learn and teach discernment. In the past, you prostituted your gift for power and possessions. Those whom you served and sacrificed then will cross your path again. Remember—honor, integrity, discernment."

A moment later, I was back in my body, sitting propped against pillows on my bed. The connection was still in place.

I knew it was time to ask precisely who this compassionate source was. I projected the thought-question: "When will I hear the voice of my Higher Self?"

I sensed amusement as the source responded: *"You have been listening to your Higher Self for quite a while. Be at peace. All will be well."* In a few minutes, I was deeply asleep.

The next day, I shared the guidance with Marc and asked him not to speak of it to anyone. Nor did I. Since I was acutely aware of the popular trend to fantasize about former lives, my stance on the subject was one of caution and reservation. I had no problem with believing that I had "blown" a life; it was the drama of the scene and setting that troubled me.

Tempted to discard the guidance, but not certain that I should, I turned within. Displayed on my inner screen were pages and pages of lined notebook paper, the kind of paper that accompanied me from middle school through twelfth grade. I recognized the sheets by the doodles thereon: stone coffin after stone coffin, some with lids in place and others without.

Fourteen years later, I would form a meditation group in Gulf Breeze, Florida. We would become exceptionally bonded, personally and spiritually. An unpredictable development would give us reason to consider a past-life association, and for the first time I would speak of the guidance about Egypt.

Marc and I reached our peak in harmony during the time we attended the Gateway to Light services and classes. We were caught up in common goals.

When Marc learned that a neighbor's son was dying from leukemia, he visited the young boy often, to bring him comfort and whatever healing energies were in divine order.

Although the boy made his transition, the experience was a rewarding one for the boy's family and for Marc. From that time on, he worked with the healing rays whenever an opportunity was presented.

In January 1972, Rev. Rita Sellman fell ill with bronchial pneumonia. She knew she would need three months to recover. Rita had been working with Fr. Di Benedetto as a spiritual counselor, giving psychic readings for the federally funded NARA II program. The clients of NARA II—which stood for Narcotic Addict Rehabilitation Act—were men and women recently paroled from prison. They had been incarcerated as a result of drug-related charges.

The NARA II clients were beginning to respond favorably to the program. Fr. Di Benedetto wanted someone to fill in for Rev. Sellman. My brother Bill was doing well in Rita's class, but he was encumbered by a demanding job, as were most of the other students.

For the previous two months, I had been giving psychic messages in the Gateway to Light Sunday service. I had also begun a six-month leave of absence from the Indian Housing Authority. I needed time away from the internal political pressures that had prevailed the previous year.

I was drafted by Fr. Di Benedetto for NARA II.

Rita never returned to the work with the drug abuse rehabilitation program. When she was well again, she and Lloyd concentrated on classes and other Gateway to Light activities. Six months later, the Sellmans were guided to move to Tucson to start a chapel there.

"Coincidental" with the conclusion of my work with NARA II at the close of 1972, my telephone rang regularly for private reading appointments. "The work I came to do" was under way.

My self-esteem and self-confidence had improved measurably during my time with NARA II. Regardless of the positive feedback I received from the people I read for, however, my pre-reading anxiety did not abate. Because of my out-of-the-body visit to the pyramids in meditation, I now understood what was going on deep within my subconscious: I was terrified of misleading people, of erring in the attunement process, and rendering false guidance.

For the next few years, I struggled with the anxiety affliction. At times I felt nauseous prior to a reading. I always hoped the seeker would cancel the appointment—few did. On a crisp fall day in 1975, a man I didn't know appeared at my door. He said his name was Dick Bell, that he was from San Francisco, and that my very good friend Theodora in Santa Fe suggested that he visit me.

We talked about psychic counseling. Mr. Bell spoke the magic words: "There is no reason for you to be so apprehensive about your work. You can relax. You are properly connected, and you do not mislead people."

As he was leaving, I asked what hotel he was staying at. He said, "the Sheraton." After he left, I thought how nice it would be for Marc to meet Mr. Bell. I thought perhaps he'd like to return that night for dinner. I called the Sheraton Hotel. No Dick Bell registered. I called the Hilton Hotel; no Dick Bell there either. I called Theodora. She said he was a stranger to her when he popped in unannounced, and she didn't know where he was heading. However, "something told her" to give him my name and address.

I never heard from Dick Bell again, but I had reason to bless him. From that day on, I was free of my pre-reading paranoia.

*GOD GAVE EVERYONE A
DIRECT LINE FOR GUIDANCE*

*THOSE WHO ARE "GIFTED"
HAVE MERELY CALLED HOME SOONER*

**Meditation
July 1993**

Beetles, Buses, and Babies

BY SUMMER 1976, MARC AND I HAD ENJOYED OUR spiritual growth agenda for nearly six years. I continued to give several psychic readings a week. Our Saturday night meditation was well attended. I taught three eight-week psychic development classes a year. We were contributing members of several small metaphysical centers. Whenever we traveled, we scheduled meditations, seminars, talks, or classes, if feasible, in the town or state we visited.

The Alliance for Health and Wholeness took a large chunk of our time and energy, as we remained committed to the ideals and purposes adopted in 1972. I had served as secretary-treasurer from the beginning, and Marc had held various offices as well.

All of these activities were in addition to our full-time jobs. I was now employed by New Mexico Blue Cross and Blue Shield as a department supervisor, having resigned from the Indian Housing Authority to accompany Marc on an out-of-town assignment in 1974.

A considerable number of people moved in and out of our days and our lives—particularly young women.

I wanted desperately to hold my marriage together in spite of Marc's occasional flirtations. I had no evidence that the attractions progressed beyond the talking stage. I didn't want to know.

When the pretty college student we'd hired as Shannon's sitter walked out, telling me later that Marc had made advances toward her, I chose to accept his denial. "She was smoking pot and imagining all kinds of things," he said.

Every such incident hurt, but I would put it behind me and move on. My dream was that as Marc's self-esteem grew with spiritual awareness and service, his need for extramarital excitement and the admiration of women would diminish. I felt that our spiritual compatibility was rare and remarkable. I didn't want to lose it.

I donned blinders and stubbornly refused to take them off—until one fall morning when the telephone rang rather early. Marc answered it and with a stricken demeanor motioned me to sit down.

"That was Candy. There's no easy way to tell you this, so I won't beat around the bush." He sat down near me and reached for my hand. I moved away. I knew I wasn't going to like what he had to say. I took a deep breath, but panic already had a stronghold. Soon it engulfed me.

"I told you I went over to her apartment last night to work with her in meditation. Well, we lost control and ended up in bed. This morning, her herpes was rampant. She called to recommend that I see a doctor now, since it is highly contagious." When I didn't speak—my mind was trying to absorb the shock as rage was racing to the surface—Marc went on. "I swear, Barb, that I didn't know she had herpes, and I didn't expect to have sex with her last night. And now I might have infected you. I feel rotten about this."

The world's wimpiest woman went wild.

A few hours later, my children and I were on our way to El Paso. Marc was to move out while we were gone. I *knew* that I would receive help from Higher Consciousness in prayer and meditation, but I needed earth-type spiritual resources as well. Dr. Di Benedetto and his wife graciously offered their love and hospitality.

I drove south on I-25 past the Organ Mountains of New Mexico, dropped Lisa and Chris off with friends in Las Cruces, and continued east on I-10 to the mile-high Franklin Range. I exited onto Transmountain Road, boomeranged, zig-zagged, and curved through the pass and down into the northeast quadrant of the city. God's handiwork—which always had entranced me—now seemed to be warning: "Wherever you go, there will always be obstacles, immense and looming. You can't escape life."

Throughout the next few days, my frame of mind swung between frenzied, flailing thoughts and the listless lethargy of despair. By the end of the week, Roméo's and Vicki's healing ministrations and my time in the Silence enabled me to center myself and to marshal the strength to go on. On the drive home, I focused on thinking constructively about the future.

As I turned the corner onto our street, I saw Marc's truck in the driveway. I steeled myself and went into the house. His jackets were still in the front closet. He was in bed with an ailing back. "Why are you still here?" I demanded, as I slammed the bedroom door shut. He told me that as he began to pack, he had an overwhelming feeling that God was not pleased with him. He didn't want to jeopardize his spiritual progress.

His words caught me off guard. I had no rebuttal. Undoubtedly, I wasn't ready—I wasn't strong enough yet—I wasn't able—to choose health and independence for myself. My energy suddenly drained out . . . I listened lifelessly as Marc told me that my possessiveness and need to control our lives was responsible for his wandering ways. Somewhere in my head a voice wanted to be heard, but I was too numb. I couldn't think or react.

For the next few years, I was intimately acquainted with self-torment, suspicion, denial, and defensiveness. Marc agreed to be monogamous until I "could comprehend that an occasional liaison would actually benefit *our* relationship." I knew that such a time would never arrive. Our union became a battle of wills: his will for an open marriage versus my will for exclusivity and trust.

The irony of my dilemma did not escape me. I had been unfaithful to my first husband. Now I was reaping—many times over—what I had sown. I intellectualized that this was my karma, the payback I had earned. I recalled the advice given me by a psychologist whom my son saw for a few months when he was twelve. "They're better off with Marc—a strong father figure—than with no father at all." I had my rationale for staying with Marc.

In December 1978, we went to Hawaii for three weeks to visit Bill, now an editor with the daily newspaper in Hilo. Bill and his second wife had just welcomed their first child. It was wonderful to spend time with them in such a lovely setting.

But back home, it was our daily routines, as usual, that caused the most problems between Marc and the kids. A frustrated organic farmer, Marc converted our back yard into an impressive vegetable garden. He was particularly successful with Kentucky Wonder pole beans. Several rows of flourishing foliage adorned tepee-type structures abundant with life: beans and bean beetles.

Chris and I were "detailed" to the garden every morning.

Our assignment was to locate the bean beetles on the undersides of the leaves and mash each leaf with our fingers to kill the beetles. We were allowed an option: we could also take the indoor-outdoor vacuum to the garden and suck those poor little beetles off the leaves.

After a few days of feeble attempts, I realized that neither Chris nor I had the stomach for such a massacre. I risked the wrath of Khan, who ranted and raved, but I stood my ground and adamantly declared that we would not do battle with the beetles.

Chris got a break from such routines when the Wesley Choir to which he belonged took on a volunteer project in Calexico, California. The teens would travel by bus, stopping at various Methodist churches along the way to put on a musical program.

When Marc and I drove Chris to the church to board the Greyhound for the tour, I was surprised to see that the driver was none other than Ralph Paulin, a friend from my days with the BIA. Disenchanted with indoor confinement in a management job, Ralph opted for the lure of the open road—again. I knew that his first love was the railroad; he had been an engineer until the diesels came in. His next best recourse was driving charters across the country.

As months passed, the pressures within the family became a way of life. None of us measured up to Marc's standards. Friends commented that Marc was more considerate to strangers than to us.

I did not recognize the warning signs with regard to Shannon's emotional health until she started first grade. A very perceptive school counselor called and urged me to withdraw my daughter and keep her home for another year. It seemed that Shannon would not answer when called on; she stood by her desk and stayed silent.

A diagnostic interview was conducted to determine if she could be mentally disabled. The interview went poorly. Shannon did not respond to the white-jacketed clinical psychologist holding up the illustrations of a policeman, a fireman, and a doctor. Shannon was to identify their professions.

The counselor believed that Shannon simply was not ready for school. Withdrawing her would prevent the system from applying an unwarranted negative label that would follow my daughter all the way through high school. We took her out that very day.

Although extremely shy, Shannon was a normal six-year-old child, capable of first grade work and well able to communicate. When I asked her why she had not answered the diagnostician, brightness and logic were evident in her response: "Mommy, that lady's questions were so silly. If she didn't know who the people were in the pictures, I wasn't going to tell her." When I asked why she didn't answer her teacher, she said, "I was scared I'd say something wrong and get yelled at, like Lisa and Chris do with Daddy."

For some time, Shannon had been whispering rather than speaking in a normal voice. In my busyness and with my tunnel vision, I was oblivious to the damage being wrought. Unusually sensitive from infancy, Shannon shrank back, trying to be invisible, when her siblings were censured. She was afraid of her father.

I tried to communicate with Marc about his austere tone of voice, imploring him to request or instruct rather than demand and command. He didn't change. I became more protective. Shannon continued to whisper. Life went on.

Years later, I recognized the seriousness of *my* contribution to Shannon's distress: passivity and my "peace at any price" way of life. While Lisa and Chris were aware of my fear of confrontation, it didn't seem to trouble them as deeply as it did my youngest child—the daughter who most mirrored me.

In late 1978, I resigned for good from outside jobs. I had recognized for several years that my heart was no longer with the business world. The spiritual focus, along with our life as a family, was all I wanted and needed for fulfillment. I wanted to give more readings a week, to "be there" for more people in pain.

Marc maneuvered me into a multilevel marketing program, which he promised to manage himself. A month later, he transferred to an out-of-town engineering project. He would be home only on weekends. When his boss inadvertently told me that Marc had volunteered for the assignment, I was furious, but I did not confront him on it. Instead, true to my nature as a record keeper, I created and maintained a ton of paperwork.

The added pressure took its toll on me. In December 1979, I fainted while visiting a friend in the hospital. I regained consciousness in the emergency room. Another friend drove me home.

An hour later, I discovered that I was hemorrhaging. For some unfathomable reason, I expected the bleeding to cease on its own. By the following morning, I had lost over half of my body's supply of blood. Marc took me to Bataan Hospital where I was admitted immediately to the intensive care unit. The gastric ulcer I didn't know I had had ruptured an artery at the bottom of my stomach. The doctor was not optimistic.

My intractable husband was staunchly opposed to healing by surgery. When asked to authorize an operation, Marc demurred. He proceeded to enlighten the doctor as to alternative treatments that should stop the hemorrhage and help salvage my stomach.

After I lazed six days in a dreamy haze, the surgeon made *me* an offer I *couldn't* refuse: a subtotal gastrectomy or death. I signed the form, surrendered forty-eight percent of my stomach, and removed my blinders. Permanently.

Lisa and Chris dedicated hours to making me laugh, in effect shaking my stapled stomach and bringing tears to my eyes. However, whenever Marc walked into the room, my abdominal muscles went into spasm—but not from humor.

Afraid that it would happen again, I asked the doctor how

to better cope with stress. He replied, to my astonishment, "Your ulcer had nothing to do with stress." I *knew* that it did. I had swallowed too much toxic emotional stress and my stomach finally rebelled.

Two months later, Shannon and I flew to North Carolina to be with Lisa for the birth of Danica and Devon. The delight of holding and caring for my first grandchildren was tantamount to the relief that Shannon and I felt by being "out from under" the taskmaster's thumb.

I spent hours walking among the tall pine trees, contemplating my options. I knew I needed to be free of my marriage. It was difficult to let go of the illusion—the dream of "what might have been." But my body—long past the reflection phase—had manifested excision, the only decision.

During our remaining time at Lisa's, I felt as though a dark cloud were overhead. I sensed it as an indication of death, and—still shaky from the surgery—I wondered if it was to be me or my marriage. In meditation, I was given:

> *"An illness or emotional crisis often precedes a significant change in spiritual perception and awareness. You chose to stay. It is not enough to choose to stay unless one has a will to live. Otherwise, the body will continue acting out the death wish, slowly."*

I knew that this time, *my* will had to be involved. From the place of peace deep within, I drew healing and strength for the beginning of the rest of my life.

Two days before we were to leave—we had been with Lisa for almost three months—Shannon walked through poison ivy. Her body's reaction was swift and severe, and her flight home miserable. Perhaps Shannon, on an unconscious level, did not want to return home.

Marc met us at the airport. Later that night, he asked me for a divorce. Suddenly, from somewhere deep, deep within, an old script surfaced and anxiety reigned. A week earlier, I had visualized my freedom. Now, in a matter of minutes, I couldn't see myself UNmarried, independent. I tearfully asked Marc to reconsider.

He agreed to a few individual sessions with a marriage counselor, but it proved pointless. When I learned on July 4, Independence Day, that someone was waiting in the wings for Marc to be free, I filed for divorce.

Surprisingly, despite tumultuous thoughts and feelings, I was able to achieve a clear connection in meditation. One evening, my mother came through to assure me that I had *"happier days coming than you have ever known."*

Gradually, my emotional turmoil settled into healthy anger. I attended a divorce recovery workshop held by a Methodist minister. Through determination, hard work, and the encouragement of Higher Consciousness, the anger dissipated and acceptance took hold.

Nevertheless, my self-image as a woman was badly damaged. I needed to know I was still attractive. I wanted to know that I'd not be single the rest of my life. I liked marriage. Who would be interested in a twice-divorced woman with three children?

In late August, I received a call from Ralph Paulin. He wanted to thank me for the sympathy card I had sent when his wife died in June. He suggested that we get together and commiserate about our losses. Chris urged me to go. I did.

We found that we had more going for us than metaphysics, although that alone was an immense plus in my mind. Ralph was as attentive, affectionate, and considerate a companion as I could hope for. The more that Chris and Shannon saw of Ralph, the more they enjoyed him, another huge plus.

My need for validation and his need to be needed propelled us into a committed relationship. We talked about marriage. I was concerned that stepparenting might throw Ralph a curve since he and his wife had been childless. The prospect did not daunt him.

Faced with another major life choice, I bypassed the outer sanctuaries in favor of the temple within. I fully expected my optimism and happiness to meet with profound relief and joy on the part of Higher Consciousness—relief that I'd made a right decision *at last* and joy that Ralph was the right mate.

As the words began to flow across the forefront of my mind, "We would advise caution, my child," I abruptly closed the door from my side, slid out of the meditative state, and spent the remainder of the day convincing myself there had been an unavoidable (unprecedented) miscommunication. I didn't open again *for guidance* until the deed was done. And, of course, *"they"* honored my right to continue learning the hard way.

My divorce was final on December 11, 1980. I married Ralph Paulin the next day.

◆ ◆ ◆

YOU MUST FIND JOY IN LIFE

IN ORDER TO FIND HEALTH.

Meditation
North Carolina, March 1980

The Dynamics of
Psychic/Intuitive Counseling

Stage One–1972 to 1982

I GAVE MY FIRST PSYCHIC READING IN JANUARY 1972 and the "last" reading in 1994. Excluding the twenty months between May 1983 and December 1984 (an "inner mission," or the period of time needed for intense personal healing and growth work), I gave from 150 to 200 readings a year.

This span of time, twenty-two years, divides quite naturally into two distinctly different stages of experience.

At the beginning of Stage One, my personal insecurities were dominant and my physical health reflected my inner turmoil. My understanding of the dynamics of psychic work was skimpy at best. I was able to attune to the seeker and *give* a reading, but I really didn't know *how* it worked. Being thrust into the NARA II experimental project early on may have been providential, as I didn't have time to worry about my limited understanding of the process.

Few books had been published on psychic development in the early seventies, and those available focused on remarkable results rather than the mechanics of the psychic/intuitive connection.

With role model Edgar Cayce on "the other side" and mentors Betty Bethards and Rita Sellman at a distance, I learned how to be a good instrument by trial and error. In retrospect, experience was truly my best teacher. The more uncomfortable the psychic session, the more determined I was to master the lesson involved. Such lessons included preparation, protection, detachment, and discernment.

I did not need to advertise. The Universe and word-of-mouth kept people calling for readings. If I were away or needed a break, telephone calls decreased. On my return, calls accelerated. Whenever the waiting list grew unwieldy—that is, close to fifty people—I asked Higher Consciousness to slow the calls down, and it did.

The anxiety I felt prior to a psychic session—the awesome responsibility should I guide wrongly about a critical choice and my underlying fear that a seeker might be angry enough to cause me harm—proved groundless. When a reading was over and I was "back to normal" (and not "spaced out," as my family called the altered state afterburn), I often walked on air for hours, thanking God for giving me the chance to help others.

Perhaps the reading appointments were especially successful because I insisted upon being "spoon fed" guidance word by word. I was determined to ensure purity however I could. I refused to translate "spiritual shorthand," which included images, symbols, and thought forms. If the message wasn't spelled out, the message did not get relayed.

A psychic session involved up to two hours, often longer.

I saw people in my home unless inconvenient. At those latter times, the minister of the First Church of Religious Science, for whom I had read, offered a room at the church for my appointments.

In 1973, I began to give "absentee" readings for people at a distance. As with in-person readings, I preferred not to know concerns in advance. I asked that questions be sent sealed in an inner envelope. On a designated date, I would "tune in" to the seeker's energy and tape-record and mail the reading. Absentee readings were more difficult because I did not have the advantage of immediate confirmation that I was well attuned to the seeker.

My procedure was the same for all readings. An hour before the appointed time, I put aside whatever I was doing and quieted my mind so that I could shift mental gears. When ready, I went into the Silence, not for guidance but to accrue adequate energy.

When the seeker arrived, I took time to establish a rapport and review the procedure. Next, we sat in the Silence together for up to ten minutes, during which time the person could mentally tell God that he or she wished to cooperate. This enabled me to move more easily into the client's energy field and to commence attunement.

As I merged with the seeker's energy field, a feeling of semirigidity, posturewise, took hold and prevailed until the reading was over. I held the microphone in my right hand. The only movement I made of my conscious intent was to flick the switch on the mike on and off. If the reading was difficult or lengthy, and I was running low on energy, my head would tip slowly to the right until I closed down. In extreme cases, I would lean with my upper torso to the right. My posture upon closing down would be quite peculiar. This circumstance lessened and was rare at the end of Stage One.

When I sensed the presence of a Source (a specific origin for the guidance, that is, my Higher Self, the seeker's superconscious, or the Keeper of the akashic records), I challenged. I would mentally ask if the Source were "of God." If I received the right response (*"Yes, indeed I AM of God. You may proceed."*) and I was aware of an overshadowing of love and peacefulness, I invited the seeker to join me in the Lord's Prayer.

Next, I asked for the white light of Christhood to shield the seeker and me from errant thought forms or mischievous influences. In the early years, I didn't realize that the seeker's *sub*conscious or strong will could also influence me. This I learned later.

Until 1977—midway through Stage One—my initial contact for a reading was with *my* superconscious. In this capacity, it served as a "doorkeeper" or liaison to properly connect me with the superconscious of the seeker or another component of Higher Consciousness. After that point, I was able to link up directly without my superconscious in the role of middleman. I can only assume that time and experience were required before I could adapt—without help—to other vibrational frequencies.

After the prayers, I described to the seeker those impressions I had derived by moving into and through his or her energy field, particularly the subconscious. Sharing the initial perceptions gave me an opportunity to determine the quality of our attunement. I asked for feedback. If the seeker confirmed my initial impressions, we moved on to questions. If the seeker could not identify with the thoughts expressed, I had a potential dilemma. More often than not, however, the seeker reconsidered what I had given and allowed that there was adequate relevancy for the reading to continue. As the seeker relaxed, the reading improved in accuracy and clarity.

Some readings simply did *not* go well. I groped and struggled, prayed and implored, but my inner screen remained blank and the Source was silent. I did not realize that the seeker could be conflicted about having a reading or perhaps was "holding back" on his or her energy. I was very hard on myself. In such cases, my deeply entrenched sense of responsibility triggered automatic self-blame.

I persisted in my efforts to break through the opaque veil—which is what I saw when attunement was blocked—for up to three hours. As a result, I'd eventually receive *something* in the way of guidance for the seeker, but my exhaustion and the seeker's weariness nullified the reading's worth, at least in my mind. Fortunately, blockages this firmly imbedded were rare.

When the seeker was comfortable with my initial impressions and all seemed in readiness for deeper attunement, *I* relaxed somewhat. The word-by-word responses to each of the seeker's questions entered my mind through my right temple. Each word, phrase, and sentence would glide slowly across the inside of my forehead as if on a conveyor belt or ticker-tape. I spoke it out as I perceived it.

Nevertheless, it wasn't unusual for me to be thrown by the first few words of a thought coming through. I'd say to myself, "There's no way that this beginning can develop into a sensible and positive-sounding statement." My mind would race past the incongruous words to see what lay ahead, usually to no avail. The Source would say, "*Speak out what you've been given and we will give you more.*" Since I had little choice, I spoke out—and the sentence would somehow surmount my dismal forecast.

Conversely, the Source often spoke with such uniquely inspiring or clever, amusing, and utterly creative phraseology that I'd want to pause and savor the moment. But the ticker-tape traveled on, and so did I in my role as an intermediary.

Time and experience proved me not the best assessor of what the seeker needed to hear. Occasionally while delivering guidance, I'd think to myself, "That's unrelated to his question!" or "She won't be happy with that." Later, if my rapport with the reading recipient was good, I'd ask about it. More often than not, my own supposition was entirely wrong and the guidance was entirely right.

At times the guidance coming through seemed puzzling, as though a piece were missing. If the seeker confirmed that he or she understood, I continued on to the next question. I knew that some guidance needed to be vague to preclude the seeker's embarrassment.

Seekers would often ask if I had received anything I was reluctant to give them. My answer was no, as I believed that whatever I was given was intended for the seeker, or it would not be given at all. I did not have the right nor the need to know any more.

If the reading was tedious or prolonged and if my energy was depleted, I had a hollow feeling in my chest. Another indication of overuse was a scratchy throat, as though my vocal cords had been strained. Such symptoms of psychic fatigue lingered for hours.

The most effective way to rebuild energy—aside from going into the Silence—was to partake of nature's beauty and life force. I hugged trees, planted flowers, or sat quietly in lovely parks. If the park had a pond, so much the better, as water is a powerful conductor. With a dearth of ponds and lakes in Albuquerque, I took to trailing my fingers in the fountains at malls whether or not I was low on energy.

Later, in Florida, I happily discovered that walking barefoot on the beach and putting my feet in the emerald green, clear waters of the Gulf of Mexico *rapidly* renewed me. Apparently, the water and the crystallized white sand yield potent kundalini energy from Mother Earth, rekindling vitality in a matter of minutes.

Stage One also "favored" me with several stressful tests of discernment. More than once, in a fit of frustration and embarrassment, I said to God, "I resign!" Without fail and within a few days, someone in despair or with a heart-rending crisis drew me back to the work. The emergency reading—along with the loving, gentle encouragement of

Higher Consciousness once I calmed down—helped me to understand and accept the learning experience that had triggered my attempted resignation.

Tests of ethics, integrity, and discernment also occurred in my "off hours." One afternoon, I was browsing in a bookshop, feeling rather smug, when I overheard another customer tell a clerk that her husband unexpectedly had surgery that morning. I unfurled my psychic antennae and drew the thought, "kidney stones." Few people were in the shop, and I decided to test the accuracy of my reception. I asked if it had been a kidney operation. The answer was a curt and cold no. I apologized, stammered something incomprehensible, and left the store—vowing never again to violate anyone's privacy. From that time on, I made it a rule to attune only at the clear request of the subject.

It is easy to be in awe of this marvelous gift—the ability to attune to and for others—but a life *away* from the work is also vital. From studying Cayce's life and listening to my other mentors, I know that continuing personal growth is as critical to our progress as is service.

The responsibility inherent with the majority of readings was intimidating. Seekers not only contemplated marriage, children, divorce, relocation, and career changes, but whether or not to stay with potentially abusive partners, sell homes, start businesses, settle lawsuits out of court, or have high-risk surgery. When asked a question of this magnitude in the middle of the reading, it was my practice to pause and confirm my attunement with a brief prayer.

Whether readings were heavy or lighthearted, almost without exception the guidance left my mind within hours. I saw two distinct advantages to this "automated erasure." First, it guaranteed the seeker that I would not remember his or her personal business forever. Secondly, it saved me from fitful nights of worry about seekers in sorrowful circumstances.

The span of time covered in a reading was anywhere from

one through ten years. I urged seekers to listen again to their tape a year or two down the road. Many people did, and most were surprised at the relevance of the guidance to later times and events.

I never knew what to expect in a reading. Spontaneous "visits" from loved ones in spirit usually elicited an emotional response by the seeker. The first indication of a loved one's presence was the appearance of a face on my inner screen. Concurrently, goose bumps and a chill would travel up my arms or even my legs. If the loved one's personality had been charismatic, a peculiar tingling sensation—it hurt, yet it didn't hurt—would pervade my ears.

At times the loved ones spoke directly to me; in this event, their words seemed to originate on the left or in the center of my forehead. If the loved ones had experienced an arduous or too-recent crossing and were still in a state of rest or acclimation, their superconscious frequently gave the seeker—through me—a report on their status. Such a report could be, *"She is fine. She is adjusting to the change and preparing for the review process. A beloved pet* (usually described) *is with her. She sends you her gratitude for your prayers."*

Most loved ones were anxious to express or ask for forgiveness and prayers. Another priority was to reassure those left behind of the "departed's" *continued* love and support. Not infrequently, they implored the seeker to "Please let me go; your grief grieves me."

Even in Stage One, those were the readings for which I felt I'd been groomed, both by personal losses and developmental experiences. My heart resonated with their need to understand where and how their loved ones were and if the loved ones knew how missed they were. Many times after an exceptionally moving encounter of this nature, I told God that ALL of my hard work and times of sacrifice were worth it, to see this one seeker's heart light go on.

By the time I was able to bring through a loved one without becoming emotional myself, Stage One was nearly a memory. The ability to be *"healthfully, lovingly detached,"* as Higher Consciousness described it, proved to be more a process of evolution than the result of conscious effort. Detachment could not be forced. It "happened" in my eighth or ninth year of service. Thereafter, my compassion and empathy remained earnest, but I observed rather than participated in the emotional exchange between the seeker and the loved one. That is, most of the time.

Readings in which a departed loved one relayed a poignant message and the seeker responded in kind exacted a greater toll on my energy. Equally taxing were those readings in which the seeker asked about many friends, foes, or family members—in which case I was required to tap into a greater number of energy fields.

When past-life information came spontaneously—the exception and not the rule—it was pertinent in some way to the present life. Most often, it explained the debt owed, major lessons and obstacles to be confronted, and urged perseverance. Without fail, the seeker was given positive reinforcement of his or her ability to overcome negativity, expiate karma, and achieve goals.

If not relevant, past-life information was not volunteered by a source, since such awareness could easily become a liability. Nonetheless, many curious seekers asked. A typical reply was:

> *"You've had lives of prominence and lives you'd as soon not know about. If important, trust in your Higher Self to release from your subconscious a glimpse or memory that will enlighten you."*

Energy

When I began giving readings, I knew that it was important for the people involved to contribute positive energy. I didn't know then how dramatic the impact of a negative environment could be until I agreed to read in 1972 for two NARA II clients who were in jail. It was only with patience and Fr. Di Benedetto's assistance as a battery that I was able to rise above the heavy atmosphere.

A few months later, at Fr. Di Benedetto's request, two other Alliance members and I went to the New Mexico state penitentiary in Santa Fe to address the Narcotics Anonymous group of inmates. We each were to talk on a metaphysical subject. When I concluded my talk, I was asked to demonstrate a psychic reading.

I knew I'd be damned if I did and damned if I didn't, so I steeled myself and selected an inmate-volunteer to sit across from me. We were in a large recreation room with portable chairs. The last image recorded in my physical vision was that of sixty-five pairs of intensely scrutinizing eyes, as the men crowded around me.

The room was rife with a volatile mixture of emotions. I felt as though the "vibes" would swallow me up. I prayed that the floor would open and engulf me. Quickly.

I started with a rendition of the Lord's Prayer—audible but not coherent. "Our Father, which art in heaven, hallowed be Thy name ... " I could *not* remember what came next. All I could think of was how to gracefully get away from the guy who was breathing down my neck. "Give us our debts and forgive us this day ... " And so it went. Although the volunteer seeker seemed to be a quiet, kind young man and we did achieve something of a rapport, the reading was understandably short and not outstanding. The Universe, even with its cosmic clout, couldn't pull that one off satisfactorily.

From that time on, I did my best to arrange for a room consistently imbued with good energy whenever I planned to do psychic work or teach a class. I tried to avoid rooms with television sets, wet bars, or a depressing decor.

Emotion—*energy in motion*—lingers. The longer it lingers and the more it is reinforced by people or activity, the more likely the energy will become an enduring part of the scene or environment. The energy of negative emotion is particularly powerful. Clearing is best accomplished by people in prayer.

Phenomena

My experiences with the phenomena of energy sounds, such as knocks and cracks in walls and ceiling or flickering lights, have been without exception innocuous, yet helpful to some degree in confidence-building. Paranormal incidents in this context seem to be a customary step along the way in psychic development. Phenomena are *not important in themselves,* but may be considered at times a supplemental means of "underscoring" or calling attention to guidance.

My first exposure to phenomena came with the NARA II experimental project. Readings were routinely accompanied by inexplicable sounds (knocks and cracks) in whatever room we were using. The intent seemed to be as an emphasis for specific guidance.

Phenomena were less frequent during private readings. One of the more interesting incidents took place during a psychic session with Mrs. Edna Wood Grier, a widow from Seattle. She wanted to know how her husband was doing. We were alone in my home.

I reached Mr. Grier quite easily. Through me, he said that he was doing fine, he encouraged his wife to take better care of her health, and then he said that he had to get back to "the shop." Suddenly, we heard a series of loud noises similar to heavy footsteps. They seemed to emanate from the ceiling of the hall which led to the front door. Next, we heard a door slam.

Startled out of the altered state, I opened my eyes to see a weeping, laughing widow. "That *was* my husband!" she cried. "He was a butcher. He always came home for lunch. When he left to go back to the butcher shop, he would stomp down the hall and slam the front door—nothing he did was quiet!"

◆   ◆   ◆

My most unforgettable paranormal experience occurred during a reading for Hillis and Wandi Dille of Albuquerque. Hillis asked how his mother Peggy was doing on the other side. I was informed by Hillis's mother—or her Higher Self— that "*She says she keeps busy. She is crocheting up a storm.*"

A little later, as the reading drew to a close, I said, "She touches your shoulder, Hillis, and says she must get back to her work." At that precise moment, lightning with thunder hit the pole directly behind the house. (It had not been raining, nor had there been any thunder and lightning that afternoon.) At the same time, the dog broke her chain and crashed through the screen door, the telephone rang, and the electricity went off.

The sounds of thunder and lightning were audible on the tape of the reading. The tape was later stolen, but the Dilles and I remember this particular event as though it were yesterday.

In a letter dated July 21, 1994, Hillis Dille had this to say about the above reading:

"To us, the phenomenon was a synchronism, like a giant exclamation point, to emphasize the validity of Mom's (Peggy's) being on the other side. Of all the people we told about the experience, Wandi's mother Leona was probably the most impressed, as it changed her from 'a firm believer in the physical resurrection' to the belief that 'we cross over and continue on.'

"In October 1977, we arrived at her home in Kentucky during a thunderstorm. She was sitting in her wheelchair on the porch, waving her arm and yelling, 'Give 'em hell, Peggy!' Leona crossed over in December 1977."

From 1980 on, I noticed phenomena only when I was unsure of my perception of the guidance coming through. On rare occasions, a seeker denied a circumstance that the Source assured me was valid. This circumstance needed to be acknowledged by the seeker for growth purposes. If phenomena occurred as the Source reiterated its guidance, I felt confident in asking the seeker to reconsider the guidance when time permitted. At such times, it was helpful to have confirmation through moderate, unsensational sounds that my interpretation was correct. I seldom called the seeker's attention to the sounds.

Overall, it needs to be remembered that a phenomenon is a means and not an end. It should never become a distraction or obsession.

The Source's Side of Spiritual Counseling

The *nature and quality* of the guidance remained constant in the entire twenty-two years of my psychic work. From the very first reading for NARA II in 1972 through the most recent private reading in 1994, the guidance and its sources were spiritually stable and steadfast, offering:

   a. An understanding of God's law;

   b. Evidence of the continuity of life;

   c. Specific help with the challenges and choices of this life; and

   d. Assistance in clearing the path for the seeker's personal connection with his or her Higher Self.

I was occasionally pressed by seekers to ask why predicted dates or specifics regarding events were often "off." I placed the question before Higher Consciousness. Immediately a clear, well-defined image projected itself onto my inner screen. The illustration was of the train table my father had constructed in the 1940s for the family's pleasure at Christmas time. The table, set up in our basement, measured eight feet by eight feet. We had two Lionel® train sets on 027 tracks, with two engines on line and two tracks with switches. One of the engines had a smokestack and when a tablet was dropped inside, puffs of smoke were emitted.

The layout on the table was elaborate. We had miniature people, houses, farms, villages, two train stations, a stagecoach with horses, and a large pond with live goldfish in it—until my cat Suzi went fishing one night.

The nostalgia I enjoyed as I viewed this scene—one of the happier memories of Adams's family life—was interrupted by an incoming, unfolding scroll as it caressed my mind:

> *"See the woman in the village at the north end of the table. Now look to the south and find the gentleman in front of the country store. Do you see all of the highways and detours, schools, businesses, vehicles, traffic signs, and other people weaving their way in between the two who are trying to meet?*
>
> *"Viewing you from our vantage point is much like looking upon the scene you are so fondly remembering here. It can appear likely that two people will meet in a certain period of time, but there are many variables beyond our control. (For instance) the free will of another, and yet another, and yet another, all who are crossing the paths of the woman and the man. And the two themselves—one or both—may decide to disregard the voice of intuition.*
>
> *"At our best, we can only prognosticate what seems likely based upon our awareness of character and drive. But humans do indeed have free will, and Universal*

*Law does not permit us to interfere with that, nor would
we choose to do so. Keep this in mind when you serve as
an instrument of Light."*

Meditation, 1976

The following questions were placed by Fr. Di Benedetto
during the tenure of the NARA II experimental project,
January through December 1972.

Question: Can you elaborate on the role of angels
and the role of guides in furnishing spiritual guidance?

*Source: "The angelic realm is far above my quarters. I
can only tell you this: that they are God's true messengers, His right-hand men and women, so to speak, and
are endowed with divine prescience of mind. They are
there to help, but they are there at His direction. It is not
for me to say when or how they could be placed at your
disposition, but only that the Almighty Father antici-
pates your every need and sends those He cherishes most
and those of us He loves, who want to progress, to be
with you in your need.*

*"You must respect God's all-knowing. Your guides
and teachers are very willingly assigned to you—and
usually there has been a past relationship in earth life
(with you), unless you are a very highly evolved one—to
help you progress and to help themselves progress. They
have their guides above, in a higher plane, who can also
look down upon you. As your aspirations go, so goes
your guidance. As you are ready to progress, your guidance progresses. The angelic realm has a different
mission. They do not need to progress, but they often
choose to help. Can I put it more simply than that?*

*"You want to know, can you call upon an angel or
archangel or guide at any time, night or day? By all
means, do so, if you sincerely want their help, but you
will find that God has anticipated your every need and*

sends those in whom your care is entrusted. Give Him your faith; you will be taken care of.

" ... for we here long to guide, not that our knowledge is insufferably paramount to yours ... but we have the benefit that you have not of foresight and sight in retrospect, and overall evaluation. We have help, also, from higher planes, just as you who are receptive have help from us.

"We try not to lead you astray, for it is only by your progress that we progress; we have said that before, and it is unalterably true. We do long, desperately, to help, for we must all return to God one day; not one of us can make it alone."

Question: Please explain the nature of the difficulty you had in locating (individual's name withheld) for the absentee reading.

Source: "We must locate the aura, the mental, physical, astral, and etheric bodies. We can, at times, tap into the akashic records without being able to perceive the aura, but we prefer not to do so for reasons of our own. In order to locate the aura and to perceive this and the vibrations of the soul, we should know where the physical body is at. We are also hindered by the state of mind or by the shutting off at times of points of entrance that you call the psychic centers.

"A person's awareness and Light come into play. One with more Light is more easily found. Those who live in a closed box all their life are most difficult to find; their aura is most difficult to perceive. We also respect the soul's free will, but this is another matter."

Question: Can you provide guidelines for tapping into the akashic records?

Source: "It is not nearly as vital for those of you making the sojourn on the earth plane to become cognizant of what is retained on those ledger pages as most people would think. Only in special, certain cases are we al-

*lowed to relay that information. For instance ... where
there is an impediment to progress because of a soul's
blockage, where a soul is—because of pain, imagined
or real, mental or physical—consciously unable to remove the block.*

*"We will then slip in, but otherwise it will serve no
purpose but to confuse the issue.*

*" ... Many times those seeking to reach akasha out of
a false need, selfishness, or curiosity will reach instead a
pseudo akasha, located in one of the lower planes. Most
likely the seeker will be enthralled by the knowledge of
'who' they were, whereby another obstacle has been laid
in their path. When we permit this, it is for growth, but
it is not always our way of enabling growth.*

*"Asking first that it be God's will will always ascer-
tain a truthful answer. Be not dismayed if entry is
disbarred. Better it be so than too many backward steps
be undertaken because of this."*

In 1972, as I entered Stage One—the first ten years—of
my psychic work, I was beset by an identity crisis, confusion, and emotional fragility. The psychic counseling work
gradually, very gradually, gave me self-confidence and self-
esteem. Working with people in all walks of life and all states
of mind helped me to become nonjudgmental, less critical,
and more content with my own lot in life. I began to have a
sense of who I was.

With the blessing of experience and loving help from
Higher Consciousness, my acute anxiety about the work
and my aptitude for it had been dispelled. In its place, more
often than not: life-reinforcing exhilaration.

YOU ARE A CHALICE INTO WHICH GOD POURS LIFE

YOU SHARE THAT LIFE WITH HUMANITY

*YOUR CHALICE IS NEVER QUITE
FULL AND IT IS NEVER QUITE EMPTY*

FOR LIFE IS ALWAYS MOVING THROUGH

Meditation
June 1977

An Inner Mission

MARRYING RALPH PROVED TO BE AN ENORMOUS blessing—but very much a blessing in disguise. The blessing part was marvelous. The disguise part nearly did me in.

Within the first six months of our life together, Ralph drew my youngest child, Shannon, out of her shell. Soon, her habit of whispering to avoid her father's attention was a symptom and a memory of the past. Ralph had extended talks with Shannon which equipped her to work through her longstanding fear of her father's harshness, as well as her resentment of my pathetic passivity.

Where Ralph's sensitivity and good-naturedness served

to bring about Shannon's comfort with males, his whole-some sense of humor and generosity endeared him to Lisa and Chris. Whatever he had was theirs, no strings attached. Whatever they needed, he wanted to provide. He had the same attitude with regard to me.

My heart's desire was a career of psychic/intuitive counseling and teaching work. Momentary satisfaction and recognition came with the responsible jobs held during my thirty years in the business world, but I needed more than that. I needed to know that my life mattered. I wanted God to assure me that I was worthwhile. The only genuine feeling of fulfillment I had experienced was with the birth of my children. The only inner peace I had really known came through meditation and spiritual work.

Once Ralph knew that I was not playing a fortuneteller game, he had little problem with my aspirations. Initially, he worried that the Paulin name would be sullied and he'd look like a fool to his family. However, as more people told him how valuable their reading had been, his apprehension lessened and enthusiasm grew.

With unwavering joy, I resigned my job and retired my panty girdle—forever, I hoped. That was the first day of the rest of my life, as the saying goes.

Luxuriating in my rose-colored world, I did not see Ralph's insecurities. Neither did I realize that he was an alcoholic. Although I knew that he drank every day, I seldom saw behavior or heard an attitude expressed that shouted "intoxication!"

Seven months after we were wed in my living room, surrounded by white poinsettia and friends, Ralph used his vacation to drive to North Carolina. Because of the tensions at home prior to my divorce from Marc, I had permitted Chris to live with Lisa and finish high school there. He had graduated, and he needed someone to bring him and his cherished motorbike home.

Ralph left on a Sunday. On Monday I answered the telephone to hear utter dejection in his voice: "I want you to keep both houses. I'll bring Chris home and then I'll go away. The last thing I want is to humiliate you." My mind raced through several scenarios. He went on. "I'm in Shamrock, Texas. I spent last night in jail."

The police had watched Ralph's truck weave for ten miles before pulling him over. They saw the six-pack of beer on the seat beside him and an open fifth of rum in the camper. He told me he had drunk a few beers, but he was more tired than drunk. As was Ralph's pattern, he had "pushed it," going fifty miles farther and then another fifty when he should have stopped to sleep. The Breathalyzer® indicated a blood alcohol level of .11, but Ralph was sure that the officer had manipulated the gauge. He was cited for DUI and escorted to the town tank.

I knew for certain he'd never had a DUI before, but I wasn't at all certain that the gauge had been manipulated. His despair grabbed at me nonetheless, and I assured him that we'd work it out. I knew it could have been worse . . . much worse.

I bought Ralph's story that he usually did not drink while driving. When he subsequently reduced the amount he drank at home, I convinced myself that the DUI had been a one-time episode. For the sake of my sanity, I had to believe that it would not happen again. The prospect of spending the remainder of my life dealing with everything that alcoholism comprises was overwhelmingly stressful.

Our marriage survived the "Shamrock shame" and we continued to enjoy our life together. The eleven-year age difference did not interfere with our compatibility. Ralph and I shared many memories of the "times" in which we were reared. When he was home, we often talked until the wee hours of the morning.

Early in 1982, Ralph told me that he planned to retire when he reached sixty in two years. When we applied for an insurance policy to ensure college for Shannon, we were turned down. Startled, I called my agent, who told me that Ralph's urine test showed "sugar." He was diabetic.

Reeling, I asked my husband to see his family physician. There, I learned that Ralph had developed adult-onset diabetes mellitus (non-insulin dependent diabetes) at least ten years earlier, probably as a result of years of alcohol abuse.

When Ralph went outside to have a cigarette, Dr. Levin urged me to try to motivate him to quit drinking. "I've pleaded with him for years," he said. "If he doesn't quit now—completely—it's going to be very bad. I would give your husband no more than five years to live, Mrs. Paulin. Ralph's liver is in bad shape."

I hesitantly repeated Dr. Levin's counsel as we drove home. Quite sharply, the man I had married for better or for worse replied, "Don't ever ask me to quit drinking. I don't abuse you and I don't spend household money on booze. I can control my drinking. I'm not an alcoholic." I bit my tongue and changed the subject.

The day finally arrived when I had to acknowledge my naïveté. With Ralph out of town, I called AA. I spent two hours talking with someone whose knowledge about the disease was maximal: a recovering alcoholic, a man a few years older than my husband.

This authority said that oftentimes as an alcoholic approached sixty, tolerance for the drug decreased. The personality—so cheerful and congenial—would then become morose, manipulative, faultfinding, possessive, and even paranoiac. The physical body would begin to show the damage done. This gentleman was as psychic as I, even more so: he was one hundred percent accurate.

The predicted changes in tolerance and temperament became obvious in the summer of 1982, shortly after we relocated to Olathe, Kansas, a work-related move. I soon accepted that my husband drank more heavily than he wanted me to know. He was inebriated to some degree during most of his off-duty hours.

My fix-it fantasies found a physician right away. Dr. Eidt echoed the same diagnosis and prognosis: "Only a few years left on the liver if your husband keeps on drinking. Better build a life of your own, Mrs. Paulin." I enrolled in a diabetes management class and diligently designed a diet that took both conditions—diabetes and cirrhosis—into consideration. Ralph continued to drink.

After a few weeks of dress rehearsal in my mind, I nervously confronted Ralph with my belief that he was indisputably an alcoholic and that Shannon and I planned to attend Alanon and Alateen meetings. My husband was not pleased about being "labeled." He said he would stop drinking, and he did—for three months.

At my first Alanon meeting, I was asked to "tell my story." I started with a statement that underscored my magnanimous attitude: "I'm here to find a way to help my husband quit drinking." Everyone smiled. They, too, thought that Alanon would help them to change the alcoholic and soon learned that they could only change themselves. By the time the meeting was over, Ralph Paulin was no longer my magnificent obsession: I was.

Ralph's alcoholism was the catalyst and Alanon the springboard for a dive into the depths of my being. The symptoms of menopause, moderate the first year, were now intensifying—as were the symptoms of my deeper distress. Beneath these lay root causes, ready to surface from a subconscious storage tank. That the intense phase of personal healing was upon me was inescapable.

I stopped doing the absentee readings by which I'd maintained my skills and self-esteem. (I had chosen not to cultivate a Kansas clientele for readings since our stay in Kansas was only temporary.)

My husband's retirement nearing, we wavered between returning to Albuquerque or settling in a lovely part of northwest Florida, an area we'd visited the previous summer. While there, we had impulsively scouted houses for sale. The decision was easy to make when I had a dream in which the words "Camille" and "healing" were highlighted. Retirement day arrived. We moved into the house on Camelia Circle in Gulf Breeze in April 1984.

My most urgent unresolved issue was the fear of another highway death, despite the fact that almost twenty years had passed since my mother's fatal accident. The decision to marry a man who loved and lived to drive—train, bus, or automobile; it didn't matter as long as he was at the wheel—must have been engineered by a force greater than my conscious mind. And Ralph was routinely drinking and driving now that he wasn't working.

A physician we saw in Florida determined that the notorious liver would not be viable beyond two to three years. All three doctors—in Albuquerque, Kansas, and Florida—had predicted that I'd be a widow by 1988. Ralph chose not to believe the prognosis. He rationalized that he felt stronger than the doctors gave him credit for and that he was still physically active. Several years later, he would tell me that his alcohol-logged brain had blocked comprehension of the truth.

Anxiety and severe depression dictated my days and numbed my mind. Without the energy or the willingness to deal with confrontation, I felt trapped and helpless. I was in too much anguish to meditate. All I could do was pray.

Lisa called. She had a grapefruit-sized cyst on one of her ovaries; it had to be removed. Her twins were visiting their father in Tennessee. She planned to drive there before having surgery.

I called her surgeon who said curtly, "That cyst could rupture at any moment!" I pleaded with Lisa to have the operation first and recover fully before attempting such a trip. No dice. Danica and Devon had to return home to New Mexico first. She promised to call me every day while she was on the road. It took all the energy I could muster to block from my mind the image of her car in a ditch or worse—her body on a stretcher.

The first night: no call. The second day: no call. If Ralph was the catalyst, Lisa was the trigger—and dread, the missile—of my undoing. Nothing in my world made sense. I stood for what seemed an hour, fingers welded onto the edge of the kitchen countertop, feet frozen in place, and mind suspended in sanity-saving space. For the first time in years, I considered suicide.

Although Lisa's trip and subsequent surgery were successful, I was unable to stabilize myself.

Somehow, Shannon was spared from full awareness of the trouble I was in, for which I thanked God profusely. Thirty minutes after Ralph left to drive Shannon to the airport in Atlanta for her six-week visit with Marc, I checked in at Baptist Hospital's Stress Center. We had been in Gulf Breeze for three months.

I had made the arrangements in advance. Ralph agreed with my plan, but I had not shared my desperate wish to be free of his alcoholism—or, if necessary, to be free of my marriage. I laid the bulk of the blame on my fear of highway deaths and menopause. In retrospect, I was conflicted by a desire for—and fear of—freedom and independence.

My first few days in the Stress Center were filled with constant tears, a feeling of hopelessness, and hibernation when possible. Dr. Goldwater, the psychiatrist to whom I'd been referred for admittance, initially diagnosed me as being depressed and anxious. No news there. She prescribed Imipramine®, a tricyclic antidepressant. When the medication gave me "cotton-mouth" and caused me to stutter, she lowered the dosage. A relatively safe drug, Imipramine proved effective in helping me to bridge the depression and thus be able to work on issues and root causes.

The Stress Center's carefully structured treatment program was developed to help with a multitude of diagnoses. Nevertheless, the patients shared a common denominator: life's complications had become so overwhelming that we were, in varying degrees, sick.

I had two private therapy sessions daily, one with the psychiatrist's assistant and the other with a Stress Center mental health counselor. Group therapy sessions were also scheduled on a daily basis. I saw Dr. Goldwater three times a week in relatively brief sessions. Interspersed among these opportunities—for indeed that's what they were, effective opportunities to do the hard work, the "real" work—we had meals, exercise, crafts, and programs on achieving good mental health.

The therapy sessions were exhausting. Most of the patients were eager to go to bed at night. I took afternoon naps as well.

At the end of my first week, I was told that I was "codependent." I had never heard the term before. I thought I was being called a co-alcoholic. I pushed through my depression to register a vehement protest. That done, I stopped crying and started listening.

According to the counselor, the characteristics of a codependent person include: passivity; low self-esteem; an excessive sense of responsibility; valuing the opinions of others more than one's own; judging self by another's standards; and, the core of the disease, dependency upon another person or some other external for *personal validation and assurance of self-worth.* Codependent people tend to remain in troubling relationships far longer than is wise. Although my self-esteem had greatly improved over the previous ten years largely because of my spiritual work, I *was* codependent.

The "co" in codependency pulls in the partner, the accomplice in this unhappy, unwholesome way of life. Frequently, the partner has an addictive personality or another type of emotional disorder.

The two codependents indulge their respective diseases until one achieves mental and emotional health and wants out of the union.

After acknowledging my codependency, I moved into the painful work of probing for the reasons why I was codependent.

The dreaded role-playing exercise, exceedingly uncomfortable for me, produced a key insight about what was going on in my subconscious. Cast in the role of my father, I was to tell Barbara (myself)—played by another patient—what I thought of her. The words that I heard myself speak shocked me. They bespoke an indictment I had long forgotten: "You weren't born to us; we found you in a garbage dump and felt sorry for you, and so we brought you home. If you aren't careful, we'll take you back to where you came from."

Fragments of scenes, strained through a sieve in my mind, anguished me for days. I knew then that my father's ill-thought-out threat had created a script I'd adhered to all of my life.

Other insights were netted and given a preliminary examination during my four-week stay in the hospital. Another key or two would come almost three years later, dressed as dreams by my Higher Self.

Without doubt, my years of meditation and metaphysical study had transported me a long way on my journey to health and wholeness. The Stress Center experience, the best gift I'd ever given myself, provided the earth-type tools plus a critical key needed for acceleration of the healing process. I believed that the worst was behind me; now, I had a map to follow. I knew where I was going.

A year later, Ralph would voluntarily enter Baptist Hospital's Care Unit—an alcoholism treatment program. Albeit he would regress in six months, the program introduced concepts on self-healing which, years down the road, Ralph would draw on for the attainment of—as he puts it—"a sensible life," a life without alcohol.

◆ ◆ ◆

Through the end of 1984 and the first few months of 1985, I had weekly appointments with Dr. Stephen Quackenbos, a therapist in private practice. We focused on loosening the grip that codependency had on my life. We worked on resolving the repressed memories and emotions that had surfaced in the hospital. And we explored further insights as they evolved in the private therapy sessions.

As the azaleas in Gulf Breeze erupted into brilliantly hued bloom with the advent of spring, the seeding and gardening of my growth began to yield fruit. I was able to see the full range of codependency's negative effects on my life.

An eye-opening example of a negative pattern of the past was my self-sabotage, careerwise. I went to work for the federal civil service system three different times and quit each job just a few months short of the three-year mark when I would have attained the advantageous "permanent status."

Correlating with these and other job resignations was the clear awareness—in retrospect—that I had also sabotaged my potential for independence. With each resignation we may have been out of debt, but we were then unable to build a savings account. Without money in the bank or an adequate-paying job, I had mind-easing "justification" for staying in a miserable marriage.

Discussing my younger years was especially stressful because of personal regrets. Some of the regrets resulted from inconsideration and immaturity on my part. Other feelings of contrition were not warranted. Nonetheless—justifiable or not—it was not easy to release the remorse that arose as the clearing process continued.

Another traumatic area in therapy involved my ingrained need to observe the commandment, "Honor thy father and thy mother." Dr. Quackenbos helped me to understand that this divine principle may in reality mean: "Honor your parents by living a noble and worthwhile life" and not "Do not see their shortcomings and never criticize them." Understanding this enabled me to more willingly talk about the hostilities and unhappiness in the family home.

One night during this phase of therapy, I dreamed that three or four men I didn't recognize were playing volleyball in back of my family's house. I was about seven years old. I walked into the yard and one of the men tossed the ball to me, inviting me to play. I intentionally did not catch the ball. Instead, I turned and walked away. That was all there was to the dream.

My therapist asked me to draw the scene. When he examined the picture, he asked if I knew any adult males who had injured their left forearm. He pointed out a dark circle quite prominent on the left arm of the stick figure holding the ball. I did not recall until later in the week that my father had badly injured his arm while working on an automobile when he was twenty-three. I did not attach any meaning to this dream, and I arrived at the next therapy session with a full agenda of other topics to be addressed.

Dr. Quackenbos intuited that I was avoiding—or not wanting to confront—the next issue, that of emotional damage from probable mistreatment of a sexual nature. He believed that the signs were there. In an effort to break down my resistance, he changed his approach from supportive to confrontative, a technique I saw as a maneuver to incite my anger (presumably with my father) and project it onto him. This irritated me. I didn't cooperate.

We had reached an impasse. My position was that we had accomplished a great deal in less than a year and, if further exploration was required, I'd be guided by my super-conscious when the time was right. I was feeling very well. Dr. Quackenbos, surmising that I needed a break from weekly sessions, agreed, and I left therapy.

Fortunately, because of the therapist's skills and my determination to break the cycle of codependency (which I now saw as having imprisoned my mother and her mother before her), I had moved forward in my quest for health. And I had grown.

Shortly thereafter, Ralph commented: "You are much less a puppet and more your own person." He added: "It's not as convenient for me, but it's a change I'm really happy to see."

FOR NOW WE SEE THROUGH A GLASS, DARKLY;

BUT THEN FACE TO FACE:

NOW I KNOW IN PART; BUT THEN SHALL I KNOW

EVEN AS ALSO I AM KNOWN.

I Corinthians 13:12

The Dynamics of Psychic/Intuitive Counseling

Stage Two—1983 to 1994

I RETURNED TO PSYCHIC/INTUITIVE COUNSELING work in late January 1985. It had been six months since my emotional breakdown.

One of the overriding features throughout Stage Two was the difference in the overall thrust of the readings I gave. More than a few seekers or their situations clearly mirrored either what I had overcome, what I was currently going through, or what I was trying to attain. As a result, portions of the guidance those particular seekers received were directly helpful to me as well. I saw this as a remarkable blessing.

The first readings I gave were for people from Unity Church of Christianity, of which Ralph and I were members. Before long, word-of-mouth referrals kept me scheduled with up to six in-person readings a week. Requests for absentee readings, almost nil during my twenty-month sabbatical, began to trickle in.

Soon thereafter, I formed two weekly meditation groups, one on a weekday morning and one on Saturday night, both held in my home. It wasn't long before I was invited to speak and give seminars and classes at Still Waters Centre and later for other groups.

I had no difficulty in resuming the work. It was almost as though I had not taken any time off, with a favorable exception: enhanced clarity and accuracy. The work I had done in the Stress Center to clear old scripts from my subconscious had also cleared the communication conduit. Nevertheless, I continued to insist on receiving guidance word by word (I called it being "spoon-fed").

Higher Consciousness acquiesced for another year or so. One bright summer morning, as I was resting in the tranquillity of a deep meditation, my Higher Self said—and not for the first time:

> *"You have such a strong tendency to make the work harder than it should be. Relax. Do not struggle so hard. Open up and wait for the guidance to come, to flow. Tap into the INTUITIVE level and begin . . . Trust your inner knowing."*

Gradually, the Source weaned me from the energy-consuming spoon-feeding I had needed for nearly thirteen years. Higher Consciousness knew that it was time for energy-*conserving* methods of communication, such as "spiritual shorthand." The transition to the new methods turned out to be quite stressful.

The chief difference was that instead of a voice speaking

words one by one into my mind, an idea or thought was projected onto my mind. The deliberateness of words, with little need for interpretation, had enabled my confidence in a superconscious origin. Conversely, an idea or thought often seemed tentative or vaporous. I found myself frequently tempted to "flesh it out," but afraid that I could mislead by doing so.

Indeed, in some cases, added description on my part proved helpful to the seeker. There was a troublesome fine line between intuitive analysis and my conscious supposition based on personal experience. On many occasions, I crossed my fingers—out of sight of the seeker—hoping for relief-giving, spontaneous validation.

My dilemma was compounded by the increasing number of seekers whose questions might have been my own. The incidence of such sessions had been sporadic in Stage One. Now, I noted—at times with amazement, always with appreciation—that whenever a crisis or difficult decision was at hand in my life, a seeker with a similar situation would surely sit across from me within a week.

I asked in meditation if I was interfering with guidance in those particular cases. The Source responded word by word:

> "The thoughts that are becoming infused—and there are some on occasion—are those which only heighten and magnify God's love and wisdom. It is advice coming from your Higher Self. If ever contrary to our purpose or to the detriment of the subject's life, we will alert or stop you."

Eventually, I became comfortable and more confident in giving primarily intuitive readings. Apparently satisfied with my instrumentality, Higher Consciousness gave me every consideration possible. When I felt it essential for the guidance to be definite and specific, the Source rendered it word by word. Whenever I became discouraged after two con-

secutively tough readings, I could count on a divinely or-
chestrated reading, easy and inspiring, to be next on the
schedule.

I was now ready for spiritual shorthand. The premise was
that in saving a hundred words, an image or symbol—if accurately interpreted—would also save energy. Energy was
an ongoing concern of mine and a concern on the part of
Higher Consciousness as well. I was told repeatedly that
sources must consider the welfare of the instrument above
all else.

The unwritten agreement between me as an instrument
and Higher Consciousness as an overseer was that I would
build energy in healthy, wholesome ways and use my energy wisely. The overseer would do what it could to protect
and conserve my energy without violating my free will. In
more than a few sessions, all of which were draining or prolonged, the Source abruptly ended the reading with: *"The
instrument's Light is waning. We must close the door."*

From this point on, Higher Consciousness utilized a
blending of methods: shorthand, intuitive impressions and
ideas, and word-by-word sentences. I entered the seeker's
energy field through the subconscious. After noting what
was ready to be reckoned with, I moved upward, into the
superconscious. I did my best to bypass the conscious mind
so as to avoid contamination of the guidance.

Spiritual shorthand included symbols, images, and a
graph on which light and dark patterns or colors were reflected. The graph indicated events, moods, and circumstances at various periods in the seeker's past and present,
and probabilities for the future. When combined with the
energies and emotions accessed as I began the attunement
process, the shorthand equipped me with a good start and
foundation for the reading. It also provided information I
could not have consciously known about the seeker. This
evidential material served to give us confidence in my attunement.

Although all of the abbreviated forms could be surprisingly pertinent, the most reliable were feelings. Emotions I typically observed included joy and excitement, grief, yearning, missing someone, apprehension, fear, regret, confusion, resentment, disillusionment, deep anger, and depression. The emotions were often negative since they correlated with unfinished business.

Intuitive impressions, ideas, and thoughts comprised a sudden "knowing," an insight—or an entire thought which all at once permeated my mind.

Midway through Stage Two, the Source began to draw upon *my* life to render guidance-by-association. For instance, if the seeker had an unresolved issue with a parent, my mother's or father's face would flash before me. I might simultaneously *sense* the nature of the issue involved. If someone in the seeker's life had a problem with alcohol, I'd see my Uncle Bill's face and form. A quiet, shy man, he was the most overt alcoholic in the family. Sometimes the associative image was not a person from my past, but an incident.

One of the more unusual associations occurred during the attunement phase of a reading. Bernice, a lifelong friend who had been stricken with polio in 1946 at the age of twelve, appeared on my inner screen. I knew nothing about the seeker, and there were many options for a possible point of relevance in my friend's life.

Suddenly, I saw the image of an iron lung. I asked the seeker if she could relate to that. She replied, "Yes. There is an old iron lung in the basement of the school for nursing in which I'm enrolled. I'm fascinated with it." This wasn't an important association, but it helped both of us to breathe easy about our connection.

At the wind-down of any reading, the Source conveyed a warm and supportive statement, such as *"I AM with you every day in every way . . . "* This was the one part I didn't need word by word, as I had heard it so often, but word by word it came. The precise phrases varied at times, but love, compassion, and encouragement were never omitted. Both the seeker and I were blessed by the unconditional love and acceptance which enveloped us as the reading concluded.

The next challenge took me by surprise. It involved my lack of confidence in my ability to establish a *quick* connection with a source in the event of a crisis. On this particular occasion, my friend Norma called from New Jersey to say that her son was severely depressed and possibly suicidal. His father had died two years earlier from kidney failure. Along with uncompleted grief work, Norma's son was burdened with guilt over his impatience with his dad. Norma asked me to give him intuitive guidance then and there.

I had never attempted a telephone reading. I saw my program of preparation as essential to a pure and safe connection with Higher Consciousness. I demurred, saying that I'd tape-record a reading the next day and send it by overnight mail.

Since it wasn't easy to take my conscious mind out of the picture when reading for friends or family, I went to unusual lengths to prepare. When I connected with Higher Consciousness, a stream of convoluted thoughts made its way into my mind. I recognized the essence of the message as being comforting and appropriate, but the sing-song packaging was both confusing and annoying.

Try as I might, I couldn't obtain an explanation or a change in the delivery. Although embarrassed, I mailed the tape to Norma. The next time we talked, she said her son would have been put off by the tape, so she didn't give it to him. I couldn't blame her. I did blame myself for the disappointing result. The redeeming grace was that when speaking with Norma the day she first called, I urged her to have her son seek professional counseling, which he did.

I suspected that I was being given a message by Higher Consciousness, probably because I had erred in some way. In meditation, the Source said:

"You are an instrument of Light. You can trust your-self to help under any conditions. Do not hesitate again to meet such a need at the time it is needed. We will be with you. We are sorry for your embarrassment, but discomfort seems to be necessary to gain your full attention."

From that time on, I trusted Higher Consciousness to help me connect safely, quickly—and on the telephone, if necessary.

In the same period of time, I was given the following guidance about my preparation for a reading:

"You should not hold a crystal in your hand for readings because we do not want your vibrational frequency rate or energy altered. You do not need any tools or special arrangements—just yourself and body as a vehicle, as pure and healthy as possible.

"There will be times when you will be called for healing and other work, and we do not want you to feel impaired as an instrument because your 'implements' are not available.

"Hold a glass (not plastic) of water in your hand. Do not use ice cubes. The temperature of the water should be equal to your body temperature. One half-hour prior to a reading or healing work, observe bodily status. Eat nor drink hot nor cold."

By now, I had a better understanding of the higher purpose and dynamics of the work. While I knew that different psychics had different specialties, I also knew that spiritual guidance overall was intended to emancipate, not to enslave.

I saw many people who gladly and gratefully would have sought a reading every few months for years. Perhaps they were dependent by nature, or they lacked confidence in their ability to meditate. I made it a practice to limit appointments to three, with a minimum of six months in between, except in a crisis. Higher Consciousness must have agreed with me, as there seemed to be a subtle change in the tenor of a seeker's third reading, whose superconscious was not as accommodating. At times the Source hedged, suggesting that seekers *think more* on their quandary. This was particularly evident in readings for clearly codependent people.

Energy

Sixty-to-ninety-minute readings required a significant amount of fuel. If fairly healthy and calm, the seeker contributed energy to the cause. A number of seekers, however, were depressed or physically unwell and generally unable to contribute.

As Stage Two progressed, I noticed that I was not able to recoup and rebuild energy quite as efficiently as before. I was now in my fifties. I didn't know how much effect age had upon energy replenishment, but I decided to make some changes in my work.

The most overt change was to limit the amount of time in which I'd struggle to break through a seeker's depression or resistance (conscious or unconscious). If my spontaneous impressions at the beginning of the reading were not relevant, I offered the seeker the option of calling off the reading. If the seeker wanted to go on, I agreed to "try" for ten more minutes (one or two questions).

If still unsuccessful, I would terminate the reading.

Another change was to shorten the spontaneous impression phase of the reading from an average twenty minutes to ten.

During the giving of readings for which I needed supplemental fuel, certain family members, especially my husband—and my son, when he lived with us—were drafted as batteries by the Universe. I'd emerge from my reading room to see one of the men sprawled out, asleep, on the sofa. On one occasion, my son—who was not a metaphysical student—was astounded to *feel* his energy being siphoned out the soles of his feet as he lay on his bed watching television.

Ultimately, I arranged to link up with a woman friend who could serve as a battery in dire situations. She did not need to be in my home as I gave the reading. She usually was aware when she was being pressed into service as she would feel led to sit down and relax. Later, I occasionally served as a battery for her.

Supplemental energy made a tremendous difference when I read for friends and family. For those sessions, if feasible, I asked two to four people who understood the process to sit in on the reading as batteries. This almost always enabled me to "rise above" the emotional ties and my conscious awareness of their situation.

Sessions in which I reached a departed loved one used the most energy; it took longer to rebuild afterward. Some seekers inquired about a number of people on the other side. At times, I felt like a "cosmic chameleon" as I moved through countless energy fields, trying to acclimate to each for a brief, shining moment or two.

Audible sounds of energy surges inexplicably "developed" on several tapes of readings in Stage Two. Two different seekers reported that they could hear chanting—Buddhist in one case, American Indian in the other—in the background. The baffling phenomena served to lure one of the seekers into meditation. A college student, Tina Brown, was so skeptical and private-natured that I'd been unable to break through for her. She subsequently changed her focus in life to a more predominant spiritual path. I felt intuitively then, and still do, that one day Tina will contribute something of worth to our understanding of the vital life force.

When the replica of the Vietnam Wall came to Pensacola,

Ralph and I went to see it. My family had not lost anyone close in Vietnam, and although I was empathetic toward families who had, my interest was quietly casual.

I must have been twenty-five yards away when the emotions enveloping the Wall hit me where it hurt: my heart. Tears streamed down my face and my steps faltered. As I slowly drew closer and my eyes took in the poignant mementos—dried and forlorn flowers, tear-stained letters, heartfelt poems, black and white ragged-edge photos, personal items such as hair combs and handkerchiefs, and candles—which lined the base of the Wall, I sobbed uncontrollably.

Never has a profound realization come to me in such a devastatingly emotional way. When I was able to compose myself, it was clear to me that those who were grief-stricken had left a part of themselves at the Wall. I walked through the energy fields of thousands of people in mourning, not all of whom were in physical form.

I never doubted the power of energy-in-motion after that.

Midway through Stage Two, I felt lovingly led by unseen conspirators to preface my pre-reading meditation with a new affirmation. I do not know its origin, but I do know that it brings me confidence and a sense of divine order.

I hold a glass of water in both hands and taking a sip with each phrase, I say:

"With this holy water, I cleanse and heal myself. With this holy water, I purify myself. With this holy water, I become one with all life, everywhere."

As Stage Two drew to a close, I knew that my apprenticeship was complete.

IF I CAN STOP ONE HEART FROM BREAKING,

I SHALL NOT LIVE IN VAIN:

IF I CAN EASE ONE LIFE THE ACHING,

OR COOL ONE PAIN,

OR HELP ONE FAINTING ROBIN

UNTO HIS NEST AGAIN,

I SHALL NOT LIVE IN VAIN.

Emily Dickinson
"The Last Word"

Problems and Pitfalls:
Guidance Gleaned, Lessons Learned

THE PURPOSE OF SPIRITUAL GUIDANCE IS TO *enlighten*: to lessen our load, not add to it; to *encourage*, not to destroy vision and hope; to strengthen faith in ourselves and to bring forth the desire to follow the *path of Light*.

This does not preclude the giving of constructive, cautionary advice or warnings, but it does preclude the giving of personal guidance which states or implies that a situation is hopeless.

In early 1992, one of my clients was told by a psychic in another city that her daughter would commit suicide in August, her mother would die in six months, and her husband would have a heart attack by the end of the year. Understandably upset, she called to ask my opinion on the reading's validity. Based on my experience, I believe that Higher Consciousness does not work that way. I urged my client to disregard the "guidance" completely. As of early 1994, the dire predictions had not materialized.

The understanding I have been given by Higher Consciousness is that even at the last moment, a soul can petition God to grant an extension of time here. The petition and the purpose, therefore, are the business of the soul and the Almighty, and not ours.

Another sensitive issue is information that the seeker was someone famous in a former life. In 1972, I gave a reading for a husband and wife in which the guidance that came through was both inspiring and practical—until I was told that they had been Caesar and Cleopatra. The former existences were popular ones. How many reimbodiments of Caesar and Cleopatra can there be in one century? I'd heard about a number of them.

I was confused and frustrated. I had prepared well to give the reading and I strove for the highest guidance I could attain. I closed down and asked the two seekers to hold the guidance in abeyance until I could confirm or correct it in a few days.

A similar incident had occurred the previous month. Toward the close of the reading, it was given that the seeker had been Sigmund Freud in her last life. The lady gently advised me when I was out of the altered state that she had been two years old when Freud died. The bulk of the reading was helpful and largely verifiable.

Since the seeker was somewhat depressed at the time and I was discouraged about personal matters, I reasoned that adequate energy had not been available to sustain a valid connection through the *entire* reading. Nonetheless, I was troubled.

And now it had happened again. This time I told Higher

Consciousness that I would not do another reading until I understood what had gone wrong.

Higher Consciousness explained that I had been tested on my alertness as to random reception of false, ego-flattering information. The Source had these thoughts to impart about giving guidance that one had been famous or a great achiever in a past life:

> *"Think. What useful purpose could such knowledge serve? Would not the awareness that one wasn't living up to the potential of the past be a source of continual dismay? All have been on top occasionally and at the bottom of the barrel as well. One life at a time, one persona at a time . . . "*

This is not to say that all such guidance is false; certainly, there *are* people who may have the right *and a need to know* about prominence in a past life. I believe those cases are rare, but if the criteria of common sense and intuition have been applied and prayer yields a yes by word or sign, the guidance may well be true.

Discernment was also critical in regard to the seeker's inner voices and emotions, such as wishful thinking or fear. The greatest challenge was to elude a seeker's romantic goals and to reach clear attunement with the Higher Self. The desire for a compatible, loving mate can be all-consuming. Odd as it may seem, I have found it difficult at times to tell the difference between the seeker's intense yearning and authentic guidance coming through.

With the advent of 1992, I became acutely aware that giving a reading tired me more. I needed a longer period of time for "reentry" into conscious alertness, and it was far more difficult to recoup my energy and build a reserve for the next reading.

At one point, distressed by my frequent fatigue, I had a vivid dream in which I saw a baby grand piano sitting in the middle of a busy intersection in my hometown. A voice in my dream said, "*The piano's underpinnings have been rup-tured and other damage was done by the pounding and battering of forceful energy over the years.*"

I knew that the piano was a stand-in for me. My need for word-by-word guidance for thirteen years, my *"making it harder than it needed to be,"* as my Higher Self said, had taken its toll.

On one occasion, after I delayed starting an absentee reading for several hours because of tiredness, I asked my daughter to help. During the meditation, Higher Consciousness said that the reading would now be *"fairly light and easy."* It was—for me.

Shannon unsealed the envelope and began to voice the first question. Instantly, she started to sob and tremble, an uncharacteristic reaction despite her sensitivity and compassion. Although I was tempted to disengage from attunement to comfort her, I felt led to wait. I knew instinctively that Shannon had been pulled into the seeker's energy field by virtue of the woman's emotions. When I heard the query in full, I understood. My client sought information about the biological mother who gave her up for adoption when she was an infant.

I heard the force field, I received the guidance, and I had a moderate drop in energy about a half-hour after the session, but I did not need to deal with the emotions anchored in the seeker's subconscious. I assume that my Higher Self wanted to help me conserve what energy I had and to send Shannon a message: she could develop her own abilities quite easily should she choose to do so.

The most hazardous pitfall for an intuitive counselor is to neglect his or her personal growth. Unresolved business, *ready to surface* but unacknowledged and perhaps unrecognized, may be automatically *projected* onto the seeker during the course of a reading. This troublesome maneuver of the higher mind can be subtle. The only reliable means of ensuring that it does not happen is to be continually faithful to one's own personal and spiritual growth.

Projection's cousin *self-protection* may have deterred me in certain cases from complete attunement in readings for men. This came to light as the result of my 1991 survey for feedback from recipients of absentee readings. Two of the eighteen replies stated that the guidance had not been especially helpful and one claimed that the reading was totally inaccurate. All three seekers were men.

Puzzled, I went to my files for the seekers' questions and the reading tapes. I was startled to see that in some way each man had clearly indicated a struggle with deep inner anger or rage.

I realized then what may have happened. Notwithstanding the steady progress I had made toward achieving emotional health, I was still afraid to expose myself to another's anger, especially if the person was male. Some part of my consciousness had acted to shield me from deep attunement in such situations.

In assimilating all that accompanied this invaluable insight—that I had not yet *completely* released or transmuted my fear of male anger—a further question came to mind. I had given each man a full-length reading. There were no interruptions to the flow of the guidance. Did I on some level fabricate the thoughts that substituted for my picking up on the anger? Higher Consciousness told me not to worry about this, adding *"all was as it was meant to be."*

Whenever quiet time was available over the next few weeks, I confronted this long-existing, crippling inhabitant of the fear frontier. I recalled to mind the various occasions in which I had sidestepped exposure to someone's anger rather than trying to calm the person. I made notes about the incidents and contemplated what the likely results would have been if I'd remained or responded. Of particular help was the realization that although unpleasant, the experience *would not have brought me actual harm*. The apprehension was worse than the "ordeal" may have been.

The last step in the overcoming process was to use the Silence in several meditations—a powerful time, as my subconscious was open and available to me—for the absolute release of this fear. For this step, I designed a firmly and confidently worded affirmation: "*I AM not afraid to experience anger—either my own or that of another. I respond to anger in constructive, healthy ways. I AM successful in transmuting anger when its right purpose is done.*"

In the three years since, all indications have been that my inability to confront and deal with anger is finally resolved.

Guidelines for Seekers

There is a time and place in which a psychic/intuitive reading may be of value to you. The relevance and helpfulness of the type of guidance described in this book is as dependent upon you, the seeker, as it is upon the psychic. Your motivation should be sincere and serious, whether you are striving for self-understanding; for assistance with choices and forthcoming decisions; help with relationships; or for assurance of divine order and grace in your life.

The first pitfall encountered when one decides to seek a reading is to choose the wrong counselor. Different psychic/intuitive counselors have different specialties:

1. Some psychics are drawn to giving the type of reading which they themselves needed in the past. This can be wise, as they would be better able to understand where the seeker "is coming from." The focus here would be on personal and spiritual growth.

2. There *are* good psychics who read with a light touch, who entertain, and yet who well may sow valuable seeds.

3. Certain psychics are able to help the police solve crimes and to find missing objects and family members.

4. Some psychics specialize in past-life readings, others

in health and overcoming; and others in career or material matters.

To find the right counselor, word-of-mouth or personal referral are the best resources. If these resources are not available, try to ascertain the prospective counselor's motivation for doing this work. Be wary of counselors who rest on their laurels and relax their attention to personal growth.

I would caution that you not run from one psychic counselor to another and thus become a "readings junkie." The quality of guidance may deteriorate with each successive session, particularly if you have not absorbed and fully worked with guidance from prior readings. I have found that Higher Consciousness prefers seekers to go with*in* for guidance and won't countenance counselor-dependency.

When you find an intuitive counselor whom you feel you can trust, know that compensation—the exchange of energy—is appropriate. The form of the energy is not as important as the ensuring of balance: one needs to give in return for what one receives. Also, *"the labourer is worthy of his hire."* (Luke 10:7)

An appointment with a conscientious counselor is an appointment with Higher Consciousness; the psychic is simply a skilled intermediary. The wise seeker will carefully consider the questions. Inadequate preparation can quickly sabotage a reading.

There is a delicate line between clearly stated questions and overfeeding of information. My rule of thumb is for the seeker to be specific, but to avoid telling me what his or her own intuition is saying. An example of a good question: "I'm considering a career in computer sciences, education or business administration. Which would be in divine order for me?" Overfeeding would include, "I'd like to teach history at the junior college level, but I can't tolerate kids who think they know more than the teacher."

The ideal is to phrase the question clearly enough that there is no doubt what you are asking. Write—write—write your questions in advance. In this way, your mind will not need to race ahead during the reading to try to recall what you planned to ask next. Just as the instrument's mind should be calm, so should yours—if you truly want an up-lifting, growth-producing experience.

You do not need to close off your conscious mind during the reading. Your conscious mind is not being read. Your subconscious storage facility is being scanned, but it is your superconscious or Higher Consciousness that will provide the guidance.

A serious seeker should insist that the reading be taped. With an hour-long session, it is scarcely possible to remember all of the guidance with its shadings and subtleties. An in-depth reading normally encompasses three to five years of guidance.

Guidance that may seem literal but not relevant at the time may turn out to be symbolic and applicable to developments a year down the road. This is one reason why it is helpful to periodically rehear the tape.

Keep an open mind, but remember that *your* intuition is the bottom line.

◆   ◆   ◆

THEY THAT BRING TO EACH SOUL NOT COMFORT,

NOT AS EARTHLY PLEASURE, BUT THAT WHICH IS

SPIRITUALLY CONSTRUCTIVE IN
THE EXPERIENCE OF A SOUL,

ARE WORTHY OF ACCEPTANCE

Cayce reading 5752-5

The Seekers: From Heavy Hearts to Light-Filled Lives

OVER THE YEARS, PEOPLE FROM ALL WALKS OF LIFE have entered my reading room. No matter their age, race, social status, profession or life style, most all were seeking solace and a way to make sense out of life.

Since meditation is *my* Light-sustaining, guidance-achieving means of choice, I prodded and persuaded who-ever I could to "Practice the Presence in the Silence." If meditation worked for me in spite of my merry-go-round mind, it could work for anyone.

To this end, I did my best to keep at least one weekly meditation group going for serious seekers to attend. I led one or two groups a week—usually, one in my home and the other at Unity Church of Christianity in Pensacola or Gulf Breeze. When a group grew too large for my moderate-sized house, we met at a metaphysical bookstore after closing hours.

During a talk at Still Waters Centre in 1986, I offered to start meditation groups in other people's homes. I would lead the group for eight weeks and then turn it over to the host or hostess. Six couples responded and for the next few years, four to six meditation groups met weekly in Pensacola, Gulf Breeze, and Midway.

My recommendation to people who were sincere in their quest for inner guidance was to meditate once a day at home, if feasible, and once a week with a group. The pooled energy of the group accelerated progress. Aspirants who were faithful to this discipline eventually broke through to their superconscious. When a breakthrough occurred, I was as jubilant as the meditator.

A number of successful meditators looked toward further development so as to become more intuitively responsive to the people and challenges in their lives.

Katrina J., in an absentee reading in January 1991, asked how she could grow spiritually and psychically (please note that "psychic" means "of the soul-mind"). The response by Higher Consciousness is noteworthy for any seeker of Light.

H.C.: *"Meditation is the key—group and alone. First giving self over to that part of you, that part of self, which is OF GOD . . . It is important to shift gears and get yourself out of the way . . . To want the knowingness, the intuitive knowingness, the words from your Higher Self, to come to you as a being, as a soul in incarnation. Not for any kind of ego satisfaction or recognition, but as a soul in your entirety so that you can be guided from within. (To want) your faculties—psychic, physical, intuitive to be balanced and used for the furtherment of your own life and growth, and in service to other people.*

"Ascertain your motivation first. Write it down, place it in your Bible or in another holy place and pray on it. Then lift your heart to the Light, to God, to Creation as it should be—with everyone filled with love for everyone else. Recognize oneness and that energy blends, and you will have the foundation to begin.

"Know what your own moral law is and honor it in every way, even when no one is looking, even when no one hears. Honor that moral, ethical, spiritual code or law you live by. You will enhance each and every part of self—the emotional, the physical, the mental, the spiritual. You will enhance the vibrational quality of your being, for you are indeed electromagnetic Light. You will enhance your intuitiveness, and you will find the empowerment that comes from within from knowing you are a part of God."

When the right motivation and dedication were in evidence, I recommended that successful meditators further refine their natural intuitiveness through learning how to attune on behalf of others. I offer the following extracts from letters not as testimonials to *my* help, but as encouragement to those readers who are ready to reach for personal and spiritual health and empowerment.

Karen B.: "You have opened doors for me that I believe will lead me to wholeness. There are no words in any planetary language that can express how grateful I am. How do you thank someone who has given you life? . . . who has given you more than all the treasures on earth? . . . who has given you your birthright?" (1989)

Linda Clara: "You have taught me, given me confidence, listened to me, consoled me, gently led me along the spiritual path, and at the right time challenged me to take that step out on faith that no one ever thinks he or she is quite ready for . . . By encouraging me to go beyond what I thought were my limitations, you have given me a whole new world and you have given me *myself.*" (1990)

Teresa H.: "I cannot begin to explain the enormous impact you have had on my life . . . I don't know how you've put up with me. Dragging me, moaning and groaning, to a higher expression of self had to be grueling at times. Thank you for not letting me quit . . . (and) for sharing all that you devoted a lifetime to. It will serve me well as I grow into my own adventure. The greatest tribute I can give you is to share the gifts you have given me with others. Through your loving guidance, I have centered into an enlightened existence, a better member of the Universe and a more willing worker devoted to service and growth . . . you have changed my life." (1991)

Linda Louise: "I have listened to the tape (of the reading) several times. You told me I was very close to direct communication with my Higher Self and the Collective Unconscious, so I have been practicing the meditation you suggested . . . I used to get so frustrated trying to 'break through,' and setting a twenty-minute limit has been very helpful . . . I know I can do it myself and I really want to! I feel I am divinely guided in knowing what it is I came here to do . . . to understand why I think and feel the way I do, (and) to feel a validation of *myself.*" (1993)

Unfortunately, the greater number of people who sought readings were in too much inner—and often outer—turmoil to think constructively about meditation. They needed guidance *now.*

I looked on my life's work as twofold: teaching meditation and reading for people in pain. I knew that if I could connect to Higher Consciousness in a seeker's behalf, help would come. My files contain many letters which attest to the wonders wrought in a seeker's ability to cope, to have hope and a measure of peace in heart and mind. These are the people I have reached out to. These are the people I want to convince that the strength is *within* and that the inner voice can be heard.

◆ ◆ ◆

What follows are portions of guidance received in response to different needs as voiced by different seekers, to whom I have given pseudonyms.

Georgia: Searching for Her Biological Mother (1992)

H.C.: *"My child, it is not quite time for the location to be made, but made it will be within a matter of a few years—and quite happily so, for she longs to see you as well as you long to see her.*

"The young woman ... who bore you to infancy was but a child herself ... She felt it was in the best interest of all—but in particular, this tiny soul she carried in her womb—to give you up for adoption, to know that you had been placed with loving parents who perhaps could not have a child of their own. She gave a gift, and to her it was indeed a treasure.

"There is no history of mental illness nor malnutrition that would have caused any defects of which you could possibly be unaware at this time. There were no drugs involved. You came from a fairly stable background. There are no skeletons in the closet for you to worry about."

The reading went on to give Georgia specific information on her biological parents' lives after the adoption took place. I spoke with Georgia in mid-June 1994. She said her search had led her to a courthouse in Texas where she was told that the records must remain sealed until she has a "compelling" need to know. She feels intuitively that she will know when the time is right to proceed. For now, Georgia is letting the matter rest.

Melinda: Remorse over an Abortion (1991)

Sensing the presence of a little boy in spirit around Melinda, I asked if she had lost a child by miscarriage or abortion. She replied that she had indeed had an abortion several years earlier.

It was not unusual for me to "pick up" a child in spirit around a woman. In most cases, the soul was either waiting for conception to take place or, if a pregnancy had been terminated, wanting to reassure the mother of its continued love and support—especially if the seeker were burdened with grief or guilt.

I told Melinda that the child was in the room with us and he was every bit as much alive as we, if not more so. Melinda's Higher Self then spoke into my mind:

> H.C.: "... and could not love you more had he remained on the earth plane and followed through with what seemed to be the plan, but was not. Let go. Let go and let God and let good prevail. What occurred was perhaps not the best choice and may have seemed like the only choice, but was known as a part of your plan before it happened. And thus the soul that hovers is aware of the decisions that will be made, yet chooses to come into your life to imbue you with love and bonding to draw upon for the time being and to play a role in the lesson ... You have earned no eternal damnation ... and it is time that you forgave yourself, as God, at the moment the wrong choice is being made, forgives you."

In a meditation in October 1987 in Hobbs, New Mexico, Higher Consciousness gave me a unique perspective on one of our most tragic conditions: the drug abuse epidemic.

In the Words of a Source

"We take time over here for our own form of spiritual nourishment and upliftment to help gird us for the work that we are required to do, especially now that the earth plane is in so much turmoil with physical conditions of deprivation and suffering. Not that the earth hasn't been in this shape before—for indeed it has—but never have there been so many all across the globe who have created a hell of their own making for selves by turning over their minds, their power, and their control to chemicals so that they are halfway suspended in and out of the body, in and out of the world a good deal of the time."

◆ ◆ ◆

Kathryn: Relevance of a Past Life to This Life's Tragedy (1992)

Kathryn's twenty-eight-year-old son killed her mother in March 1992. Gary was a substance abuser; he began using illegal drugs when he was twelve. Gary had lived with his grandmother for several years, and he obviously loved her very much. She, in turn, doted on her grandson; in effect, enabling his addiction, as she could not use "tough love" precepts.

All Gary remembers is that he was in the shower when "the walls started caving in" on him. He was "coming down." He later described the drug he used as similar to LSD. Gary has no recollection of killing his grandmother. He does recall leaving the house that night with her credit cards and car.

A week later, a relative found the grandmother's body hidden in a closet. She had been stabbed by someone in a rage.

Although a psychologist concluded that Gary may not knowingly have killed Kathryn's mother, Gary was found guilty of first-degree murder and sentenced to death. Later, the sentence was changed to life imprisonment. He will be eligible for parole in 2032.

That her son murdered her mother was a nightmare of horrendous proportion for Kathryn. She never stopped loving Gary and she hurt desperately for him, but she also loved and missed her mother.

Kathryn was tormented by the question of her own responsibility in the formation of Gary's personality and values. She suffered intense guilt and anguish over the emotionally unstable family environment of Gary's childhood. Her daughter, reared in the same home, had been able to avoid emotional and behavioral difficulties. Kathryn wondered what made the difference.

All I knew when I sat down to do the absentee reading for Kathryn in August 1993 was that her son Gary had killed her mother. I did not want details or circumstances in advance. After working my way through the deeper emotions in Kathryn's energy field, I was startled to see on my inner screen a scene far removed from the topic of death. It looked much like a holiday greeting card with an illustration of an old-fashioned Christmas complete with horse-drawn carriages, holiday revelers, and carolers standing under a gaslight. My description of the scene follows:

> I see a small boy running alongside a carriage, pounding on the door for it to stop. He is pleading with an older woman inside: "Grandmama, Grandmama,

please come back, my mother needs you, my mother needs you!" The old woman inside is very stern. She looks straight ahead. The driver of the carriage looks down and she calls to him, "Go on, go on. Pay that child no mind!" Again, "Pay that boy no mind!"

The driver takes his heavily booted foot and pushes the boy away. He falls down in the middle of the icy, snow-packed street and weeps his heart out. People tell him to go home, for it is Christmas Eve. Desolate, he stumbles up the steps. His mother is in bed nursing the babe she had birthed the previous day. She is very weak and wan. She reaches out her hand to stroke his cheek and asks why the tears.

The child tells her that he tried to bring Grandmama back. The young woman in the bed, old and worn beyond her years, manages a half smile as she whispers, "It will be all right." He cries, "We have no food to eat! We have no wood to burn! The children are hungry!" His three stair-step siblings are in an adjacent room. The woman had borne a child yearly for five years. Her husband abandoned them because she had not done away with this last little hungry mouth to feed. He wanted no more hungry mouths to feed.

The boy, eldest of the children at seven and the apple of his mother's eye, knows there is no money, and he fears that she will not again be well. The doctor said that Mother needed an operation, although its success could not be guaranteed. Without it, her survival was greatly at risk.

The gravely ill woman had sent a message to her mother asking for forgiveness. She had married in opposition to the older woman's will. The Gran'dam came and looked around and said to her suffering daughter, "You made your bed, now lie in it!" She did not know that the man had left, nor of the doctor's admonition.

The older woman's pride fortified her harsh words

of judgment. She pronounced sentence by walking out and leaving them in their sorry plight. By morning, the children's mother was dead.

The hatred that was kindled that night stayed with the little boy who loved his mother so. Hatred for the man who abandoned them so cruelly; hatred for his Grandmama.

My screen went blank as word-by-word guidance began.

H.C.: *"What's done is done and cannot be undone, but there is a balancing and there is a plan. That plan has now been met and did not end as it might have, in forgiveness all around. But it is done; it is over. Love, forgiveness, acceptance, and peace must now become the foundation for the future. We are ready for questions."*

K.: My son, my second child, who was into drugs, killed my mother. He was convicted of murdering her. Was this a karmic issue, then? What more can you tell me about this?

H.C.: *"This question has been answered, as you by now are aware. (Word unintelligible) desolation, rage, and also some guilt affected him and then affected her. She volunteered to come back and to try to reach him with all of the understanding that she could muster herself, leaving it up to your son to decide if he could forgive her neglect.*

"He blamed her for your death, you see. Such a young boy to reason so lastingly. All has been resolved now, not in the way we had hoped, but your mother, who sees from her vantage point the story back for generations, completely forgave him and sends him love. (She) is working on herself so that such a travesty could never occur again, and she speaks not of her death, but of yours.

"Understanding more about life itself and the nature

of consciousness, she knows now full well that when we
withdraw our love because another could not meet our
demands, we are using—in the most deplorable way—
the power God puts in our hands."

While Kathryn knows that present-life circumstances
undoubtedly contributed to the tragedy and that *the former
life experience does not justify this life's violence,* the guidance helped her to make some sense of it. In realizing that a
certain amount of destiny was involved, Kathryn was able
to step back and view the events with *spiritual detachment.*
The reading helped her to let go of her overwhelming anguish and feelings of personal guilt and to move ahead with
her life. It also brought Kathryn a measure of peace of mind
for the first time since the tragedy.

◆   ◆   ◆

The Taylor Family: The
Afterlife-Aftermath of Suicide (1991)

Jarold Taylor was twenty-six when he took his life.

Five months later, Jarold's family asked me to try to reach
him in an absentee reading. Understandably, they were bewildered and disconsolate.

As I attuned to Jarold's energy prior to the questions, I
was able to ascertain what his mental, physiological, and
emotional state had been at the time of his suicide. I also
perceived specific information that may have contributed
to his flawed thinking. After I described Jarold's progress on
the other side, Higher Consciousness took over the microphone with word-by-word guidance.

The following extracts from the reading may be of general interest. Intensely personal passages have been omitted.

H.C.: *"In his heart, he simply wanted to go home. Indeed he will not be and is not damned, for God understands the longing. God can see into the heart; He counts the rhyme and reason that are there. He understands us through and through.*

"There is no eternal damnation; there is no fire. There are no consequences of one's shortening his or her life span other than certain 'rules and requirements' that are not mandatory, but are urged for consideration upon those who have taken this route.

"The first of two requirements for atonement or, to put it a different way, 'at-one-ment,' is that the soul who left you perceives the grief, the hurt, the disappointment, and the confusion that the act generated. Is this not 'punishment' enough? Few souls who shorten a particular experience ever shorten another one, especially when they see the trail of tears they left behind.

"The second is that the soul serve out at another time the number of years by which it shortened this experience . . . and dedicate the new life to others, that others may find the courage within when they are feeling hopeless and helpless."

Q: (Addressed to Jarold) What would you like for us to know? How can we heal?

J.T.: *"Try to see a bright Light whenever you think of my name . . . No need to wish you had told me this or that while I was still there, for I hear you now. I've heard you speak with tongues and speak with hearts since the day I left. I'm so grateful that you miss me, and that the love was so deep.*

". . . I have had a glimpse of what life holds for all of you and for the earth itself, only a glimpse, but when time passes it will be magnificent. Maybe not before this century is over, but later. They say up here that time has to pass before it all can be right, but you don't grasp time—it isn't important here. I have to keep telling my-

self (that) it is *important there.*

"... All of the good that God has promised will come to pass. I see that now, as I am guided through this maze of loving, healing helpers. They call this plane "The Resting Place." They say it's an interim location. The colors are unimaginable. The lightness takes some getting used to.

"When I was first here after I woke up, I kept reaching for a wallet, a set of keys, a drink, and even the telephone. And then I had to laugh. I'd like to laugh more often, and I'd like you to laugh along with me. Don't cry. Every tear hurts and reverberates.

"Your pain haunts me ... and it is very difficult to forgive myself for that. If I could wipe away the tears and have this choice all over again, I'd rather be a cripple, deformed, deaf and dumb, and in prison than to have left you in the way I did.

"Forgive me, forgive me. Let me go to the Higher Realms where I will wait for you."

◆ ◆ ◆

As rewarding as the foregoing readings were for me, I also found noncrisis sessions a source of personal fulfillment, particularly when the seeker *truly* wanted to grow. The following unsolicited letters represent two such individuals. Michael is a counselor; Glen is an associate professor of psychology.

June 12, 1994

Dear Barbara:

I hope all is well. I am writing you to tell you of my experiences with the guidance you have given me.

My first reading with you was in 1987; it was my first experience with any type of guidance. I was very re-

luctant, but when I met you, I became very much at ease. In the session, I was overwhelmed with encouragement.

The connection we had that first time was extraordinary. Everything you tapped in on was accurate. I have always felt there was a purpose to my life in helping others. You confirmed this for me. Through you I found what this purpose is.

As you already know, I am HIV-positive. I believe I have this disease because I'm here to help others deal with their HIV status. If I wasn't infected, I would not have been so accepting of people. I have been HIV-positive for nine years now without any symptoms at all, and my CD4 cells have been consistently high.

Through the years of counseling people on their disease, I have realized how lonely people are and how much they need to feel a part of something. I believe that *my* lesson to learn in this life is loneliness.

The first thing I tell people is that they are not alone and they are not "bad" people; also, that they will be all right and that they're loved—being all right in the spiritual sense, not the physical sense. I tell them not to worry about the disease, to ask for guidance, and be able to accept what might be in store for them.

The second reading was a distant reading (absentee). There was not as much information, but it was reassuring that the path I was on was correct. It again confirmed that I will not be disabled by my disease for the next ten years or so—and that depends on what I do with myself and how I handle my life. This, too, I already suspected, for—again—my purpose is to help others deal with their mortality and to take control of their disease.

I try to live in the Light. By saying to myself, "I am of the Light, I am in the Light, I am the Light," I find comfort in knowing that the down feelings will pass. I pray for guidance from God not for things or to keep me healthy, but to help me deal with whatever life has in store for me.

My job of counseling HIV-positive patients is going well, but I find myself even lonelier. I am not able to let the staff or the patients know about my HIV status, and I must live in silence . . . I have told a few patients who are having the most difficult time.

The staff is extremely judgmental . . . Little do they know that I'm there and working for the patients just as well, if not better, than they. For now, I live my life cautiously and quietly; not as free and comfortable as I'd like.

Barbara, I thank you for your help. Your intuitiveness is astounding and enlightening. I hope you continue to be of great help to many people and that they may seek the guidance of their own Super Being and find solitude. Good luck and God bless.

Michael

◆ ◆ ◆

March 1, 1994

Dear Barbara:

About three years ago, I had my first reading with you and it changed the direction of my life. I experienced the most profound and clear contact with the spiritual world I had ever had. While sitting with you, it became clear to me that I was being spoken to by God or His messengers through you. The effect this had on me is impossible to describe, but when I think of it, your words *"and the peace that passes all understanding"* come immediately to mind. That phrase best describes what I experienced, although words are not able to communicate the depth and power of peace that I felt.

I also had a strong feeling that I was exactly where I was supposed to be in life. The combination of these feelings was so profound that when I went to work several days later, I received comments like "What happened to you—you look so peaceful and calm." The first of these comments was made to me as I walked down the hall long before I even spoke to anyone.

That reading was a turning point in my life. My spiritual awareness was increased immensely and my journey of spiritual growth began in earnest. Many difficult and wonderful things have happened to me since then, too many wonderful things to mention now. The changes of that day have enabled me to withstand the difficult days and to fully enjoy the good days and the great days. I have also been able to help many others in the last couple of years and this has been a great joy to me.

I now know you well enough to know that you will not take the credit for what happened, but merely for being an intermediary. Thank you from the deepest part of me. Thank you for being willing to give of yourself and, in so doing, enabling me to receive a genuine and profound blessing through you. I will never forget that day with you. It changed my life forever.

Glen

If I was able to bring through guidance that helped seekers to change their lives for the better, those seekers and their stories helped me, in turn, to heal and change my life as well.

◆ ◆ ◆

We *are* all a part of each other *and* a part of the whole, as an Anglican priest penned so eloquently in the seventeenth century.

◆ ◆ ◆

NO MAN IS AN ILAND, INTIRE OF IT SELFE;

EVERY MAN IS A PEECE OF THE CONTINENT, A PART OF THE MAINE;

IF A CLOD BE WASHED AWAY BY THE SEA, EUROPE IS THE LESSE,

AS WELL AS IF A PROMONTORIE WERE,

AS WELL AS IF A MANNOR OF THY FRIENDS OR OF THINE OWN WERE.

ANY MAN'S DEATH DIMINISHES ME,

BECAUSE I AM INVOLVED IN MANKINDE.

AND THEREFORE NEVER SEND TO KNOW FOR WHOM THE BELL TOLLS.

IT TOLLS FOR THEE.

John Donne (1573-1631)
"Devotions XVII"

The Peace That
Passes All Understanding

ON THIS CLEAR AND COOL EVENING IN EARLY
February 1987, Still Waters Centre was anything but still.
The atmosphere positively crackled as the brigade of Light-
seekers charged toward the hard-wood, hard-on-the-
bottom pews and standby folding chairs. By a miscalcula-
tion in timing, I'd arrived early enough to secure a seat up
front. The quaint country church, its edifice erected with
the timber of the time, had been squeezed out of service by
the concrete block, brick, and stone institutions of inspiration that now saturated the Myrtle Grove area on the west
side of Pensacola.

John and Carol Pepper, private citizens, had acquired the grounds and building for the purpose of "promoting the study of ancient philosophies and reviving the lost art of thinking in the Higher Realms." Still Waters Centre launched many a speaker and seminar in the Southeast, including me.

People hurried down the center aisle to compete for pillows and floor space on the platform. Several sat in a semilotus position around the podium. The sanctuary, which safely seated 100, was bulging at the seams. Later, it would be known that 350 pair of feet had entered this night. It would also be discovered that the subflooring of the vestibule had broken under the weight of the people above it.

Tonight's guest lecturer was an eighty-year-old retired attorney from Georgia, a Mr. Harry Bromley. He had traversed the globe many times in search of spiritual truth and inner peace and would talk about the marvels he had seen.

I craned my neck to see how many people I knew. Vivian, a member of my psychic development class, waved. Behind her, Laura and Rocky, who regularly attended my Tuesday night meditation, were settling into their seats.

Never a table-hopper, tonight I decided to sally forth and chat with my friends across the aisle. Little did I realize as I maneuvered my way over to Vivian's pew that this stroll would set in motion the resolution of ages-old karma. As I drew near, I was suddenly immobilized by a muscle spasm. One of my hands flew to my abdomen. Almost simultaneously, the other hand reached up to cover my mouth as a cough commenced. The cough graduated into a series. I felt as though dried oregano flakes were lining my throat. The abdominal muscle continued to contract.

I couldn't talk. Vivian offered a pocket package of tissues; I accepted. Laura rose and bent toward me, a roll of cough drops in her hand. I took two and tossed them in my mouth. Nothing changed.

By now, I was drawing a small cluster of sympathizers and

repelling the people in Vivian's pew. The overhead lighting dimmed; the program was ready to begin.

Once I was back in my seat, the spasms and the coughs abated. For the next forty-seven hours, I didn't need to cough nor did a muscle seize a moment in the spotlight. Confounded by the Saturday night episode (I seldom had colds, coughs, or sore throats any more, and I didn't have one now), by Monday morning I had relegated it to the file of nearly forgotten incidents.

But this flustering experience was not to be a one-time ordeal. It would happen several times over the next two weeks. I didn't suspect then that cosmic conspirators were involved.

My Monday evening meditation group met at The Friary, formerly a retirement home for monks. This serene setting, eight miles east of Gulf Breeze, now housed a residential rehabilitation program for substance abusers and their families. Although patients and staff were invited, most of the meditators were nonafflicted residents of nearby neighborhoods.

That Monday evening I began to cough, a hacking type of cough, shortly after the Silence ended. A muscle in my torso grabbed, but the discomfort was moderate. Still, I had no idea what was happening to me.

Tuesday night arrived and the Gulf Breeze meditation group gathered at Susan Lightfoot's house. Pennye had also meditated at The Friary the previous night, as was usual for her. This particular group was exceptional in that we had bonded from the beginning. Although diverse in age and profession, each of us was dedicated to our quest for Light. The warmth and support that resulted was wonderful. Few people missed attending on Tuesday nights.

I hurried into Susan's living room and headed for my favorite chair. Everyone else was there, quiet and ready to "Practice the Presence." I had scarcely sat down when a muscle spasm wracked my body, nearly taking my breath away. I started to cough, but by this time I was mad—at my physical being. I inhaled deeply, held the tickling torment in my throat at bay, and gave the opening prayer.

The spasms accelerated during meditation. I spent much of the time bent over, my forehead on my knees. The room was fairly dark, and I managed not to cough or otherwise disrupt the Silence. When it came time for the healing prayers, no one moved into the middle of the circle. I couldn't understand that, as I knew that one of the meditators, recovering from the flu, had planned to do so.

Higher Consciousness caught me off guard. *"We'd like you to prostrate yourself on the floor in the middle of the circle now."*

Aghast and hoping that I hadn't heard right, I replied, mentally but distinctly, "Why should I do that? There's hardly enough room. These people will be floored. They won't know what I'm doing. I'll look like a fool!"

The response was immediate: *"You must prostrate yourself before these people."* That more-evolved, noble, and less self-conscious part of me, my Higher Self, may have said that I *"must,"* but false pride didn't agree, and I did not comply. I left shortly after the closing, unnerved and bewildered.

I dreamed all that night, as I had been doing for several days. The next morning as I was emerging from the twilight zone, Higher Consciousness finally explained:

"Fourteen from your present life were with you in Egypt in the life of which we once spoke ... "

My mind raced back to October 1971 and a meditation that took place in the middle of the night. I had been escorted by a Higher Being on an out-of-the-body journey to the pyramids in Egypt. There, I learned in a dramatic way that I had been placed in a sarcophagus while still alive. The closing of the lid took my life from me. How long had it been since I thought of this? Had I believed it? I'd never spoken of the experience except to Marc.

"You betrayed your vows and these people by your lust for power, possessions, and carnal pleasure. You misused the sacred silence. Others in the temple clamored for your life to be taken. Those who are with you today did not protest but for one. They all are to go with you through a cleansing and a reconsecration. There needs to be forgiveness by and between all."

I sat alone for hours on Wednesday morning, contemplating the experience of the past five days. I knew I had not fabricated the story nor had I induced coughing spells and stomach spasms. With a dislike of center stage, I had nothing to gain and much to lose—particularly my credibility—if my mind was playing tricks on me.

If the guidance were true, it followed that the regular members of the Tuesday night meditation group were with me in Egypt and had either taken part in—or observed—my demise.

It never crossed my mind to ask Higher Consciousness for the time of history or the location of the temple. When or where didn't matter to me. If the story of a past life together was valid, it was only important that I rectify the wrong that I had done. And if that were the case, the sooner the better.

I went into prayer. I promised God that if the guidance I had received was of Him, I would honor it. I asked Him to stop the physical manifestations immediately if the guidance was not valid. I gave Him my complete trust.

Late that afternoon, I had an answer. Kathy and Richard, members of the Tuesday night meditation group, came for the reading they had scheduled weeks earlier. I coughed spasmodically throughout their reading. They were distressed for me. I said nothing of the guidance I had received about Egypt. I simply apologized.

Two other Tuesday night meditators "coincidentally" had reading appointments that week. With one reading, the

coughing episodes were pronounced and I had some difficulty with abdominal muscle contractions. With the other
reading, I coughed only at the start. I concluded that the
severity of the physiological symptoms identified for me the
people who had been closest or most condemning. This
"identification process" would continue for nine days.

The most violent contractions and coughing occurred on
Thursday night at the beginning of the psychic development class. The minute that Vivian arrived, fierce stomach
cramps assailed me and I sank doubled over into a chair.
The coughing was more like deep retching. I couldn't talk; I
could hardly catch my breath. The four participants left. It
was obvious that there would be no class.

I surmised that Vivian had played a pivotal role in the dis-
closure of my indiscretions and the misuse of my gift in
Egypt. Later, when she and I shared our intuitive guidance,
I was heartened to hear that her act did not result from a
personal vendetta, but out of a concern for the people
served by the temple. She had sought my discipline, not my
death. It was understandable, then, why Vivian had been
unable to meditate with the Gulf Breeze group. She had attended once but later spoke of her "discomfort" when in
the Silence with us.

The next step was to explain to the rest of the group about
my 1971 out-of-the-body trip to ancient Egypt and to tell them
that recent guidance had placed us all in the life described.

When I did, Kathy gasped and exclaimed, "That clarifies
the dream I had two weeks ago! . . . We were underground. I
could see stone stairs leading upward and then a room . . .
there are hangings of Egyptian origin . . . one large (hanging), pure gold with pictures hammered out in it . . .

"Below that picture is a sarcophagus . . . There are people
standing around, ten—maybe twelve—people, very solemn . . . Suddenly I see that there is someone in there . . .
someone who is still alive . . . Some (of the people) are se-
cretly joyful, others are genuinely sad. As the dream ends,

the top of the sarcophagus is closing."

No one spoke for a few minutes and then several spoke at once. Although they had not had time to fully absorb the guidance, the meditators—because of their intuitive sensitivity and trust in me (for which I was immensely grateful)— were willing to consider the experience as an authentic karmic revelation. Nevertheless, I was reluctant to ask any but Susan and my husband to be with me when I rededicated my life as I had been asked to do. I felt awkward and vulnerable about the entire subject.

Ralph declined my invitation, saying that he was not comfortable with the idea. Torn between his belief in my integrity and his intense dislike of attention-securing activities, the dislike won out. It was compounded by his skepticism of "all the people who publicize claims of past lives in ancient Egypt." However, Ralph continued to support my work in all other ways.

On Saturday, March 7, 1987, Susan and I went to Unity Church of Christianity in Pensacola. Susan, at my request, had designed a simple but appropriate ceremony, drawing from a book of spiritual inspiration. I would lie face down on the floor of the sanctuary while Susan read the passages she had chosen. She would then ask me to repeat the words of a vow by which I would reconsecrate my life to God's work.

Our unseen companions from the Higher Realms arranged for the surprise appearance of the church pianist, who "happened" to be a Tuesday night meditator. Disconcerted at first because I had hoped for no audience, when Jean offered to contribute music, I accepted. Her uplifting selections made the ceremony even more meaningful.

The muscle spasms and coughing spells ended as abruptly as they had begun. All of the disconcerting developments over the preceding two weeks melted into distant memory, replaced by a feeling of exultation when I heard in my next meditation:

*"Your spiritual karma has been balanced. You are
free. We are proud of you. Go with God, my child."*

Three months later, in a reading I gave for the group as a
whole, we learned more about our history and the purpose
for our coming together in this life. The origin of the guidance was identified as *"Ahmentorhep, the voice of the group
conscience."*

*"... You have been brought together at this time and
given the awareness of your togetherness so that you
may create for selves the platform through which the
One Source, One Power, One All may speak, may move,
may manifest blessings. This is not your first experience
together, nor is it total yet.*
   *"... You were together before, in Greece at Delphi, in
the temple there where the oracles were housed and
consulted. You were together in Egypt . . . at the time
that God sent Edgar Cayce as one of His spokespersons
to bring together peoples and heal the divisiveness, that
the true religion may be founded and well grounded."*

(Note to Reader: According to the Cayce readings on file
at the A.R.E. in Virginia Beach, one of Edgar Cayce's incarnations was as Ra Ta, who became the High Priest in Egypt
some 10,600 years before "the entry of the Prince of Peace
into the earth." Ra Ta was sent by God to instruct the people
in the ways of the Law of One, as Egypt had been determined to be the spiritual center of the Universal Forces in
the earth. A detailed account of that era may be found in
Many Happy Returns: The Lives of Edgar Cayce by W. H.
Church, Harper & Row, Publishers, 1984.)

*"You were part of his party as he journeyed hither
and yon, but you were not in the inner circle . . . You
returned to Egypt in the experience of which you have*

been apprised... The spiritual dharma, the bond which will allow you to serve as a group, is very strong.

"It remains now up to each and every one to decide for self where the service commences and when, in whose name, and how it shall be done. We cannot give you a detailed plan to execute, for your free will needs to be part of the decisions and choices made.

"There must be no coercion, no undue pressure, nor any feeling of resentment if some reject the work. There cannot be a dissenting vibration when the platform is put together. Not at this time, not in this life.

"Whether or not the work commences and the gifts are pressed into service is not as critical as is the choice that you each need to make in your own life, in your own way, and about yourself. For that is what your coming together is all about.

"Each of you now has the capability of reaching the Temple within to hear your inner voice, the voice of your Higher Self. If it were not so, we would not be allowed to tell you this. This is the first mansion of which Christ spoke, and it is a mansion full of glory, bathed in Light.

"By your coming together, a blending of your energies, and the willingness that you have exhibited to help one another, you have opened that passageway more clearly, irrevocably, and sooner than you might have otherwise. You stand on the fringe of spiritual selfhood and the integration of the earth life with the beingness of you as souls created in the image of God.

"... There are many ways to serve. By listening, by speaking, by touching, by healing, by teaching, by supporting, by drawing away from at times. Let yourself be guided by your intuition... Allow the ideas that we now loose and set free to pervade and permeate ... Those ideas will bring you the mode of service, the opportunity, and the resources to develop and to give.

"... Know that there are hopes that ride with you ...

You are not in your location solely by your choice... For the waters that surround you are regenerative and healing ... From this day on, there needs to be no further agonizing nor painful plagiarizing from the past. Begin anew."

In response to a question placed by Diane, the voice of the group conscience had this to say: *"... From this day on, those who remain with the group in heart, mind, and soul are no longer only individuals but part of a task force consecrated in Light."*

The Gulf Breeze meditation group continued to meet weekly for another year. Although we shared the desire to bring into materialization a center of healing and service in northwest Florida, we were unable to progress past the brainstorming stage at that time.

One might think that the foregoing events were personal drama enough, but a higher hand continued to implement a custom-designed program of revelation. Next on the agenda: the completion of my personal self-healing work.

During the two-week period in February when I was "gifted" with muscle spasms and coughing spells, I had two dreams that were critical to my self-understanding and the overcoming of my codependency. Both dreams came "out of the blue."

The first dream was short and shocking. I saw myself at age fourteen slowly stepping—as though I were blind—down the stairs to the basement in the Liberty Street house where I had lived in 1949. At the halfway point, I lifted my eyes from my feet to a higher level on the right and my feet froze in place. I felt as though a cannonball had hit me in the stomach as I saw my grandfather's head suspended by a rope from the ceiling over the coal bin... It seemed to me he was gently spinning a quarter turn in each direction . . .

The dream ended without any further movement or thought on my part. It had been thirty-eight years, almost to the day, that my grandfather had hanged himself with my jumping rope. For the next six months, I worked through the stages of grief that I had unconsciously deferred, beginning with anger at being "abandoned" by this man who meant so much to me, the only nurturing male in my life at the time.

While visiting New Jersey in the summer of 1987, I went to the grave site of my grandparents, and—I could have done this *anywhere*—I railed at him through tears of grief and frustration, and then I forgave. I know he heard. Peace enveloped me. I was able to accept my grandfather's suicide.

The second dream concerned my relationship with my dad as it was when I was a child, the period up to age eight—years missing from conscious memory. I recognized the house. In the dream, I saw my father lying on his bed. My mother must have been on an errand. A little girl, perhaps three years old, toddled past the doorway. He called her to him, swooped her up onto the bed, pressed his torso against her, and masturbated himself.

I awoke. I knew that what the dream depicted had really happened. I remained calm but pensive all day. In mid-afternoon, when everyone was out and the house was quiet, I went into the Silence. I asked: "Do you have any more to show me?"

A different scene from my childhood came into view on my inner screen. There was no voice-over. The scene showed the same little girl, a few years older and in the same house, standing at the top of the cellar stairs. She was looking down toward the bottom of the steps, where my dad was waiting. He called to her to "come down and see the puppies." She did. She held each of the four beagle puppies, one at a time. And then her little hand was guided to encircle, to stroke, and to place in her mouth another "puppy."

I acknowledged the scene as truth. It faded. I knew there were no other scenes to view.

Insights came: a blending of the voice of the heart, a memory from deep within the Pandora's box of the soul, and the wisdom of the higher mind.

I saw that my father had tried, perhaps unconsciously, to establish the emotional bond with me that he could not with my mother. When I was eight and my mother threatened to leave (I'm not certain what the catalyst was), he must have comprehended that boundaries were in place for a purpose. He drew back from closeness and became ambivalent in his attention. I was no longer "special."

The next day as rage stormed the citadel of my conscious mind, I packed and stored all of the photographs of my parents in a dark closet. I called Susan Lightfoot and Cheryl Malone, both being good friends of mine and by profession mental health counselors. Susan and Cheryl alternated two months of Saturdays in working with me to process and resolve my anger and resentment.

We role played; I was both my mother and myself. It was incredibly painful. I asked her (my mother), "Did you know? Why didn't you . . . " I listened to my voice speak for my mother as a reply came: "My father, too . . . The same thing happened to me."

Months later, when I surveyed the landscape of my life with my father's sexual trespasses and emotional abuse in mind, I understood the neediness that had plagued me. Had his behavior also sabotaged my self-esteem *as a woman?* Or did I, on some level, blame myself? Why, for forty-some years, had I felt and behaved subservient to men? What was it about independence that alarmed me? Was it the thought of life without the "protection" of a man?

Whatever the root cause of my inability to value and assert myself as a woman, the clarity with which I could now see my life worked wonders—but not overnight. I recognized my worth on the intellectual level. I knew that making these final changes in reactions and patterns would take a little longer. But I had waited too long already for complete health. The past few months had been power packed with guidance and revelations. It was already May. The year 1987 was rushing by. I needed to strike while the iron was hot.

I located a respected treatment program for codependency in Tennessee, applied for admittance, was accepted for early July, and then—six weeks later as I started to pack for the trip—the facility notified me of a problem with insurance. The snafu had occurred five weeks earlier, but no one from the program had called me.

My next move was to meditate to see behind the scenes, as I was by now quite proficient in sensing cosmic intervention. This is what I was told by Higher Consciousness:

> *"Because you were willing to go to any lengths to make of yourself a clear instrument with no impediments, you have been allowed to finish the healing process on the higher planes. You and your father have been in contact. You will not consciously remember the dialogue, but all is well. He is free to go on to progression.*
>
> *"You do not need to enter another recovery program. You are in a state of grace. Healing of the past has taken place."*

The box of family photographs came out of their dark repository into the light once more. As the days lightened with summer, so did my frame and density of mind until all sadness and unknowing were gone. When I think of my dad, it is with compassion and healthful, loving detachment. I see the soul and not the personality.

In September, I spoke at Still Waters Centre on "The Healing Nature of Psychic Guidance." My planned talk was replaced through the persistence of my Higher Self with a more personal talk about healing. My anxiety level was high—unusual for me after so many years of talks and seminars—but when the night was over, I intuitively knew that *through public acknowledgment,* I had taken another critical step in the recovery process. I could move on.

The health and wholeness I had struggled to attain for over twenty years were in sight.

In the seven years since the foregoing events took place, I have written of the changes in myself and my life in journals, letters, notes, and in the margins of books. I have beeñ. in awe of the remarkable difference in my feelings and attitudes.

Until 1987, I often said to God, "Send me the remaindeɪ of my karma and lessons, because I want *this* to be my last life on the physical plane!" Now, much to my amazement, I look forward to coming back—particularly with those I love—to continue my growth and to be of service, if possible.

The liberating, enlightening changes in my being and in my life include more than a few of major significance.

Most important, my physical, mental, and emotional health is greatly improved. I seldom need to see a physician, and since I rarely get "bent out of shape" any more, I seldom visit a chiropractor. I'm happy almost all of the time, I have an optimistic outlook, and my self-esteem and self-confidence are very good. (I've lost my interest in a facelift, as I feel that my face fits my life: full of hard-won, customized character.)

Clearly a change of enormous benefit: I am no longer addicted to the approval of others. What is essential is that I keep my life in divine order.

I'm assertive when it is appropriate, and if mine is the lone dissenting opinion on a panel, I offer it clearly with the courage of my conviction. I am no longer a comfortable conformist.

My strong need to control the choices of others in accord with what I believe to be best is gradually diminishing. I no longer jump into a readiness mode when I spot a chance to "fix" another person's life, and I know that I can't be everything to everyone.

I can look authority figures in the eye. I can confront. I look forward to success and not sabotage. I cope exceedingly well with life's little mishaps. I'm O.K. without "producing" every minute. Leisure time appeals to me and is no longer "undeserved."

There are times when I say no without feeling guilty, and I don't have to justify—or apologize for—my decision.

I am as independent as is healthy and right within a marriage. Should life put me "on my own" one day, I am confident that all will be well. My faith in God and the Universe to guide and provide a way is unshakable. My health and life are proof of this.

> *Best of all, I'm no longer codependent.*
> *I'm free to be me and part of a family.*

When a family member changes in such a dramatic way (granted it was gradual), there is a natural impact. My family views my health as wholesome, not as a threat. Each in his or her own way mirrored for me where I wanted to go; each helped me to arrive; and each gained by watching me grow.

Shannon

Shannon, my youngest, was the most likely candidate for codependency. Watching my struggle helped her to derail and obviate a pattern prevalent on my maternal side for generations. Exceptionally insightful, she has matured beautifully into her own personhood. Shannon graduated from college with a degree in sociology in spring 1994. She plans to attend graduate school in 1995.

In a recent conversation, Shannon had this to say: "I feel very lucky that I incarnated into the family that I did, that you were able to instill metaphysical beliefs—or, as you would say, 'To help me remember what I know as a soul.' I look at my friends who are coming into this philosophy now, who didn't have this advantage while growing up. They envy me.

"It would be marvelous if in some capacity I can combine my spiritual beliefs with my profession. I consider myself a humanist. I want to be in service to humankind. I may focus on women's and minority issues.

"I'm spiritually equipped to deal with painful issues. I feel equipped to handle anything that comes up because of watching you. It didn't come from any specific instance of guidance per se, but by observing you live by—and implement—what you believed in.

"What I learned from you is an overall way of life."

Chris

Chris came to live with us in Florida in 1986 while recovering from a fracture of his left leg. He planned to return to New Mexico when it healed. He is still here. Chris fell in love, not only with the water that surrounds us, but with a lovely young woman, Patricia, who became his wife in 1990. Chris pilots a towboat on the intercoastal waterways from Florida to Mississippi.

I believe that Chris's exposure to metaphysical philosophy plus my work enabled him to respect and *express* the natural feelings of love and affection that most men keep in check. I am very proud of the values he holds and the principles by which he lives.

Lisa

Lisa's profession is accounting. Her personal and spiritual priority continues to be family. In 1992, Lisa and Terry adopted two darling little girls, ages one and three, through the state of Florida. Kayleigh and Anne, born to a Caucasian mother and a black father, are thriving. Their teen-age brother and sister, Danica and Devon, are proving to be wonderful role models. The twins have not encountered racial prejudice to date.

Lisa and Terry are considered an ideal couple by the Florida Department of Health and Human Resources. Caseworkers call every month or two to ask if they could adopt another child. Lisa and Terry know that a little boy is somewhere, waiting. Their family will then be complete.

My eldest child was *born* with her values and direction—and an independent spirit—intact. When I asked Lisa what she learned from my path, she replied, "Unconditional love," and added that all of the guidance I gave her from her Higher Self made an indelible impression. She has more confidence in *her* natural intuitiveness than she might have had otherwise.

Lisa emphasized how helpful it is to understand that "There is a definite reason and a spiritual purpose behind everything that happens to us." She assured me that this awareness helps her to accept unpredictable and challenging developments with patience. Time and time again, this adage bears out as the purpose comes to light. *"Endurance is but acceptance,"* her Higher Self advised.

Ralph

In mid-1992, after several five- and six-month-long periods of sobriety and slippage, Ralph drew the strength and confidence from *within* to reject alcoholism as a way of life. He and his liver are doing well.

Ralph was not a novice to metaphysical philosophy when we married in 1980, but he was new to meditation. He credits the support and encouragement he received from his Higher Self with enabling him to achieve a healthier and happier life style.

I look on our union as an outstanding example of *positive* karma. The support we gave each other in defusing and destructing our minefields—his, alcohol; mine, codependency—was undoubtedly part of a larger plan. We are at a good place now. We married out of emotional need; we remain together out of choice.

As a Source once said, *"Letting go and letting God does not mean losing."*

My Brothers, Barry and Bill

Barry, who lives in New Jersey, is in charge of vehicle maintenance for the U.S. Postal Service. He'll retire in another year. He and Lorraine have three grown children and three grandchildren.

Barry's religious orientation is different from mine, but his words are familiar: "I don't believe anyone can overcome the trauma of childhood or the trauma of tragedy alone. I believe that you need divine intervention, divine guidance, to bring you through.

"Listen to your inner voice and inner peace will come."

If Barry's story (chapters 3 and 7) can be of help to someone dealing with a traumatic event, he would be happy to hear from you. He believes it is time to share the comfort he received.

Address your letter to Barry Adams, c/o A.R.E. Press.

Bill has been a counselor at a shelter for battered women in New Mexico for over ten years. He is healing his deeper scars by helping others to heal theirs. He is married to Cynthia; they have a little girl. Bill spends every weekend with his two children from a prior marriage, ensuring that they have a nurturing dad.

He is the author of *War Between Two Houses,* a two-act play based on the relationship between Emily Dickinson's brother Austin and her friend and editor, Mabel Loomis Todd. The play was first produced by the Old Lyceum Theatre in Clovis, New Mexico, in 1989.

Bill recently told me that while he no longer uses his psychic abilities to give readings, he knows that the door to the higher planes remains open. He believes that much of the comfort and guidance he gives to people in pain comes *through* him, not from him. At those times, Bill is aware that he renders, in a conversational manner, spiritual sustenance in a secular vocabulary.

A few mornings ago, I had an urge to meditate at an unusual time. When I closed my eyes, I saw a sleek, shiny, and modern railroad train swiftly cross my inner screen from right to left. Always before, the train had moved from left to right. I pondered over the scene for a moment and then the light dawned. For the first time, I am able to travel through the past—this life's poignant and painful memories as well as my mistakes—without getting stuck in sadness or taking on obsolete burdens of guilt and regret. It is a marvelous way to feel.

Just prior to the writing of this chapter, my brother Bill brought his family to Gulf Breeze for a five-day visit. Barry, who had not seen Bill in eight years and then for only one all-too-fleeting day, flew down to surprise him. The three of us were reunited for the first time since our mother's funeral in 1964.

Toward midnight on our final evening together, Barry, Bill, and I walked to Shoreline Park and then out to the end of the pier. We stood silently for a few minutes, each recall-ing priceless memories of another pier, another time.

Then, as we reclined under a luster-laden sky, hearing the gentle waters of the Sound lapping at pitch-coated pilings, the gifts and griefs of our growing-up years subtly shifted into spiritual perspective. We shared our thoughts on life and love—love for each other, our families, and God. It was a healing moment that will forever be precious.

For we must heal ourselves and the family as a micro-cosm of the Universe before we can hope for the healing of our planet in its entirety.

◆ ◆ ◆

Looking back on my life, I see my entrance as a Type A personality: A for *afraid*.

I'm now striving to become a Type S, S for *serene*. I'm not there yet.

But I'm still on the path . . .

THE PATH OF PROMISE, THE PATH OF PEACE.

◆ ◆ ◆

Appendix
Melissa in the Morning

An Afterdeath Experience

IN THE EARLY MORNING HOURS ON APRIL 7, 1989, nineteen-year-old Melissa Soderman was found dead by her estranged husband. Their two small children were at home with their mother, but neither had been physically hurt. This event occurred in Wichita Falls, Texas.

Melissa's aunt, Linda Stephens, was a neighbor with whom I shared only a "fringe friendship" (when on the fringe of our front yards, we waved or exchanged pleasant amenities), since both of us led busy lives. Late in the afternoon of April 7, I was hand-watering a flower bed when Linda approached, her face ashen. She told me that she had received a call from her sister, Joy Smith, by which she learned that Joy's daughter Melissa was dead. Joy had just been notified and few details were available. When the brief conversation ended, Linda did not know how Melissa had died.

Linda was aware of the nature of my career and was fairly conversant with metaphysical philosophy, but we had never spoken about either. She asked me if I would be willing to do a psychic reading regarding the tragedy in the hope that comforting guidance could be given to the family in general and Melissa's mother in particular. Linda was leaving the next morning to meet her sister in Texas.

We had the reading at 8:00 in the evening, less than twenty-four hours after the death. I was very surprised to be able to reach Melissa so soon, as previous experience had led me to conclude that the departing soul usually needed more time to complete the transition and acclimate to the changes. Information came in the reading that neither Melissa's aunt nor I could have known. An example of this is that Melissa was pregnant at the time of her death, a fact which no one in the family knew until the autopsy report was issued. Joy Smith subsequently validated much of the guidance and requested a reading with questions about Melissa's assailant and the location of evidence, such as the murder weapon.

This next reading took place on April 26 with Linda again sitting in for Joy Smith. I contacted Melissa, but she was more interested in communicating reassurance and a measure of understanding regarding her life, its challenges, and her present state of being than in providing evidence to identify and support indictment of her assailant. Higher Consciousness did not counteract Melissa's intent, and thus this reading contained a mixture of valid and nonhelpful, even perplexing, guidance.

The third reading took place on May 20. Joy was present along with Linda. Joy's questions continued to relate to Melissa, her death, and the custody of her children. This is a particularly beautiful reading, one that I feel will be a blessing to readers who may have lost a family member "before their time."

The case remains unsolved. A new investigator was appointed by the Wichita Falls Police Department. He indicated to Melissa's mother that he was open to any leads.

When I began giving readings in early 1972, I wanted to be used primarily to help people in pain. In retrospect, I presume this was because I empathized so naturally—and often intensely—with people experiencing grief, anxiety, or an overwhelming feeling of hopelessness. I wanted to share this marvelous resource that I had found in hearing an inner voice, so that others could begin to heal their lives as I was healing mine.

Higher Consciousness took me at my word, and over the past twenty-some years I have read for a great many people in trauma or emotional turmoil. Anguish afflicts all types of people in all walks of life. Social, professional, or financial status makes no difference. We all hurt when our children hurt, we all have our regrets or feelings of guilt when someone dies unexpectedly; and we all have our secret sorrows and shame. Tragedy does not discriminate; it can hit anyone at anytime, and it can hit hard.

In this particular experience, I gave three readings within a six-week period for the family of a young woman who was murdered while her two babies slept in the house. Because of the length of the readings, I have omitted my prayers, repetitive statements, and guidance not relevant to the family's loss. It was also necessary to exclude information that could jeopardize future prosecution of the case. The guidance presented has not been altered, nor has its meaning been changed by the omissions. Verbatim guidance is italicized; interpreted guidance is not.

In the course of writing "Melissa in the Morning," I realized the value of an unvarnished overview of the guidance received in the readings, specifically as to helpfulness, validity, and nonvalidity. Melissa's mother and aunt were wonderfully cooperative. The numerals in parentheses found in the main body of this appendix correspond to comments made in subsequent evaluations.

A word about readings: in the delivery of guidance, little attention is paid by Higher Consciousness to proper sentence structure or grammatical rules. As the intermediary relaying the guidance, I am more concerned about "getting it right" than in saying it right. Your patience and perseverance as the reader will be much appreciated and, it is hoped, rewarded.

The initial reading was requested by the victim's aunt, Linda Stephens, of Gulf Breeze, Florida. Linda provides the background leading to her request:

L.S.: I received a telephone call on April 7, 1989, from my sister Joy, informing me that her daughter Melissa had "been killed." My first thought was that she must have been killed in an auto accident, and I asked if this was the case. Joy repeated, "Linda, it wasn't an accident. She was killed." We were both understandably emotional, and there was no further clarification.

I told my sister that I would join her in Wichita Falls, Texas, the next day. Before we ended the conversation, Joy said several times that she didn't know how she was going to make it through this unless she could know that Melissa wasn't lost somewhere in between earth and heaven, because it had happened so quickly. She also needed to know that someone, perhaps our father who had passed over two years earlier, was with Missy to help her. I was heartbroken for my sister and I kept thinking, what can we do? What can we do?

I remembered that my next-door neighbor, Barbara, was

a psychic. We had neighbor-type conversations when we were outdoors at the same time, but had never talked about her work. Now, I wondered if perhaps she could reach Melissa and give us some reassurance about where and how she was.

I walked outside. Barbara was in front of her house, watering plants with the garden hose. I held back, thinking that perhaps this wasn't what I was supposed to do, and I decided to take care of a few errands. If she was still outside when I came back, I'd take that as a sign that I should ask. I was gone considerably longer than I expected, but Barbara had not budged from her spot.

We had the reading at 8:00 that night. All Barbara knew in advance was that Melissa was nineteen, and she had been killed less than twenty-four hours earlier. I brought a photo of Melissa taken at age twelve. Barbara quickly glanced at it and laid it aside, face down, on her coffee table. She explained that she preferred not to look at photographs.

Melissa One

Initial Reading for Joy Smith, April 7, 1989

B.P.: What I found myself tuning into was Missy voicing the word, *No*, several times, turning her face away, turning her head away, trying to either avoid the blow that was coming at her which apparently was on her left (1), and I could see her turn her head completely down to the right. All of a sudden, everything froze; the scene froze, I felt nothing hit, I felt nothing connect. I felt no pain, no jar, just absolutely everything went still and stayed frozen, which I didn't quite understand at first. I felt my head aligned with her head.

Something *may* have struck, but she was apparently lifted out of the body so quickly that she could feel nothing. Although there was a momentary state of numbness that didn't last but thirty seconds, I found her all of a sudden looking up from having looked down as she was avoiding the confrontation.

(She was) looking up, seeing Light, very beautiful Light in front of her, enveloping her, and a smile came to her face. I found myself smiling, tears of joy have come to my eyes and I still have them; they are not tears of anguish nor tears of pain. It's as though the pain were prevented. The blow which probably was struck was coming in from the left, not directly but at an angle, northwest I would say, but she was lifted out of the body and immediately enveloped in Light.

I do not see her going very far away, but I know that she recognized an angelic being at that point and saw very misty Light, all-encompassing around her, and a beautiful smile came on her face. All of a sudden the muscles of her face relaxed, because she knew that she was safe. She very much knew that she was safe.

Now that sensation, those physical feelings, my being in the physical body with her at the moment of that particular experience ended right there, but I mentally asked if we could find Missy. A voice began to relay information that is a little bit unusual: that she is in a state (similar to) suspended animation. She has not yet completely crossed over. She is very definitely out of the body. She is not sensing and feeling your pain and the family's pain or the turmoil and recriminations and the violence about the scene, because there were emanations of violence and temper and then deep, deep grief and anger. She is not able to pick up on those feelings.

What is happening is that she is separating from the feeling body for just a very brief period of time to enable her to begin the change in vibrations from being in an earth body. During the time (we) are in an earth body, since we are energy, our vibrational rate is toned down and very slow. During the transition back to pure spirit, the vibrations have to pick up and gradually quicken so that they will become rapid enough to allow the etheric to drop away. The etheric is the bridge between spirit and the physical body. She is at this moment beginning to shed the etheric.

She does have consciousness, but not feeling. Now, that isn't emotions, but sensations. Even though she has only just the last few hours seen the separation of the silver chord from the etheric and the body, there has been no reverberation or sensing of any distress or pain that the body engendered before it completely gave up its viability, its life. She was lifted out of the body, the emotional was separated, and the spirit is now in the process of separating completely from the etheric.

There will be sensory perception on her part that will allow her to attune to the family probably within the next twenty-two to twenty-four hours, but for this particular twenty-four-hour segment from the time of impact and the lifting out of the body until the next eighteen hours or so, she will be unable to hear you and feel any emotional grief being manifested in her name toward her.

Usually I pick up on people a couple of weeks after they have crossed over, with an exception once in a while. Even those exceptions are not always the same. But Missy is in this particular state akin to suspended animation. The consciousness is there so that she knows she is changing form, and she is able to communicate to a degree. It certainly will not be at length, because that takes a great deal of energy and power.

I sense many loved ones around her. A little girl in spirit, a tiny, tiny soul, almost an infant (2); perhaps there was a miscarriage or ... Joy, I don't know if maybe you had lost an infant, either stillborn or younger, just a few months' gestation, or Missy did. But there is a tiny little soul, female (2), that is near Missy and several others who appear to have been loved ones. (There is) a great deal of light that would emanate from Missy's own guardian angel and the teachers and guides that surround her.

She has not yet gone through what is considered to be

the gate from the realm of the earth's atmosphere into pure spirit. It has been delayed because of the violence, the shock that the body and even the spirit encountered. There was a suddenness that delayed the beginning of the transition even after she was out of the body. So it's like a little time warp there that she is going through.

She is very much in good hands. Again, I will say that I sense a guardian angel with her and about seven in spirit that would be considered teachers—and several loved ones who apparently may have been either not on the earth plane recently but on the spirit side and yet had known her from other lives or from a sojourn in spirit before. I do not sense these as angelic. I sense them as souls who had been in incarnation at other times, but not recently. They are not having any difficulty in being close to her because they can acclimate to her vibrations.

Those who were on the earth with her in *this* life but who are now are on the other side will need to wait until she completes her passageway through the gate, which is about another day almost from now. So tomorrow evening, she will be waking up to full awareness of where she is and, at that particular time, those who would greet her will be there. Usually this takes place on a grassy knoll, sometimes under a weeping willow tree with a brook nearby. It's usually a very peaceful scene.

I do feel a man in the distance that I would take to be her grandfather. In fact, I'm told there are two, two older men. The first appears to me to have been about 5'9" or 5'10" ... Now, I would be seeing him off in a distance, and this is not near Missy yet, but waiting for her to complete the initial passage through the gate, where she will then shed any semblance of the earth's vibrations. What seems prominent to me is a dark, five o'clock shadow effect, which would not be what he looks like now, but what anyone here on the earth plane would recognize. Not a beard, but there is that shadow there, and very deep-set eyes. Not too thin a face, but it is not a fat face; it is not a round face, it's a little angular. The man would appear close to seventy. Shirt sleeves are rolled up to the elbow. A thin belt, narrow, not wide, through the loops of his pants, just a shirt—looks like a white shirt—dark trousers. (3)

He is just standing there. There are two men, but I do not see . . . There is also a woman, and she is a mother figure. I know she is not Missy's mother. I don't know if she is a grandmother or not, but she is coming in a mother vibration more than a grandmother vibration. The only thing that tells me is that this was a really strong mother. This lady has a round face and very full cheeks. I don't see her frame, I only see the face. It may not be a relative. (4) It may be someone who is there to work with young people who are suddenly lifted out of the body, suddenly finding themselves in transition. That's the impression I have, someone who is there to help the soul understand because it has been so sudden.

I've been told that Missy is conscious, although again this state is kind of like someone has been able, a guardian angel you might say, to separate off the feeling body so that she will not be in turmoil at this point, because that is very devastating. When a soul gets caught up in the turmoil of its crossing, it sometimes becomes earthbound and does not go through the gate and does not continue on. Now, the souls that this happens to are those who will not listen to their teachers and will not recognize that something is occurring and that they have been released from the physical.

That is not Missy's case. She is fully aware. She knew in the moment that it looked like there was going to be an impact, she knew and accepted it, or else she would not have been released as easily from the body. She allowed the release to take place.

On the awareness and understanding level—the Higher Mind and the mind that was the bridge into the physical—she has accepted that transition is taking place. But again, she is not feeling any pain, nor is she able right now to feel the grieving that is beginning, and the anger on the earth. I'm going to ask now what thoughts, if any, can be transmitted or conveyed back.

(Note to Reader: At this point, Melissa spoke directly into my mind for the benefit of her mother and her aunt.)

Melissa: *"Please let me go. I've had a glimpse of what lies ahead and it's so much better than anything I knew down there. Take care of my little ones. But I need to go. Let me go. Don't hold me back. Don't hold on. If you could but see what lies ahead, for I have been shown . . . It's a ways off yet, but I have seen it, the Light, and it is intense, but it doesn't hurt my eyes, and the peace, the peacefulness . . . There just isn't any sadness here. All I can see around me is joy. You can see it in the faces. Just pure love and joy. And I want to reach out and touch that so badly.*

"I did not know until the last minute that it was going to happen, but now I know that there was no other way. I would have lived with fear every day the rest of my life. (5) *At least it's over now, and I know I'll never have to fear again, to be afraid again.*

"I wish I could have told you about the Light I saw three weeks ago. It came into my bedroom through the window one night when it was storming outside, and I was waiting for the rain to be over, wanting to see the sun. I was crying, and I asked if there was a God, for Him to let the sun shine in my life again because I didn't want to wake up afraid every day. (5) *All of a sudden, it was like the sun was in my room. The Light was all around me. It couldn't have lasted very long, and yet it felt like years. I didn't understand it then, but now I know it was sent to assure me that the sun wasn't very far away. It was the same Light that took me last night and brought me here.*

"There is just so much joy all around me. I can't feel it yet,

but I know that it will be mine, and I want you to have this, too. I've never been as happy as I know I'm going to be here. I want you all to know I love you so, and wherever I go I don't think I'll be that far away. Please don't be angry with me for wanting to stay. You'll understand some day.

"They are telling me now that I need to move ahead, to rest awhile, and then to go on where I can learn more. Please take good care of the little ones. I know they will be all right, because they have you. Someone is coming for me now."

B.P.: She is saying, *"Momma . . . "* She is moving away, but what she is saying sounds like *"Oh, Momma, be happy for me, and let me go."*

I see her in white, the back of a white robe. I also see her—this may be a memory that I'm picking up on; I don't know if she ever took ballet lessons or was in a school (play) maybe—with a little ballet costume on with that starchy net skirt, but I see a figure of a young girl—a lot of what I see around her is white and pink. Maybe she liked to wear white and pink. (6)

I'm definitely seeing her as a ballerina or a ballet dancer. It's the little froufrou skirt that stands out. There are ballet slippers, although I have a sense of her trying to learn tap. (7)

I don't have her now. The essence has moved away from me.

I'm told she is in very good hands.

I'm seeing someone here, a young man with a very fat face. In fact, he is heavy, overweight. (He has) sort of a snarl, a sneer or a snarl. A sarcastic tone, and then a laugh. Very changeable. Very different inside than the exterior most of the time, also. Wavy hair, I'd say probably medium brown or dark brown, but not black. I see him with a blue tux on, the kind that fellows wore to senior proms, junior proms, or maybe even getting married. Sort of an icy blue shade. It's not vivid. The impression I have is of someone that nobody really knew, inside an exterior that seemed to be one way.

You know, personality came across one way, but inside there's almost a mad . . . (8) Do you have any other questions?

L.S.: I can't think of any more. We just wanted to know that she was safe and that she wasn't lost because of the quick departure.

B.P.: She is surrounded by beings of Light, and there is a great deal of love coming toward her. In fact, she is moving now, slowly moving on up. It is quite a process, apparently, to divest oneself of the energies associated with the earth, because I think that she also has to shake off a lot of attachments, and that's part of the process as well. She has a great deal of help.

She will never have to come back to be with her husband again. It is completely over. I'm being told that now, that there will never need to be any further contact whatsoever.

L.S.: So the karma is over.

B.P.: The karma is over. He could not possibly have a hold on her again. I almost sense that he mesmerized her. Your sister will be able to confirm whether this is true or not, but it is almost as though he was able to hypnotize her, to get a hold on her mind. There was something right from the very first day when she met him, and I think she might have met him when she was about thirteen (9), even though there wasn't physical contact yet. There was a real psychic and mental manipulation taking place. That has been irrevocably broken.

I'm not sure—I think that Missy had a little girl and a little boy. The youngest one might be a little boy (10). I think that they will be protected from him. They will be protected by the state and by virtue of divine order and divine law.

L.S.: I don't know the circumstances of her husband's family, his parents . . .

B.P.: There is a possibility of a conflict there. (11) It is possible that they will want them, but, of course, he won't have them. And that is something that can be resolved later. What is important now is that all the prayers that go to Missy do release her as she requests. Of course, she will be missed, and grieving has to take place because that is therapeutic and that is part of the loosening up, the letting-go process. But it is critical that no one hold her back by wishing that she had more years or feeling as though she didn't live her life out, because she apparently accomplished what she needed to accomplish in this life.

One of the goals that she had was to break away from him. In taking the step that she took to separate, and also in mentally and emotionally trying to break the hold that he had on her, she did get the job done. I think that there was quite an arduous relationship between them in at least two other lives, and it has now been fully and irrevocably ended.

The question comes to mind, did it have to be this way? And I'm told, no, that it did not. Had he elected to go for help to a therapist, (or) to commit himself for intensive therapy treatment possibly in a hospital . . . I feel that this man almost had a breakdown about several, or seven, years ago. He knew that he was struggling with violent thoughts. (12)

Missy was not the only woman, the only girl, that he physically abused. I'm not talking about sexual abuse here as much as physical, pushing around, smacking, a fist in the stomach, up against the wall, and then the next day I feel he would not remember this happening, almost as though there were a pressure on the brain. She was very much afraid of him. (13) I do think there is some kind of a past record in this life. I'm not sure if it's for assault, or what. There have been past incidents. (14)

What Joy needs to do now is to find comfort in knowing that her daughter need not ever be afraid again, that she is in a place of great love, and that while this certainly is extremely tragic and painful . . .

L.S.: I know that sometimes through curiosity or the need to be with family, those who have just died come to their own funerals. Will this be the case with Missy?

B.P.: No, she won't be at the memorial. Her transition is going to take a little bit more time, although nothing is wrong with the process. Perhaps having had children, some of the attachments need to fall away completely before . . . so that when she does come back, it will be in full awareness that she has made this transition and that there is no true separation when there is love. However, she will not be tempted to attach again and not be able to release herself and go on.

So I feel there is probably what we would designate as a week to ten days before you will sense her presence, although she will send her love. The essence and the love may be felt but not her presence . . . but then she will come and go in peace. There will be really strong feelings of peace when her presence is felt, not sadness, not tears, not a quickening of the vibrations, but a sense of peace and calm and then thoughts of her. She might be able to generate an image in the mind when she is there. She will come and go as often as she can until she knows that she has been released, that there is nothing else to be done by her to effect her release. And then after that, her visits will be mainly to her children.

I think that there is a photograph which is in an ornate-looking frame. It wouldn't be a plain wooden frame or a metal frame. It's one of those fancier-looking frames. My impression of it is that it is silvertone. It's not on a wall, it is sitting on a dresser or a chest of drawers or a table. And I do see long hair. I see it a little curlier than is in this picture that you have shown me, Linda. In the picture that I'm talking about, she is older and the hair is curlier. (15)

L.S.: There is just so much that I don't know about her circumstances the last several years.

Melissa: "*I love you all, I love you all.*" Those words are still echoing down: "*I love you all. Please don't be sad. I'm going to be so very happy, and I'm going to be free. And I'll never stop loving you. Please don't stop loving me.*"

B.P.: Melissa had learned to trust God (16) and to turn within. This last couple of years she was learning that her real help came from within. She is going to help her mother understand, too, as time goes on. Right now she is not able to communicate well because it does take quite a bit of power, and she's not even fully . . . she knows she is in transition. She understands (that) she has left the earth body. She knows she's going to where she will be very happy, but in time she'll be able to be there for her mother when her mother gets discouraged and blue.

I think there have been times in the past when perhaps Joy was discouraged herself about other things in life, and Missy didn't know what to do. But the feeling I have now is that in the future, she'll be able to be there for you, Joy. You will sense her presence and there will be, maybe, telepathic thought communication, telepathic thought . . . (17)

Missy will have many, many loved ones (around her) as she goes through the gateway and then is fully aware, with the finer bodies intact, becoming whole spiritually . . . She will be fine . . . Let yourself grieve, but know that your daughter is going to be just fine.

I'm going to turn the tape off now. God bless you, and I'll keep you all in my prayers. Good night.

Melissa Two

Linda Stephens, Melissa's aunt, explains how the second reading came about:

I flew to Wichita Falls for Melissa's services, taking the tape of the first reading to give to Joy when the time seemed right. When I arrived, Joy was speaking with detectives from the sheriff's department. After they left and we had shed our initial tears together, Joy again expressed her need to know that Melissa was in good hands, not confused and frightened. I told her that I had asked my neighbor, Barbara Paulin, a psychic, to try and attune to Melissa's spirit and that Barbara was told that Melissa was surrounded by love and light.

While this comforted Joy, I knew that she needed to hear something evidential so that she could have complete confidence in the reading. I asked her if Missy had possibly miscarried a child in recent months, because Barbara had observed a tiny, tiny soul with Missy. On hearing this, Joy began to cry again, saying, "I know, I know, I know she really had Missy, because unknown to me or anyone else, Missy was pregnant at the time of her death!" The detectives, having the results of the autopsy, had just informed Joy and Missy's estranged husband of the pregnancy.

About two-and-one-half weeks after the services, Joy told me on the telephone that the investigation was not progressing because little evidence had been found and there were no leads for the detectives to pursue. We asked Barbara to do a reading, with the focus on information to assist with the investigation.

April 26, 1989

B.P.: It wasn't but a moment before I had tremendous soft, gentle, misty Light in my view, and it is such a wonderful feeling to be in this Light and to experience it. It is just so peaceful that it is almost unbearable. Perhaps what is unbearable about it is that you know you are going to have to leave it to come back to the here and now, and I don't really want to leave it.

It is similar to what happens in a deep meditation with alignment and attunement. You know whether you can sense a presence or not. The vibrations are of such accepting, unconditional love; you know this, you feel it, and you feel peace as you have never felt before.

Immediately as I went into that feeling of Light and the tears began to well up from joy and peace, then I knew that Melissa was there. She wanted me to be able to relay to you and her mother how powerful the emotion is, how completely at peace you feel with yourself in this particular place on this spectrum.

Melissa was ready and probably came back into this life just to live these few short years, even though it is hard to understand and accept. But she has gone into total Light; she is not in the transitional state (in which) I found her in the first twenty-four hours. She has just progressed beautifully.

Many people when they cross over stay three months, six months, a year of our time, in an intermediate state that might be akin to something religion terms to be transitional. But she has not had to spend that much time once she was able to detach herself with tremendous love for all of you there—and for the children, especially. Once she was able to let go and let God and to accept that she was making a transition, crossing over, back in spirit again, then it was almost instantaneous that she found herself on a realm of tremendous light.

I wouldn't call this the ultimate, I wouldn't say that she is at the seventh plane or the ultimate plane of existence, where everything has been learned and incorporated into her being, but she certainly is in a marvelous place and will make good progress from here. The review, I think, is also almost complete, the review process that a soul goes through when it crosses over. That sometimes also takes what we would perceive as months, although there is no time and space in the next dimension.

She is in a place where there is just utmost love and peace and joy, and wishes you all could be there with her, and (she) will wait for the time that you are. She will definitely be there unless she comes back into incarnation to be with people in the family another time, (with) another opportunity perhaps to serve others, and that is a significant consideration. I don't think this decision has been made yet.

Before we turn to your questions, I will ask if there is anything spontaneous to come through. I do have her in centered alignment right at the moment. Oh! There is something. I saw a gem hanging from a chain; it could be a small diamond, and it is a gold chain, perhaps 18". The gem was clear; I did not see color in it. If this is something she has had in the past, I don't know. (18)

There is somebody here . . . someone who has been with the family in incarnation many times, (but who) is *not* at the present moment, who would be like a consultant on spiritual growth for the family. Not with the family all the time, just when beckoned or needed—like your spiritual director, like a priest or a minister that you would call on in the flesh. You also have one in spirit.

I don't know, this hasn't come through before for anyone else. But that seems to be the source I have and the words that were coming a moment ago for you, Joy, in particular—but also for anyone else who is grieving—are that *"The peace of God be with you and His peace carry you ever onward. The ray of peace will be available to you and accessible throughout the next weeks and months and perhaps even years, as needed to calm the emotions when recall is made of the recent events."*

(Note to Reader: The next nine questions revolved around the investigation, Joy's job search, and personal family issues. The information given in the reading with regard to evidence did not prove valid to date. Consequently, no help was received that would lead to identification and indictment of Melissa's assailant.)

According to Linda Stephens, Melissa's husband found her body and reported her death to the police. He was cooperative when questioned and subsequently took two polygraph tests. He has not been designated a prime suspect. However, because of immaturity, temperament, and his history of drug abuse, he was not considered—by his or Melissa's parents—capable of rearing the two children.

(Note to Reader: The reading continues. Direct dialogue by Higher Consciousness is indicated by H.C.)

H.C.: *"We would say to all who hear this tape to trust in God's love and time and universal justice to avenge what needs to be avenged, to bring order and light into the lives of those who are struggling to understand and to believe."*

L.S.: Will Joy be able to get custody (of Melissa's two children) soon? Will Melissa's husband give his consent and sign papers?

H.C.: *"It will be sooner than it now looks. He will reverse his stand abruptly. She should act upon the moment, but have it done with all legal precaution. Just a moment ... He is imbued with the idea of fleeing and would like to break all ties and connections. Once she has the sense of this, although he may not say what he has in mind, it would be best to get the documents executed and recorded before he swiftly changes his mind again.* (19)

"*When that is behind her, know that any other steps to be taken will go smoothly and will seem providential . . . Those on our side who minister do so with a bond of love and commitment not seen on the earth plane, and (we) have no other distractions . . . (Joy) may trust and depend upon unlimited resources, caring and guidance from this side of the veil for however long it is needed.* (Tape turned.)

"*We will always be able to send Melissa's love and support from wherever she is at and (to) impress those in whose care they are growing with loving suggestions for her children's welfare. With this we would close. You, my dear child, are not alone. All the cares attendant upon you today—both within and without the situation at hand—will fall in place once you see the growth you are attaining and then understand that this is work you came back to do for self and others. We are very proud of what you are accomplishing and demonstrating for others. God bless you and keep you.*"

Melissa Three

Linda Stephens on the third reading: Joy came to visit me in Gulf Breeze, Florida, about eight weeks after Missy's death. We felt the need to be together to help each other with the grieving process. She asked me to arrange an in-person session with Barbara, whose readings had been immensely helpful so far. It was not until the three of us were together for the reading that Barbara and I heard Joy's questions.

May 20, 1989

B.P.: When I first closed my eyes, I knew that she (Melissa) was there and her tears started to fall. I heard the words:

Melissa: *"Mother, mother, how I wish that I could reach out
and physically touch and comfort you as you used to comfort me. Do you remember when you would stroke my face
when I was just a little girl, my cheek, my chin... Your touch
felt so good to me then. Your love feels so good to me now. I
wish that I could give back to you the strength that was always there for me, because I know that strength now, and I
am seeing the understanding which is all around me, the
light and the peace that is in people's hearts.*

*"It is so wonderful to feel love on this side of what we
laughingly call 'the veil,' because it's a love that just knows no
limit, no judgment, no fear. It's just complete with such understanding that as we talk with one another with our minds
more than with our mouths, with our hearts more than with
our hands—but the touch with our hearts is every bit as comforting and as real, if not more so—I would that you could
visit in the daytime and when you could realize that you were
here.*

*"I've seen you twice now. You've come to me. Only once
have I been able to come to you in a way that I could make
my presence known. At other times, I had to be content with
just sending my love and asking you not to grieve and asking
you to take care of the little ones. But I'm getting stronger now
and happier, and with a feeling of wholeness that I've never
known before. Some day maybe you will be able to come
across, just for a visit, with your eyes wide open. There are so
many sights I want to show you.*

*"There are many here around us, some I know to be angels
and others just seem to be friends. But you are the subject of
much conversation because not a day goes by that you don't
show your willingness to try to see with what they call the
spiritual vision, that which has others all torn up, people
who only seem to be able to cry. You are always asking for
understanding and to be led as to what to do that would be*

right. I am so proud of you. I hope that you are of me as well, because I also want to do what's right.

"*I know I need to really let go and to move on up where I can learn more and perhaps come back and be a teacher, or at least a reacher. They tell me that there is such a need down there today, and I remember well all the funny ideas that didn't make much sense then, like 'Where is hell and who goes there for eternity to suffer on and on?' How wonderful it is to know for sure that God wouldn't do that to anyone. I want to come back and be one of those who tell that when you are a child of this loving God, there is no such place as hell.*

"*I'm with you now, and for a while I can stay. I'll stand right here beside you and touch your face like you touched mine. I hope that you can feel my presence and my love and my gratitude, because it would be so much harder if you weren't doing this well. I know your heart hurts and mine would as well if our positions were reversed. I'm not so sure that I'd have known what to do and how to act, but now I do, not only from being here, but seeing you as well. I really love you, even more than I knew then. Thank you for being you. I'll be quiet now, so that others can come through.*"

B.P.: I'm going to reconnect with my own Higher Self to rise above the emotion so that it doesn't interfere, my own emotion. I'm not feeling really clear . . . O.K. I have a source that stands ready now to approach any of the questions that are on your mind . . . and to move them out of the way.

J.S.: I'm really worried about the children. I'm afraid I have not handled this well because I didn't get the documents signed. I was being nice to Melissa's husband and waiting on him, and he came and took the children. I don't think they are in imminent danger, but I think about it all the time. Every time I sleep I dream about it. I don't know what to do. I don't know if I should be there.

H.C.: *"They aren't in imminent danger . . . but there does need to be documentation as to the nature of his behavior over the years, his unpredictability and the confusion that accompanies his words verbally as well as any in writing. If necessary, approach the department having to do with the welfare of children and the courts that have jurisdiction over the crime and begin to build a case.*

" While we would not impress you with so much urgency that you felt scattered and anxious, we would say that time is becoming important, and momentum also . . . He is extremely erratic in his thinking processes insofar as what he is going to do, where he is going to take the children, what his personal plans are. He does not at this time harbor any intent to harm them, but there is always the possibility of self-harm while under the influence of chemicals or of his own dark side. In that event, the children could be either neglected or possibly injured as well. We do not foresee that in the coming three weeks or a month, as there is a stabilizing influence around him at this time, but that is not going to be there for too long. (20)

"You have every right to address this concern to the proper authorities, and they will agree with you. The difficulty will be in gathering adequate hard documentation so that the court will feel it has substantiation to act. His own mother and father may come in a sense to the rescue (21) in that they know that he is capable of extreme turns . . . (and) shifts in temperament. You may seek to avail yourself of their assistance, for these children are their grandchildren as well. If you can initiate the claim, much work can be done by telephone, for there will be others that will come to your aid."

J.S.: I am also worried about my own state of mind in that I have not worked since all this happened, even though I have looked for work. I fear that I will not be able to hold up under the pressure of the new job and still continue with my spiritual search. (22)

H.C.: *"You will do very well. You will not have any problems. There will be a strength pouring through you from those of us around you as well as from resources you don't consciously know you have. (This strength will come) while you are . . . taking care of the responsibilities of the work. It will come quite easily to you. The requirements that are necessitated on behalf of the children and with regard to other . . . legalities will not necessitate frequent travel, and you will be able to manage these. (23)*

"We would anticipate that the children will be relocated once again to the same homestead that they were at in Fort Worth/Dallas within the next few weeks. (24)

"There are several on our side of the veil who are working now with your son-in-law to try to instill in him, when the mind is vulnerable, a sense of rightness, a sense of responsibility toward those children. And he himself, without our help, has an inclination to not be saddled—as his mind would have it—with any responsibility other than for himself. (25) He feels that by taking the children back, he is creating an image that is wholesome. But this will not be conveyed in any genuineness to anyone who matters.

"We know that the situation is of deep concern and is creating the anxiety of which you speak. We also know that our words may help but cannot completely remove that concern, that only safety and protection for the children will truly serve to relieve the concern, but we are almost certain it will go smoother and they will be returned to safe and wholesome, loving arms before too long. We do, however, again advise you to begin building a foundation for the legal action in their behalf.

"On several occasions, we felt that he was ready to sign, but free will being what it is and the influence that corrupts free will . . . through the use of the toxins, the drugs, has interfered at the eleventh hour. And thus no sure guarantee can be given, but it does appear from all indications and our perspective that everything will fall in place, and all will be well.

"Again, you will do quite nicely on the new job. There is always help coming to one such as yourself who is open and (who) understands that we are all one, all a part of each other. Thus all can support the individual and the whole. That help only requires a momentary thought on your part, inviting us in."

J.S.: Can you give me any further help in accepting our loss, especially for my other children, Brian and Melanie?

H.C.: *"What you do by your composure and even at times by your tears, not only the words that you speak, but the struggle to survive and to strive for understanding and acceptance, and then freedom of thought, freedom of movement, in the Light, will do more than any other type of conveyance or communication could do to provide your children with an example, a demonstration, of right thinking, of growth, of strength and of courage.*

"It may be years before your children ... understand in full and are able to acknowledge the depth of inspiration that you are providing now. While they do not seem to have in their divine plan a similar experience ahead, there will be others in their lives as time goes on who do experience tragedy of a similar nature, and your children will need to deal with losses of other kinds.

"The greatest work a soul can do on the earth plane today is that of parenting, and the challenges are many, the responsibility heavy, the burden is not light. But the growth that can be attained through parenting with spiritual balance ... can be so fulfilling at the end of the road. Far better be it that a parent looks back and sees a child who has learned how to reason with the earth mind and intuit with the spirit, than to see a child who may have graduated cum laude from seven different universities and hold a prestige position that takes him or her to many different countries, speaking several languages ...

"Keep on keeping on. Your children will benefit as well as you, and your child on this side of the veil, the newcomer that we recently welcomed with open arms and loving hearts, for this is what she drew by coming to us with open arms and a loving heart, looking for the Light, is also gladdened and not saddened by the work that you are doing on self and on behalf of others.

"If you could but see, again from our vantage point, the Light around you and the Light you cast, compared with those who cannot let go of their loved ones, be they elderly, young, or inbetween, who hold them back, who grieve and mourn far beyond the need for healing, who build memorials of money and live for decades in memory, regrets, and guilt, then you would see yourself objectively as someone who has made others proud.

"As above, so below. The help that you are seeking you are already giving, but you know it not. The help that you are giving will draw to you the help that you are seeking. Take one day at a time, my child. Tackle one problem at a time, although that does not mean that you cannot work and at the same time expend some effort on resolving other issues . . . but do not take on the next six months all at once.

"Know that the decisions you will need to make will be placed before you, and with sureness and strength you will know where you are being led. It seemed best to us . . . to place before you the choices of job location rather than to spell out the best choice and watch you wonder if you were being led rightly, because the dictum came from another source and not clearly from within you.

"You remained open to your intuition even in your travail and pain, and that is no easy matter, for emotion can easily obscure intuition. We are proud of how well you have done. But if there is no other message than this to come through to you tonight, please accept this and keep it in . . . your mind (and) your heart at all times: You are not alone and all the help you need is there for you. Just reach with the heart and

the mind and say, 'I need help, please send help in the Light.'

"You will know that you are receiving in the Light because of the love and peace that . . . pervades your senses. There will not be an instance in which you reach out and no answer comes. It may not be immediate, and it may not be in so many words, but it will come within a few hours or . . . a few days, and always in time. Perhaps a little more time so that you will be able to develop the insights to accompany the choice, but you will never be left wanting.

"This connection will remain open to you because you reached for it from deep within at a moment when others would have cried out, 'Lord, why me?'

"My child, we feel that we can say this to you now more so than before, that there was an awareness on your part the day Melissa was born that she was to help you achieve greater growth and ultimately greater joy than perhaps any other soul present in this life with you. The thought came in an instant, but you did comprehend and then released it, knowing you could not live with the thought of possible loss. (26) It was in the divine plan, although the circumstances were not spelled out. It was hoped from the very beginning that the circumstances would not be as they were, but that the change would be of a different nature, perhaps a natural exit, although somewhat premature. For Melissa did not have a full life span to expend by karmic law this time.

"When the day comes that Melissa needs to go on, we know that you will wish her well. Love can always reach across the realms . . . There is indeed no true separation. For now, as she works with the review process and heals and strengthens, she will be near you more often and near her children. She will be learning to detach with love and spiritual understanding. This process has already begun but needs to be refined and completed.

"You do not need to fear another loss; it is not coming. Let go and let God, when those moments come and in your humanness such a thought or a sad memory crosses perhaps a

weary mind, and you would reach out and hold too tight, too close. Say to self, 'Joy, remember, you must let go and let God.'

"God keep you. We will close now. Your daughter with- draws, but she reaches out and touches and wipes away that tear. Good night."

Evaluation of the Melissa Readings
June 5, 1994

by Melissa's mother, Joy Smith, and aunt, Linda Stephens

(Numbers correspond with points in the readings.)

1. J.S.: I know that Melissa was struck on the head and had other wounds. I have not yet been able to read the au- topsy report for precise locations.

    L.S.: Melissa was struck on the left upper part of her head (the temple and slightly above). When we first viewed the body, we had to ask the funeral home to add more cos- metic cover because this particular wound still showed.

2. J.S.: I learned after her death that Melissa was preg- nant. No one knew beforehand. Melissa's estranged hus- band and I were informed by the sheriff's department detectives after the autopsy. The fetus was a boy (the read- ing was incorrect as to gender).

3. J.S.: Upon hearing the tape, I immediately felt that the grandfather figure was Melissa's paternal grandfather who died before she was born. The description fits perfectly. I have a photograph of him wearing dark pants and a white shirt with sleeves rolled up, as was his habit. He had very dark hair that never turned gray in old age. He was a church elder, a very loving and kind man, but somewhat stoic in his demeanor. He also had an angular face.

4. J.S.: This describes our maternal grandmother (Missy's great-grandmother) to a tee. She had a round face and full cheeks and was every bit the mother, not only to her own children but to others.

5. L.S.: Missy had spent the previous summer with her mother in Memphis because she said she was afraid to stay in Wichita Falls.

J.S.: She said her husband had received threats against her and the children by drug dealers, because he was an informant. After the murder, I asked the detective on the case about this, and he said that Melissa's husband had not been working with the police.

6. J.S.: Yes, Missy looked especially good in pink.

L.S.: Joy had not heard the tape at the time of the funeral, so she did not associate the predominant color of all the flowers sent to the services. They were overwhelmingly *pink*.

7. J.S.: At the time I heard the tape, I had no idea where the ballerina came from. Recently, however, Missy's daughter, who was only seven months old when her mother died, has decided—seemingly out of the blue—that she will take ballet and tap as well. I have bought her tights, ballet slippers, and tap shoes, and her paternal grandmother has bought her a beautiful lace tutu.

L.S.: I cannot help but believe that even then, so soon after the murder, picking up on the future little ballerina was to show that life *would* indeed go on, normalcy would resume, and Missy's children would have a happy life.

8. J.S.: I do not recognize the person described here. It could very well be the killer, but the description doesn't fit anyone I know to have associated with Missy.

9. J.S.: Melissa *did* meet her husband when she was thirteen. She seemed unable and, at times, unwilling to get away from him.

10. J.S.: Missy's children are a boy and a girl. The boy is only thirteen months older than his sister.

11. J.S.: There *was* a conflict as to who would take the children. We all knew that their father was not able. After several weeks, the children's paternal grandmother did come from California and take the children home with her. I realize now that this is where they belong. She and her husband are doing an excellent job of rearing them and they have legal custody. Their father cannot regain custody without a court hearing.

12. J.S.: Unknown.

13. J.S.: Brian Miller, my son and Melissa's brother, told me after her death that he had seen physical evidence that her husband had hit her. When asked about it, she brushed it off as minor. It is my understanding that although he was not consistently abusive, it was not unusual for him to strike her during an argument.

14. J.S.: Melissa's husband had a history of criminal activity. He served time in the penitentiary for attempting to rob a liquor store. His accomplice hit the owner with a hammer and ran, but he stayed and called the police himself.

15. J.S.: The photograph described is of Melissa with long hair, recently permed.

16. L.S.: Missy had done much reevaluating, especially during the last year of her life. Just a few months before her death, she had begun to attend a small fundamentalist church and had recently gone forward during the invitational or altar call and rededicated her life to Christ. The minister spoke of this with the family.

17. J.S.: There have been numerous occasions when I felt that Missy communicated and comforted me and several outstanding experiences involving electricity. One time in particular continues to reassure me when I think of it. I was driving alone at night down a curving country road, feeling especially low. This was about a year after Missy's death. I put one of the reading tapes on that Barbara made and as I often did, I said a short prayer asking that Missy was all right and doing well. Suddenly, the headlights went off, although

the switch indicated they were on. For the next seventeen miles, the car headlights went off and on, off and on. At one point, a driver in front of me pulled over and asked if I was signaling him. When I arrived home, I ran into the house and pulled my husband outside to check the car, but the flashing had stopped and the phenomenon has not reoccurred in the four years since.

18.   J.S.: This is a small pendant that belonged to Missy. I wore it after her death. It had a small diamond inset on a gold chain.

19.   J.S.: Melissa's husband changed his mind at the last moment, leaving me waiting at the lawyer's office after having at first agreed to sign over the children.

20.   J.S.: At the time the children's father took them from where they were staying in Dallas, he had met a nurse and was staying with her and her child. I believe she was the stabilizing force referred to, but this relationship only lasted a couple of weeks.

21.   J.S.: The paternal grandparents literally came to the rescue. When I telephoned to say that Melissa's husband had taken the children, his mother immediately quit her job and flew to Texas to pick up the children and take them to her home. She and her husband have provided a nurturing home for them ever since.

22.   J.S.: I have had no problem staying focused on work. In fact, those who knew my situation expressed amazement at my ability to work under such extreme emotional circumstances.

23.   J.S.: I did not have to travel. The guardianship papers were handled through the mail.

24.   J.S.: Partially incorrect. The children went to live with their paternal grandparents in California, later moving to the Midwest. The children's father has visited twice and calls infrequently.

25.   J.S.: Their father did express at times that he could not care for the children.

26. J.S.: I was always afraid of losing Missy. I would have
dreams in which our family would be walking along and
Missy would fall in a hole. These dreams filled me with fore-
boding. I was especially fearful when Missy was six, and I
would lie awake at night and cry. My fear was that Missy
would become ill and die, even though she was a very
healthy child. I never worried this way about my other children. During this period, I asked God to let Melissa live until
adulthood and have children of her own. God answered this
prayer.

J.S.: During the third reading, which both Linda and I
attended, I was astounded to see Barbara "take on" several
of Melissa's mannerisms. Two affectations were particularly
striking. My daughter had thick hair and, in particular, a
wave that usually hung down over the right side of her forehead. She would repeatedly brush or flip this wave away
from her face with her hand. Barbara did this several times
although the gesture was pointless, as her hair wasn't in the
way. Barbara also kept smoothing the skin under her eyes
with her fingers, another of Melissa's routine mannerisms.

All during this reading, Linda and I were aware of the
thunder and lightning outside. It did not rain. Inside the
room where the reading was taking place, the atmosphere
was charged with the pops and crackles of electricity.

In Retrospect, in Celebration

The readings Barbara did for me after Missy's murder
helped me immeasurably. At a time when I was feeling such
extreme loss, they helped me concentrate on the grand new
adventure that Missy had embarked upon, rather than the
horrible circumstances of her death.

I drew great comfort in knowing that persons on the
other side whom I could recognize were there to help her
and me. Knowing that Barbara did not have any knowledge
of these people, yet described them so accurately, verified

their presence. I was able to pray for Missy to move forward into the Light and learn as quickly as possible the delights of being in spirit. It has also helped me to fear my own death less and look forward to seeing my loved ones on the other side, and to be truly free.

I know that this sounds strange, and I do not completely understand my feelings, but the capture of the killer is not an objective of mine. It is as though that person is so far removed from me that I know in a spiritual way he is not even living in the same world. I have often prayed for the Light of God to shine in this person. It saddens me to think that anyone lives in such darkness when the Light is so available. I don't know if I were to meet Missy's killer face to face, with full knowledge that he/she was in fact guilty, I would be able to forgive, but I believe that by God's grace, I could.

Missy has come to me many times to offer comfort when I most needed it. She has come in dreams, in poetry and song, to comfort me and let me see her as the happy spirit she is now. I believe that Melissa and our spiritual guides and counselors have enabled me to live through this ordeal and become a more forgiving and loving person. Her death has put my life in perspective. I only wish I could share the peace and understanding that I have been given. Perhaps Barbara's book will allow me to do this.

Melissa does not come as often now, and I don't ask her to. I know she is busy learning and growing closer to God's Light.

I still cry sometimes and feel my heart will burst, but the Light always comes in my darkest hour, and I know again how much God loves me. I also know that I am well cared for at all times, whether I feel deserving or not.

Joy Smith

◆   ◆   ◆

Melissa's mother, Joy Smith, will welcome and reply to letters from readers. Please send correspondence to Mrs. Joy Smith in care of the A.R.E. Press, P.O. Box 656, Virginia Beach, VA 23451-0656.

About the Author

Barbara Paulin teaches meditation classes and has worked as an intuitive in experimental drug rehabilitation programs. She has also been featured in print and television media and spoken before business and other organizational audiences about her work and its beneficial effects.

She resides with her husband in Gulf Breeze, Florida.

What Is A.R.E.?

The Association for Research and Enlightenment, Inc. (A.R.E.®), is the international headquarters for the work of Edgar Cayce (1877-1945), who is considered the best-documented psychic of the twentieth century. Founded in 1931, the A.R.E. consists of a community of people from all walks of life and spiritual traditions, who have found meaningful and life-transformative insights from the readings of Edgar Cayce.

Although A.R.E. headquarters is located in Virginia Beach, Virginia—where visitors are always welcome—the A.R.E. community is a global network of individuals who offer conferences, educational activities, and fellowship around the world. People of every age are invited to participate in programs that focus on such topics as holistic health, dreams, reincarnation, ESP, the power of the mind, meditation, and personal spirituality.

In addition to study groups and various activities, the A.R.E. offers membership benefits and services, a bimonthly magazine, a newsletter, extracts from the Cayce readings, conferences, international tours, a massage school curriculum, an impressive volunteer network, a retreat-type camp for children and adults, and A.R.E. contacts around the world. A.R.E. also maintains an affiliation with Atlantic University, which offers a master's degree program in Transpersonal Studies.

For additional information about A.R.E. activities hosted near you, please contact:

A.R.E.
67th St. and Atlantic Ave.
P.O. Box 595
Virginia Beach, VA 23451-0595
(804) 428-3588